# The Zope Book

# Contents At a Glance

# The Zope Book

Amos Latteier
Michel Pelletier

**New Riders**
**www.newriders.com**
201 West 103rd Street, Indianapolis, Indiana 46290
An Imprint of Pearson Education
Boston • Indianapolis • London • Munich • New York • San Francisco

# The Zope Book

International Standard Book Number: 0-7357-1137-2

Library of Congress Catalog Card Number: 2001088333

05 04 03 02 01   7 6 5 4 3 2 1

Interpretation of the printing code: The rightmost double-digit number is the year of the book's printing; the rightmost single-digit number is the number of the book's printing. For example, the printing code 01-1 shows that the first printing of the book occurred in 2001.

## Trademarks

## Warning and Disclaimer

**Publisher**
David Dwyer

**Associate Publisher**
Al Valvano

**Executive Editor**
Stephanie Wall

**Managing Editor**
Gina Kanouse

**Development Editor**
Chris Zahn

**Product Marketing Manager**
Stephanie Layton

**Publicity Manager**
Susan Nixon

**Copy Editor**
Sarah Cisco

**Indexer**
Chris Morris

**Manufacturing Coordinator**
Jim Conway

**Book Designer**
Louisa Klucznik

**Cover Designer**
Brainstorm Design, Inc.

**Composition**
Ron Wise

# Table of Contents

# About the Authors

**Amos Latteier** works as a software engineer at Zope Corporation, the company that publishes Zope. He started hacking Python in the 1.3 days. He was one of the first users of Bobo, Zope's precursor. Using Bobo, he wrote Web applications for Hewlett Packard and others. Later he joined Zope Corporation and helped usher Zope into existence. Amos wrote most of Zope's initial networking and XML support. More recently, he developed training materials, wrote the online Help system, and wrote official documentation and magazine articles about Zope. He is currently planning Zope's future directions.

In his spare time, Amos builds hovercrafts, walking machines, giant potato batteries, and pigeon lofts.

**Michel Pelletier** has been a software developer for Zope Corporation since January of 1999, right about the same time Zope became Open Source. Michel likes to hike, fly, read, drink beer, play his horns, and, of course, hack in his favorite language, Python. Michel lives and works in Portland, Oregon. Before working for Zope Corporation, Michel was self-employed in a number of jobs including freelance network engineer, waiter, software consultant, beer taster, sales associate, pizza restaurant manager, starving musician, dish washer, bum, Appalachian Trail thru-hiker, and college drop-out.

# About the Technical Reviewers

These reviewers contributed their considerable hands-on expertise to the entire development process for *The Zope Book*. As the book was being written, these dedicated professionals reviewed all the material for technical content, organization, and flow. Their feedback was critical to ensuring that *The Zope Book* fits our reader's need for the highest-quality technical information.

**Tom Deprez** is an electrical engineer with post-graduate diplomas in biomedical and clinical engineering techniques, as well as a masters in networking and multimedia. A user of Zope since the separate products merged into one, Tom has used Zope in several intranet applications in the Department of Radiology at the University Hospital of Leuven, Belgium, where he is employed as a radiation physicist and an information technology project engineer. In his work he develops quality assurance and intranet applications for radiology and radiation physics. Tom initiated the ZBook project at ZDP (Zope Documentation Project) to provide general information on, and documentation of, Zope to the community. As a programmer he also has experience with Turbo Pascal to Borland Delphi. Both personally and professionally, Tom hopes to be seen by those in this world as a nice and happy guy.

**Michael Bernstein** is an information architect who has been a member of the Zope development community since early 1999, and wrote the first community-contributed "How-To" for Zope in February of that year. Currently residing in Las Vegas, he has worked for two start-ups and has built and managed various content management systems and intranets using Zope. His interests include science fiction fandom, Open Source, and other self-organizing emergent phenomena.

# Acknowledgments

We'd like to thank our community technical editors, Tom Deprez and Michael Bernstein, as well as our Development Editors, Chris Zahn and Frederick Speers, our Executive Editor, Stephanie Wall, and all the production folks at New Riders. We would also like to thank our bosses, Paul Everitt, Jim Fulton, and Rob Page for paying us to write this book, and of course, Guido van Rossum, and the dudes at PythonLabs, for the best language ever. Props for good vibes go to Johnathon Corbett at LWN, Jon Udell at `Byte.com`, Isaac King for taking a bunch of screenshots, Stephan Richter for editing the first two chapters, Andy McKay for the Perl edits, and Chris McDonough and Evan Simpson 'cuz they're our heros. Thanks to SourceForge for hosting the book during development.

We received many comments and corrections from many people, but those who stand out are Tony Tocco, Graham Chiu, Li Dongfeng, Jimmie Houcin, Richard Moon, Adam Davis, Guillaume Cordina, Tom Baraniecki, S. Condit, Danny Yoo, Duncan Booth, Doug Crozier, Hernan Martinez Foffani, Donald Braman, Larry Albert, Shaun Patston, Felix Slager, David Shaw, Lee Hunter, Joseph Schlesinger, Felix Almonte, Aadjan van der Helm, Gene Christian, Olivier Deckmyn, Dwayne Morrison, Cary O'Brien, Peter Bengtsson, Steinar Eriksen, Edwin Martin, Olivier Deckmyn, Butch Landingin, Erik Enge, Brian Takashi Hooper, Martin Hansen, Keith Larson, Alain Meurant, Larry Albert, Kathy Hester, Joel Burton, Jim Washington, Charles Y. Choi, Mats Nygren, Rik Hoekstra, Paul Winkler, Martin Wehipeihana, Scott Burton, Lars Heber, and Darrell Gallion.

# Tell Us What You Think

As the reader of this book, you are the most important critic and commentator. We value your opinion and want to know what we're doing right, what we could do better, what areas you'd like to see us publish in, and any other words of wisdom you're willing to pass our way.

As an Executive Editor for the Web Development team at New Riders Publishing, I welcome your comments. You can fax, email, or write me directly to let me know what you did or didn't like about this book—as well as what we can do to make our books stronger.

Please note that I cannot help you with technical problems related to the topic of this book, and that due to the high volume of mail I receive, I might not be able to reply to every message.

When you write, please be sure to include this book's title and author as well as your name and phone or fax number. I will carefully review your comments and share them with the author and editors who worked on the book.

Fax:      317-581-4663
Email:    stephanie.wall@newriders.com
Mail:     Stephanie Wall
          Executive Editor
          New Riders Publishing
          201 West 103rd Street
          Indianapolis, IN 46290 USA

# Foreword

Zope thinks differently about a lot of the principles of Web application development. As a result, it's a uniquely powerful tool that has built a cult following. The problem has been that, like other deeply object-oriented systems, it's hard to figure out where to start. Everything's connected to everything else—and it all makes sense—but beginners lack the necessary frame of reference.

Those of us who sensed what Zope could do forged ahead, digging through mailing lists and the source code to put the pieces together. What would have helped, and what you have in this book, is an orientation guide. The authors walk you through a number of things that I had to learn the hard way: how to connect to Zope from a WebDAV client, when to write in Python versus DTML, and how to use the security apparatus.

There's much more to Zope than this book, or indeed any book, can hope to cover. When you get serious about Zope, you'll find yourself scouring mailing lists and source code too. But thanks to Amos and Michel, you'll have a much better sense of which questions to ask, where to look for answers, and how to make the best use of Zope's many strengths.

—Jon Udell, author, consultant, and Zope user

# Introduction

Welcome to *The Zope Book*. This book is designed to introduce you to Zope and its uses. Zope is an open-source Web application server. If you are interested in writing Web pages, programming Web scripts, using databases, managing content, or doing a collaborative Web development task, then you should read this book.

## Who Should Read This Book?

This book is meant to appeal to both current Zope users and people new to Zope:

- You don't need to be a programmer to read this book or to use Zope.
- You should have some idea of how the Web works; including a basic understanding of HTML and URLs.
- You should know what a Web browser and a Web server are and should have some idea of how they communicate.

The first part of this book explains how to use Zope through its Web management interface to manage dynamic content. The concepts in these chapters are fundamental Zope concepts that show you how to use Zope to publish content on the Web.

Some later sections of this book cover advanced topics, such as relational databases, scripting with various programming languages, and XML. These chapters don't teach relational databases, programming, or XML—they simply show you how to use these technologies with Zope.

## How This Book Is Organized

The organization of this book is presented in the following sections, as well as a brief summary of each chapter.

### Part I: Introducing Zope

These chapters get the reader up and running with Zope. You learn about basic Zope objects and idioms.

### Chapter 1: Introducing Zope

Chapter 1 explains what Zope is and who it's for. It describes in broad strokes what you can do with Zope. You also learn about the differences between Zope and other Web application servers.

## Chapter 2: Using Zope

Chapter 2 covers the most important Zope concepts. By the end of this chapter, you should be able to use Zope to create and manage simple yet powerful Web applications.

## Chapter 3: Using Basic Zope Objects

Chapter 3 introduces objects, which are the most important elements of Zope. In this chapter we cover what an object is in general, and then we introduce the basic Zope objects: folders, DTML documents, DTML methods, files, and images.

## Chapter 4: Dynamic Content with DTML

Chapter 4 introduces DTML, Zope's tag-based scripting language. In this chapter we describe DTML's use for templating and scripting and its place in relation to other ways to script Zope. We cover DTML syntax and the three most basic tags: `var`, `if`, and `in`. After reading this chapter, you'll be able to create dynamic Web pages.

## Chapter 5: Creating Basic Zope Applications

Chapter 5 walks the reader through several real-world examples of building a Zope application. It provides plenty of examples showing how to use Zope objects and how they can work together to form basic applications.

# Part II: Creating Web Applications with Zope

These chapters provide a more in-depth look at advanced Zope topics. They cover the material necessary to build real Web applications with Zope.

## Chapter 6: Users and Security

Chapter 6 looks at how Zope handles users, authentication, authorization, and other security-related matters. Security is central to Zope's design and should be central to the Web applications that you create with Zope.

## Chapter 7: Variables and Advanced DTML

Chapter 7 takes a closer look at DTML. It covers DTML security and the tricky issue of how variables are looked up in DTML. It also covers advanced uses of the basic tags covered in Chapter 3 and the myriad of special purpose tags. This chapter will turn you into a DTML wizard.

### Chapter 8: Advanced Zope Scripting

Chapter 8 covers scripting Zope with Python and Perl. In this chapter we cover how to write business logic in Zope using more powerful tools than DTML. It discusses the idea of scripts in Zope, and focuses on Python- and Perl-based scripts. This chapter shows you how to add industrial-strength scripting to your site.

### Chapter 9: Searching and Categorizing Content

Chapter 9 shows you how to index and search objects with Zope's built-in search engine, the Catalog. It introduces indexing concepts and discusses different patterns for indexing and searching. Finally, it discusses metadata and search results. This chapter shows you how to create a powerful and easy-to-use information architecture.

### Chapter 10: Relational Database Connectivity

Chapter 10 describes how Zope connects to external relational databases. It shows you how to connect to and query databases. It also covers features that allow you to treat relational data as though it were Zope objects. Finally, this chapter covers security and performance considerations.

## Part III: Developing Advanced Web Applications with Zope

The final part of this book deals with advanced topics. You learn how to scale your Web applications and extend Zope.

### Chapter 11: Scalability and ZEO

Chapter 11 covers issues and solutions for building and maintaining large Web applications, and focuses on issues of management and scalability. In particular, the Zope Enterprise Object (ZEO) is covered in detail. This chapter shows you the tools and techniques you need to turn a small site into a large-scale site, servicing millions of visitors.

### Chapter 12: Extending Zope

Chapter 12 covers extending Zope by creating your own classes of objects. It discusses ZClasses and how instances are built from classes. It describes step-by-step how to build a ZClass and attendant security and design issues. Finally, it discusses creating Python base classes for ZClasses and describes the base classes that ship with Zope. This chapter shows you how to take Zope to the next level, by tailoring Zope to your needs.

### Appendixes

The appendixes provide you with references for DTML and Zope APIs.

### Appendix A: DTML Reference

Appendix A covers all the DTML markup tags and their use.

### Appendix B: API Reference

Appendix B serves as a reference for the programming interfaces for the most common Zope objects.

### Appendix C: Zope Resources

Appendix C provides a list of useful Zope-related Web sites

### Appendix D: Open Publication License

Appendix D outlines the Open Publication License.

# Conventions Used in This Book

This book uses the following typographical conventions:

- *Italic*—Italics are used to introduce new terms and to indicate variables.
- `Monospace font`—Fixed-width text indicates commands, hyperlinks, and code listings.
- ➡—Code continuation characters are used in code listings that are too long to fit within the book's margins. They should not be used in actual implementation.

That about covers it. You should be ready to explore Zope! If you have comments after reading the book, we encourage you to write to us care of New Riders. This book is designed to get you up and running with Zope. Please let us know about ways we could improve it, and we will attempt to incorporate your suggestions in future editions of *The Zope Book*.

# I

# Introducing Zope

# 1

# Introducing Zope

THIS CHAPTER EXPLAINS WHAT ZOPE IS and who it's for. It describes in broad strokes what you can do with Zope. You also learn about the differences between Zope and other Web application servers.

## What Is Zope?

*Zope* is a framework for building Web applications. A *Web application* is a computer program that users access with a Web browser over the Internet. You can also think of a Web application as a dynamic Web site that provides not only static information to users, but enables them to use dynamic tools to work with an application.

Web applications are everywhere, and Web users work with them all the time. Common examples of Web applications are sites that enable you to search the Web, such as Yahoo, collaborate on projects, such as SourceForge, or communicate with other people over email, such as HotMail. All of these application types can be developed with Zope.

So what do you get when you download Zope? You actually get a lot of things. Zope consists of several different components that work together to help you build Web applications. Zope comes with:

- **A Web server**—Zope comes with a built-in Web server that serves content to you and your users. Of course, you might already have an existing Web server, such as Apache or Microsoft IIS, and you might not want to use Zope's. Not to worry, Zope works with these Web servers also, and any other Web server that supports the Common Gateway Interface (CGI).

- **A Web-based interface**—When you build Web applications with Zope, you use your Web browser to interact with the Zope management interface. This interface is a development environment that enables you to do things, such as create Web pages, add images and documents, connect to external relational databases and write scripts in different languages.

- **An object database**—When you work with Zope, you are mostly working with objects that are stored in Zope's object database. Zope's management interface provides a simple, familiar way to manage objects that resembles the way many common file managers work.

- **Relational integration**—You don't have to store your information in Zope's object database if you don't want to because Zope works with other relational databases, such as Oracle, PostgreSQL, Sybase, MySQL, and many others.

- **Scripting language support**—Zope enables you to write Web applications in a number of different languages, such as Python (`http://www.python.org/`), Perl (`http://www.perl.org/`), and Zope's own Document Template Markup Language (DTML).

These are just some of the compelling features that have made Zope so popular for developing Web applications. Perhaps Zope's best feature of all is its friendly, open source license. *Open source* means that not only is Zope free of cost for you to download, but you are also free to use Zope in your own products and applications without paying royalties or usage fees. Zope's open source license also means that all the "source code" for Zope is available for you to look at, understand, and extend. Zope does not lock you into a proprietary solution that could hold you and your Web users hostage.

From a business perspective, the three key ideas to understanding what Zope can do for you are powerful collaboration, simple content management, and Web components. The following sections are mostly oriented toward business people making decisions about Zope, so if you are interested in jumping right in, skip to Chapter 2, "Using Zope."

## Powerful Collaboration

Years ago, Zope's core technologies were designed by Zope Corporation for an Internet service provider that provided Web pages for newspapers. These newspapers in turn wanted to provide Web pages for their customers. To scale in this environment, Zope was designed to safely delegate control to different groups of users at any level in the Web site. Safely delegating control means considering the following:

- Presenting information in an easy-to-understand way. Most people understand clicking folders better than issuing database commands, so Zope uses an interface that resembles a simple file manager, such as Microsoft Windows Explorer and other popular file managers.

- Command-line tools can be difficult to use and people are generally more comfortable using Web browsers, so Zope was designed to be used almost exclusively through a Web browser.

- Collaborative environments require tools to enable users to recover from their mistakes and to work without interfering with each other, so Zope has Undo, Versions, and other tools to help people work safely together.

These features make Zope an ideal environment for programming and authoring Web content by groups and subgroups of users.

## Simple Content Management

Many Web applications are traditionally built in three layers. Data and other information is stored in databases, the programs that drive the behavior of the application are stored in files in one location, and the HTML and other layout and presentation information is stored somewhere else.

Although this has advantages, it also has disadvantages. Different kinds of tools and expertise must be used to work with the different components. The different components may have their own maintenance concerns and may need to have their own kind of security. Many of these tools are not manageable from a Web browser or from simple command-line or Graphical User Interface (GUI) tools, such as FTP.

In Zope, all of these components are brought together into one coherent system. The components require a common set of services: security, Web-based management, searching, clustering, syndication, and others. By bringing together these concepts into one manageable system, Zope enables you to use one set of skills and one set of tools to develop complex Web applications. In addition, centralizing our model means Zope can more easily work with other external tools, such as relational databases, GUI Web editors, and other systems that can inter-operate with Zope.

### Web Components

The Web is a growing, dynamic platform. The Web has evolved enough standards and APIs that creators of services, products, and technology can think in terms of the Web as an architectural model to develop their applications around instead of just a means of distributing static HTML documents to users.

The Web is becoming an architectural model, and evidence of this is sprouting up in many locations. Microsoft's .NET architecture envisions a world of Web components running on remote systems, providing specific services to applications around the world. Frontier, by UserLand Software, pioneered a simple Web services protocol called XML-RPC to enable Web components to communicate with each other (Zope also works with XML-RPC, which is discussed in Chapter 8, "Advanced Zope Scripting"). Because of Web components, the model of a person sitting in front of the browser is no longer the only model of the Web.

## Zope History

In 1996, Jim Fulton, the CTO of Zope Corporation and a Python guru, was drafted to teach a class on CGI programming, despite not knowing much about the subject. Jim studied all the existing documentation on CGI on his way to the class. On his way back from the class, Jim considered what he didn't like about traditional CGI-based programming environments—its fragility, lack of object-orientation, and how it exposes Web server details. From these initial musings, the core of Zope was written on the plane flight back from the class.

Zope Corporation went on to release three open source software packages to support Web publishing: Bobo, Document Template, and BoboPOS. These packages were written in Python. They have evolved into core components of Zope providing the Web Object Request Broker (ORB), DTML scripting language, and object database. Zope is still mostly written in Python with a few performance-critical sections in C.

In the beginning, Zope Corporation had developed a commercial application server based on their three open source components. This product was called Principia. In November of 1998, investor Hadar Pedahazur convinced Zope Corporation to open source Principia. This became Zope, which was given its own home at Zope.org (`http://www.zope.org/`).

## Who Can Benefit from Zope?

It takes a lot of people working together to create Web services. To manage and coordinate these people on large-scale sites can be a difficult task. We've identified some common roles in this scenario to be aware of:

- Consumers use the site to locate and work with useful content.
- Business users create and manage the site's content.
- Site designers create the site's look and feel.

- Site developers program the site's services.
- Component developers create software intended for distribution.
- Administrators keep the software and environment running.
- Information architects make platform decisions and keep track of the big picture.

Zope is a platform upon which site developers create services to be turned over to site designers and business users. Component developers distribute new products and services for Zope users worldwide.

Zope can install Zope products that are focused on different audiences. For instance, Squishdot is a popular Weblog, written in Zope, that is useful right out of the box. Squishdot users will not necessarily see that Zope is underneath. Other Zope products, such as Zope Corporation's Content Management Framework (http://cmf.zope.org), take the same approach—targeting audiences that need not know of Zope's existence underneath.

## How Can You Benefit from Zope?

We've looked at the Zope philosophy and architecture, now let's survey some of the applications of Zope. All sites solve different problems, but many sites tackle a set of common issues daily. Some of the main uses for Zope are as follows:

- **Present dynamic content**—You want to tailor your Web site's presentation to its users, integrate information in databases, and provide users with searching. You would also like to make your Web site automate and facilitate your business processes. Can your Web site react intelligently to visitors to provide a compelling experience? Zope enables you to make every page dynamic. It comes with facilities for personalization, integrating information in databases, and searching.

- **Manage your Web site**—A small Web site is easy to manage, but a Web site that serves thousands of documents, images, and files needs to provide powerful management tools. Can you manage your site's data, business logic, and presentation all in one place? Can you keep up with your content, or is it getting out of hand? Zope gives you simple and powerful tools for handling gigabytes of Web content. You can manage your logic, presentation, and data all from your Web browser.

- **Secure your Web site**—When you deal with more than a handful of Web users, security becomes very important. It is crucial to organize users and be able to safely delegate tasks to them. For example, folks in your engineering department might need to be able to manage their Web pages and business logic, designers might need to update site templates, and database administrators need to manage database queries. Can your system handle thousands of users, perhaps linked to your existing LDAP or other user databases, with flexible security rules? Zope enables you to scale your site to thousands of site managers and millions of visitors. You can simply control security policies and safely delegate control to others.

- **Provide network services**—Right now most Web sites serve users, but soon Web sites will need to serve remote computer programs and other Web sites. For example, you would like to make your news items automatically available to wire service Web sites. Or maybe you want to make products for sale on your site automatically searchable from a product comparison site. Can you leverage your existing data and business logic to create network services, or will you have to start over from scratch? Zope's built-in support for networking makes every Zope site a network service. Your business logic and data can be accessed over the Web via HTTP and XML-RPC.

- **Integrate diverse content**—Your content is strewn all over the place, in relational databases, files, Web sites, FTP archives, and XML—Can you unify your data into one coherent application? Does your system support Web standards so that you can integrate content from legacy systems and add new systems in the future? Zope supports Web standards enabling you to use your existing data, infrastructure, and file systems.

- **Provide scalability**—So you struck it rich and now you're getting more hits than you ever imagined. Now you need to handle a dramatically greater level of traffic than before. Can you move your site to a different database and server platform and spread the load across multiple servers? Can your Web site grow to handle your success? Zope enables your Web applications to scale across as many machines as necessary to handle your load. Zope makes it possible to maintain a small site that can turn into a huge site overnight based on its ZEO technology (see Chapter 11, "Scalability and ZEO," for more details).

## What Zope Gives You

Let's take a closer look at the Zope features that enable you to build and manage dynamic Web sites.

- **Unique management environment**—The first thing you'll notice about Zope is that it enables you to manage your site's data, logic, and presentation right in your Web browser. This means that Zope is easy to use and is remotely administrable. Zope enables you to collaborate with others to interactively develop your Web site.

- **Built-in tools**—Zope comes with site management tools, a Web server, a search engine, database connectivity, security, collaboration services, and more. Out of the box, Zope gives you everything you need to build a powerful Web site.

- **Open standards support**—Zope excels at gluing together diverse data because of its support for open standards. Zope supports Internet standards, including SQL, ODBC, XML, DOM, FTP, HTTP, FastCGI, XML-RPC, SOAP, and more.

■ **Open source licensing**—With Zope you don't just get an application, you get the source and a community. Because Zope is open source, you are not held hostage by a single vendor; you're free to use, distribute, and adapt Zope to fit your needs. Zope also benefits from an active user and developer community. The community improves Zope's support, audits Zope's security, fixes bugs, and adds features.

■ **Extensibility**—Zope can be extended in many directions. Third-party applications can be easily created and distributed. The Zope community has produced hundreds of Zope add-ons for everything from credit card processing to Web discussions.

We've supplied you with a quick overview of what Zope is able to provide. Let's look next at how Zope compares to other Web application servers.

# Zope Alternatives

Many tools are available to help you build Web applications. Early in the history of the Web, simple Web applications were built almost exclusively with CGI programs written in Perl or other languages. Now a host of options exist, ranging from open source frameworks, such as PHP, to commercial options, such as Allaire's Cold Fusion, Java Application Servers, and Vignette's Story Server.

Zope offers a unique mix of features, some similar to, and some very different from, features offered by other Web application tools. Zope is easy to use, open source, powerful, and provides support for many different kinds of applications. The following is a short list of common Web tool drawbacks and Zope's advantages:

■ Some tools do not offer a simple file manager, such as user interface, and are hard to use. Zope has a simple user interface.

■ Some tools require complex configuration. Zope is easy to install and requires no configuration before you begin using it.

■ Some tools require using unfamiliar and proprietary development tools. Zope works with any standards-compliant Web browser, and no other tools are required to use this book.

■ Some tools don't scale the way Zope does to handle large numbers of developers and users. Zope has a consistent, powerful user management system that can scale to many users with unique, easily managed privileges.

■ Finally, most closed-source, commercial tools don't let you extend, customize, and redistribute them. Zope is open source.

## Zope Community

Zope was one of the first tools of its kind to become open source. Since opening up the code to Zope, the user base has grown tremendously.

The Zope community consists of Zope users and developers. Many of the community members are professionals, such as consultants, developers, and Webmasters, who are investing their time and money into supporting Zope. Others are students and curious hackers, who are learning how to use a cool new tool. The community gets together occasionally at conferences but spends most of its time discussing Zope on the many Zope mailing lists and Web sites. You can find out more about the many Zope-related mailing lists at `http://www.zope.org/Resources/MailingLists`.

Now that you've learned about Zope's features and history, it's time to start using it. In Chapter 2, you'll learn how to get up and running with Zope. Because Zope is free, you can download the latest version and begin working immediately.

# 2

# Using Zope

THIS CHAPTER GETS YOU UP AND RUNNING WITH ZOPE. It guides you through installing and running Zope and covers the most important Zope concepts. By the end of this chapter, you should be able to use Zope to create and manage simple, yet powerful, Web applications.

## Downloading Zope

The first steps to using Zope are to download and install it. Zope is available for free from the Zope.org Web site (http://www.zope.org). The most recent stable version is always available from the Download section at Zope.org (http://www.zope.org/Products).

Zope is currently available as a binary for Windows, Linux, and Solaris. This means that you can just download and install it without having to compile any programs. For other platforms, you must download the source and compile Zope. Zope can be compiled and run on almost any UNIX-like operating system. As a general rule of thumb, if Python is available for your operating system and you have a C compiler, then you can probably use Zope.

# Installing Zope

You will install Zope differently, depending on your platform. If you are running a recent version of Linux, you might already have Zope installed. You can get Zope in both binary and source forms. Several different binary formats are also available.

## Installing Zope for Windows

Zope for Windows comes as a self-installing .exe file. To install Zope, double-click the .exe file. This launches an Installer that walks you through the installation process. Pick a name for your Zope installation and a directory in which to install it. Click Next, and create a new Zope user account. This account is called the initial user account. This creates an account that you can use to log into Zope for the first time. You can change this username and password later if you want.

If you are using Windows NT or Windows 2000, you can choose to run Zope as a service. Running Zope as a service is a good idea for a public server. If you are just running Zope for personal use, don't bother running it as a service. Keep in mind that if you are running Windows 95, Windows 98, or Windows ME (Millenium Edition), you cannot run Zope as a service.

If you decide to uninstall Zope later, you can use the Unwise.exe program in your Zope directory.

## Downloading Linux and Solaris Binaries

The following code shows how to download the binary for your platform and extract the tarball:

```
$ tar xvfz Zope-2.3.0-linux2-x86.tgz
```

In the previous example, you are downloading version 2.3.0. This might not be the most recent version of Zope when you read this, so be sure to get the latest stable version of Zope for your platform.

The following code unpacks Zope into a new directory. Enter the Zope directory and run the Zope Installer script:

```
$ cd Zope-2.3.0-linux2-x86
$ ./install
```

The Installer prints information as it installs Zope. Among other things, it creates an Initial User account. You can change the initial username and password later with the zpasswd.py script (see Chapter 6, "Users and Security").

The Installer configures Zope to run as your UNIX userid. If you prefer to run Zope as another userid, you can use the -u command-line switch and specify the user you want to configure Zope to run as. Many books on the market contain more information on userids and UNIX administration; in general, you should check out userids and UNIX administration if you want to do anything fancy. For now, things will work fine if you just install Zope as your user by not specifying any extra command-line options.

For more information on installing Zope, see the installation instructions in doc/INSTALL.txt, and find out more about the Installer script by running it with the following -h help switch:

```
$ ./install -h
```

## Getting Zope in RPM and deb Format

Zope Corporation doesn't make Zope available in RPM format, but other people do. Jeff Rush regularly packages Zope as RPMs. For more information, check out his Web page (http://starship.python.net/crew/jrush/Zope/). Zope is also available in the Debian Linux deb package format. You can find Zope deb packages at the Debian Web site (http://packages.debian.org/zope). Generally, the latest Zope releases are found in the unstable distribution.

## Compiling Zope from Source Code

If binaries aren't available for your platform, then chances are you can compile Zope from the source. To do this, install Python from your platform sources and make sure you have a C compiler. You can get Python from the Python Web site (http://www.python.org). Although we try to use the most recent Python for Zope, often the latest Python version is more recent than the version we "officially" support for Zope. For information on what version of Python you need to compile Zope, see the release notes on the Web page for each version.

The following code shows how to download the Zope source distribution and extract the tarball:

```
$ tar xvfz Zope-2.2.0-src.tgz
```

The previous example unpacks Zope into a new directory. In the following example, enter the Zope directory and run the Zope Installer script:

```
$ cd Zope-2.2.0-src
$ python wo_pcgi.py
```

The Installer compiles Zope and sets up your installation. The Installer prints information as it runs, including the initial username and password. It's important to write down that information so that you can log into Zope. For more information, see the installation instructions in the file doc/INSTALL.txt. Again, you can change the initial user account later with the zpasswd.py script (see Chapter 6).

# Starting Zope

Depending on your platform, Zope is run with different commands. Whatever your platform, you can either run Zope manually, or automatically. When running Zope manually, you simply tell Zope when to start and when to stop. When running Zope automatically, Zope starts and stops when your computer starts and stops.

## Starting Zope on Windows

The Installer creates a Zope directory with a batch file called start.bat. Double-click the start.bat icon. This opens a window that includes logging information. In this window, you find the port on which Zope is listening. You can now log into Zope with a Web browser.

If you are running Zope as a service, you can start and stop Zope via the Services Control Panel. Zope writes events to the event log so that you can keep track of when your service starts and stops. If you run Zope as a service, you must know what port Zope is running on because you will not have direct access to its detailed logging information.

Zope comes with its own Web server. When you start Zope, its Web server starts. If you want, you can connect Zope to your existing Web server, such as IIS, but that is beyond the scope of this book. The Zope Administrator's Guide covers this kind of material (`http://www.zope.org/DocProjects/AdminGuide`).

## Starting Zope on UNIX

Run the following Start script:

```
$ ./start &
```

Zope starts running and prints logging information to the console. You should see information telling you on which port Zope is listening. You can now log into Zope with a Web browser.

Zope comes with its own Web server. When you start Zope, its Web server starts. If you want, you can connect Zope to your existing Web server, such as Apache, but that is beyond the scope of this book. The Zope Administrator's Guide covers this kind of material (`http://www.zope.org/DocProjects/AdminGuide`).

The Start script can also be edited to start Zope with many different options. How to customize your Zope startup is also described in the Administrator's Guide.

# Logging In

To log into Zope you need a Web browser. Zope's interface is written entirely in HTML; therefore, any browser that understands modern HTML works. Mozilla, and any 3.0+ version of Microsoft Internet Explorer or Netscape Navigator, will do.

To log into the management interface, point your Web browser to Zope's management URL. The management URL for Zope is Zope's base URL with /manage appended. Assuming you have Zope installed on your local machine serving on the default port 8080, the management URL is

```
http://localhost:8080/manage
```

This URL usually works, but you might need to log in to a different machine than the one shown here. To find out exactly where to log into your URL, look at the logging information Zope prints as it starts up. For example:

```
- - -
2000-08-07T23:00:53 INFO(0) ZServer Medusa (V1.18) started at
➥Mon Aug  7 16:00:53 2000
        Hostname: peanut
        Port:8080


- - -
2000-08-07T23:00:53 INFO(0) ZServer FTP server started at
➥Mon Aug  7 16:00:53 2000
        Authorizer:None
        Hostname: peanut
        Port: 8021
```

The first log entry indicates Zope is running on a machine named `peanut` and that the Web server is listening on port `8080`. This means that the management URL is `http://peanut:8080/manage`.

After you enter Zope's management URL in your browser, your browser prompts you to provide a username and password. Type in the initial username and password created during the install process. If you don't know the initial username and password, then shut Zope down by closing its window, and change the initial user password with the zpasswd.py script and restart Zope. See Chapter 6 for more information about configuring the initial user account.

# Controlling Zope with the Management Interface

After you successfully log in, you see a Web page of the Zope management interface, as shown in Figure 2.1.

The Zope management interface enables you to control Zope within your Web browser.

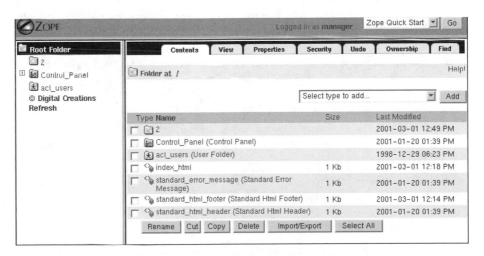

Figure 2.1    The Zope management interface.

## Using the Navigator

The Zope management interface is broken up into three frames. With the left frame, you navigate around Zope much like you would navigate around a file system with a file manager, such as Windows Explorer. This frame is called the Navigator, and it is shown in the left frame of Figure 2.1. In this frame, you see the Root folder and all its subfolders. The Root folder is in the upper-left corner of the tree. The Root folder is the "top" of Zope. Everything in Zope lives inside the Root folder.

Some of the folders have plus marks to the left of them. These plus marks enable you to expand the folders to see the subfolders that are inside.

Above the folder tree, Zope shows you login information. In this screenshot, you can see that you are currently logged in as manager. When you log in to Zope you will use the initial user account and you will see the name of this account in place of manager.

To manage a folder, click it, and it appears in the right frame of the browser window. This frame is called the Workspace.

## Using the Workspace

The right frame of the management interface shows the object you are currently managing. When you first log onto Zope, the current object is the Root folder, as shown in the right frame of Figure 2.1. The Workspace gives you information about the current object and enables you to change it.

Across the top of the screen are a number of tabs. The currently selected tab is highlighted in a lighter color. Each tab takes you to a different view of the current object. Each view enables you to perform a different management function on that object.

In Figure 2.1, you are looking at the Contents view of the Root folder object.

Another feature of the Workspace is a description of the current object's type and URL. Just below each tab is an icon representing the current object's type. The object's URL is next to that icon.

In Figure 2.1, Folder at / tells you that the current object is a folder and that its URL is /. Note that this URL is the object's URL relative to Zope's base URL. So, if the URL or your Zope site was http://mysite.example.com:8080, then the URL of the Folder at /myFolder would be http://mysite.example.com:8080/myFolder.

As you explore different Zope objects, you find that the URLs (as displayed in the management screen) can be used to navigate between objects.

For example, if you are managing a folder at /Zoo/Reptiles/Snakes, you can return to the folder /Zoo by clicking the word "Zoo" in the folder's URL.

The last frame is the uppermost top frame in Zope. This contains a pull-down box that enables you to select:

- **Preferences**—Here, you can set a default preference for your Zope session, and you can even set it to hide the top frame.

- **Logout**—Selecting this menu item logs you out of Zope.
- **Quick Start Links**—These are quick links out to Zope documentation and community resources.

# Understanding Users in Zope

Zope is a multi-user system. You've already seen how you can log into Zope via the management interface with the initial username and password. Zope supports other kinds of users:

- **Emergency User**—The Emergency User is rarely used in Zope. This account is used for creating other user accounts and fixing things if you accidentally lock yourself out. The Emergency User is both very powerful and very weak. It is not restricted by most security controls. However, the Emergency User can only create one type of object—Users. Using the Emergency User to repair your Zope system in the case of accidental lockout is discussed in the Administrator's Guide (http://www.zope.org/DocProjects/AdminGuide).

- **Manager**—The Manager is the Zope workhorse. You need to log in with the Manager account to do most of the work involved with building Zope Web sites. The initial user is a Manager, and you can create as many Manager accounts as you need.

- **Others**—You can create your own kind of users that fit into groups or are responsible for carrying out a role that you define. This is explained more in Chapter 6, which discusses Zope security and users.

## Creating Users

Managers can create Zope users in a unique kind of folder called a User folder.

User folder icons look like folders with a person on them. User folders always have the name acl_users, as shown in Figure 2.1.

Click the acl_users folder in the Root folder to enter it. User folders contain User objects. You can create new users and edit existing users. Click the Add button to create a new user, as shown in Figure 2.2.

Fill out the form to create a new user. In the Name field, put your chosen username. Choose a password and enter it in the Password and (Confirm) fields. Leave the Domains field blank. This is an advanced feature and is discussed in Chapter 6. Select the Manager role from the Roles select list. Then click the Add button.

Congratulations, you just created a Manager account. Zope shows you this new Manager account inside the User folder. Later, you can change or delete this user if you want.

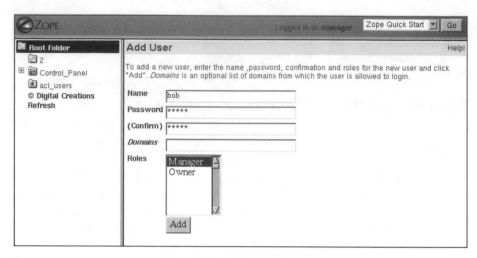

**Figure 2.2**   Adding a new user.

### Changing Logins

To change your login, you must completely exit all instances of your Web browser and then restart your browser and log in with the new authentication information. This cumbersome procedure is unfortunately necessary because most browsers cache authentication information.

To log in as your new user, quit your browser, restart it, and log in using the username and password of the Manager that has just been created.

## Understanding Objects in Zope

Zope is built on the concepts of objects and folders. The next two sections address this fundamental aspect of the way Zope works.

### Creating Objects

The Zope management interface represents everything in terms of objects and folders. When you build Web applications with Zope, you spend most of your time creating and managing objects in folders. For example, to make a new Manager account, you create a User object in a User folder.

Return to the Root folder by clicking the top-left folder in the Navigator frame.

To add a new object to the current folder, select an object from the pull-down menu labeled Select Type to Add... This pull-down menu is called the Product Add List.

For example, to create a folder, select Folder from the pull-down menu. At this point, you are taken to an Add form that collects information about the new folder, as shown in Figure 2.3.

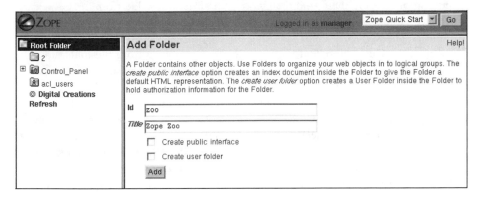

**Figure 2.3**    The Add Form folder.

Type zoo in the Id field, and Zope Zoo in the *Title* field. Then click the Add button.

Zope creates a new folder in the current folder. You can verify this by noting that a new folder named zoo is inside the Root folder.

Click the zoo folder to enter it. Notice that the URL of the folder is based on the folder's id. You can create more folders inside your new folder if you want. For example, create a folder inside the zoo folder with an id of arctic. Go to the zoo folder and choose Folder from the pull-down menu. Then type in arctic for the folder id, and Arctic Exhibit for the title. Now click the Add button. You always create new objects in the same way:

1. Go to the folder where you want to add a new object.

2. Choose the type of object you want to add from the pull-down menu.

3. Fill out an Add form and submit it.

4. Zope creates a new object in the current folder.

Notice that every Zope object has an id that you need to specify on the Add form when you create the object. The id is how Zope names objects. Objects also use their ids for their URLs.

Objects also use their ids for their URLs, for example:

```
http://localhost:8080/zoo/arctic/
```

is the URL to the artic folder.

Chapter 3, "Using Basic Zope Objects," covers all the basic Zope objects and what they can do for you.

## Moving Objects

Most computer systems enable you to move files around in directories with cut, copy, and paste. Zope has a similar system that enables you to move objects around in folders by cutting or copying them, and then pasting them to a new location.

To experiment with copy and paste, create a new folder in the Root folder with an id of bears. Then select bears by checking the check box just to the left of the folder. Then click the Cut button. Cut removes the selected objects from the folder and places them on a clipboard. The object does not, however, disappear from its location until it is pasted somewhere else.

Now enter the zoo folder by clicking it, and then enter the arctic folder by clicking it. You could also have used the Navigator to get to the same place. Now, click the Paste button to paste cut object(s) into the current folder. You should see the bears folder appear in its new location. You can verify that the folder has been moved by going to the Root folder and noting that bears is no longer there.

Copy works similarly to Cut. When you paste copied objects, the original objects are not changed. Select the object(s) you want to copy and click the Copy button. Then navigate to another folder and click the Paste button.

You can cut and copy folders that contain other objects and move many objects at one time with a single cut and paste. For example, go to the zoo folder and copy the arctic folder. Now paste it into the zoo folder. You will now have two folders inside the zoo folder, arctic and copy_of_arctic. If you paste an object into the same folder where you copied it, Zope changes the id of the pasted object. This is a necessary step because you cannot have two objects with the same id in the same folder.

To rename the copy_of_arctic folder, select the folder by checking the check box to the left of the folder. Then click the Rename button. This takes you to the Rename Items form as shown in Figure 2.4.

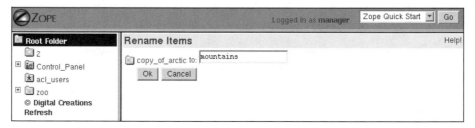

**Figure 2.4**    Renaming an object.

Type in a new id mountains and click OK. Zope ids can consist of letters, numbers, spaces, dashes, underscores and periods, and they are case-sensitive. Here are some legal Zope ids: index.html, 42, and Snake-Pit.

Now your zoo folder contains an arctic and a mountains folder. Each of these folders contains a bears folder. This is because when we made a copy of the arctic folder, it also copied the bears folder that it contained.

If you want to delete an object, select it and then click the Delete button. Unlike cut objects, deleted objects are not placed in the clipboard and cannot be pasted. In the next section, we'll see how we can retrieve deleted objects.

Zope does not allow you to cut, delete, or rename a few particular objects in the Root folder. These objects include Control_Panel, standard_html_header, standard_html_footer, and standard_error_message. These important objects are necessary for Zope's operation. Also, these operations don't work in some cases. For instance, you can't paste a User object into a regular folder.

If you are having problems with copy and paste, make sure that you have enabled cookies in your browser. Zope uses cookies to keep track of the objects that you cut and copy.

## Undoing Mistakes

Any action in Zope that causes objects to change can be undone via the Undo tab. You can recover from mistakes by undoing them.

Select the zoo folder that we created earlier and click Delete. The folder disappears. You can get it back by undoing the delete action.

Click the Undo tab, as shown in Figure 2.5.

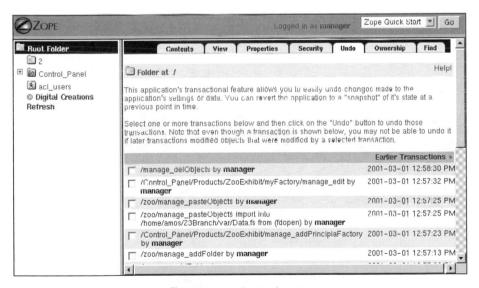

**Figure 2.5**   The Undo view.

Select the first transaction labeled /manage_delObjects, and click the Undo tab.

This action tells Zope to undo the last transaction. You can verify that the task has been completed by making sure that the zoo folder has returned.

### Undo Details and Gotchas

Undo works on the object database that Zope uses to store all Zope objects. Changes to the object database happen in transactions. You can think of a transaction as any change you make to Zope, such as creating a folder or pasting a bunch of objects to a new place. Each transaction describes all the changes that happen in the course of performing the action.

You cannot undo a transaction that a later transaction depends upon. For example, if you paste an object into a folder and then delete an object in the same folder, you might wonder whether or not you can undo the earlier paste. Both transactions change the same folder so that you can not simply undo the earlier transaction. The solution is to undo both transactions. You can undo more than one transaction at a time by selecting multiple transactions on the Undo tab and then clicking Undo.

Another problem to be aware of is that you cannot undo an undo. Therefore, if you add a folder and then undo that particular action, you cannot get the new folder back by undoing the undo.

One last note on undo. Only changes to objects stored in Zope can be undone. If you have integrated data in a relational database server, such as Oracle or MySQL (as discussed in Chapter 10, "Relational Database Connectivity"), changes to data stored there cannot be undone.

## Administering and Monitoring Zope

The Control Panel is an object in the Root folder that controls various aspects of Zope's operation.

Click the Control_Panel object in the Root folder, as shown in Figure 2.6.

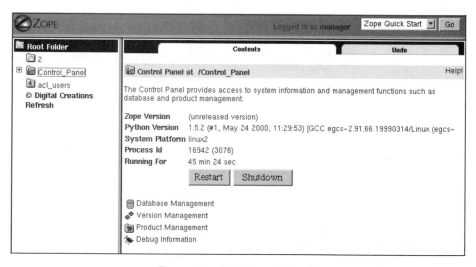

Figure 2.6   The Control Panel.

To shut down Zope, click the Shutdown button. Shutting down Zope causes the server to stop handling requests and completely removes Zope from memory. You have to manually start Zope to continue using it. Only shut down Zope if you are finished using it and have the ability to access the server on which Zope is running so that you can manually restart it later.

If you are running Zope on UNIX under daemon control or as a service on Windows, you can restart Zope from the Control Panel folder. Clicking the Restart button shuts down Zope and then immediately starts up a new instance of the Zope server. It might take Zope a few seconds to come back up and start handling requests.

On the Control Panel you will also see several links at the bottom of the screen, one of which is Database Management.

Transactions don't go away until you pack the Zope database. This means that you can undo all transactions except ones that have been removed by packing the database. When you choose to pack the database, you can specify what transactions to remove so that you can, for example, only remove transactions older than a week.

# Using the Help System

Zope has a built-in Help system. Every management screen has a Help button in the upper right-hand corner. This button launches another browser window and takes you to the Zope Help system.

Go to the Root folder. Click the Help button, and you should see what is shown in Figure 2.7.

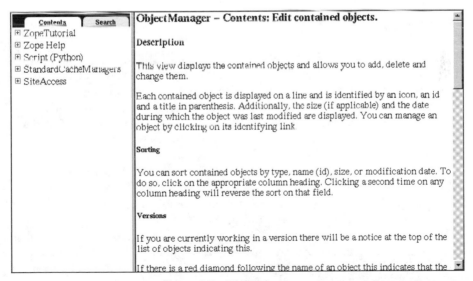

**Figure 2.7**    The Help system.

The Help system, like the Zope management interface, is divided into two frames—one for navigation and one for displaying the current topic.

When you click the Help button from the Zope management screen, the right frame of the Help system displays the help topic for the current management screen. In this case, you see information about the Contents view of a folder.

### Browsing and Searching Help

Normally, you use the Help system to get help on a specific topic. However, you can browse through all the help content if you are curious or want to find out about things besides the management screen you are currently viewing.

The Help system enables you to browse all the help topics in the Contents tab of the left help frame (refer to Figure 2.7). You can expand and contract help topics. To view a help topic in the right frame, click it.

All help on the Zope management screens is located in the Zope Help folder. Inside you'll find many help topics. You'll also find a Help folder called API Reference. This folder contains help on scripting Zope, which is explained further in Chapter 8, "Advanced Zope Scripting."

When you install third-party components, they also include help that you can browse. Each installed component has its own Help folder.

Search the Help system by clicking the Search tab and entering one or more search terms. For example, to find all the help topics that mention folders, type `folder` into the search form.

## Starting with the Zope Tutorial

Zope comes with a built-in tutorial. The tutorial guides you through all the basics of creating and managing Zope objects. To launch the tutorial, add a Zope Tutorial to the current folder by selecting Zope Tutorial from the Product Add List. The tutorial comes with several examples that you can change and copy for your own use.

If you start the tutorial and want to stop using it before you have completed all the lessons, you can later return to the tutorial. Just go to the Help system and find the lesson you would like to continue with by browsing the Zope Tutorial Help folder. You do not need to reinstall the tutorial.

If you are having problems with the tutorial, make sure to enable cookies in your browser. The tutorial uses cookies to keep track of where your example objects are. Also, if you enable JavaScript in your browser, the tutorial makes sure that the Zope management interface stays in sync with your tutorial lesson.

Now that you have Zope running, it's time to explore the system more thoroughly. You've seen how to manage Zope through the Web and have learned a little about Zope objects. In Chapter 3, you are introduced to many different Zope objects and you learn how to build simple applications with them.

# 3

# Using Basic Zope Objects

**W**HEN BUILDING A WEB APPLICATION WITH ZOPE, you construct the application out of objects. By design, different objects handle different parts of your application. Some objects hold your content data, such as word processor documents, spreadsheets, and images. Some objects control the way dynamic Web content is generated, such as how to accept input from a Web form or send email. Some objects control the way your content is displayed or presented to your viewer. In general, Zope objects take three types of roles:

- **Content**—Zope objects, such as documents, images, and files hold different kinds of textual and binary data. In addition to objects in Zope containing content, Zope can work with content stored externally, for example, in a relational database.

- **Logic**—Zope has facilities for scripting business logic. Zope allows you to script behavior using Python, Perl, and SQL. *Business logic* is any kind of programming that does not involve presentation, but rather involves carrying out tasks—such as changing objects, sending messages, testing conditions, and responding to events.

- **Presentation**—You can control the look and feel of your site with Zope objects that act as Web templates. Zope comes with a tag-based scripting language called the *Document Template Markup Language* (DTML) to control presentation.

The word *object* is a heavily loaded term. Depending on your background, it might mean any number of things. In this chapter, you can think of a Zope object as a piece of software that you can control and edit using a Web browser.

Zope comes with many built-in objects that help you perform different tasks. You can also install third-party Zope objects to expand Zope's capabilities. This chapter explains the most basic objects and how they work. You can create fully functional Zope sites using the few basic objects that are covered in this chapter.

This chapter is loosely structured around these three categories: content, logic, and presentation. Other kinds of objects in Zope that don't clearly fit into one of these three roles are explained at the end of the chapter (see "Virtual Hosting Objects").

# Using Zope Folders

*Folders* are the building blocks of Zope. The purpose of a folder is to contain other objects and to organize objects by separating them into different groups.

Folders can contain all sorts of objects, including other folders, so you can nest folders inside each other to form a tree of folders. This kind of folder within a folder arrangement provides your Zope site with *structure*. Good structure is very important, as almost all aspects of Zope (from security to behavior to presentation) are influenced by your site's folder structure.

Folder structure should be familiar to anyone who has worked with files and folders on their computer with a file manager program, such as Microsoft Windows Explorer or any one of the popular UNIX file managers, such as xfm, kfm, or the Gnome file manager. Zope tries to look like these popular programs so that you are familiar with how to organize Zope objects, which is the same way you organize files on your computer.

## Managing Folder Contents

In Chapter 2, "Using Zope," you created objects and moved objects around. In summary, you create objects in folders by choosing the name of the object you are looking for from the pull-down menu at the top of the folder's Contents view. Then you fill out the Add form and submit it. A new object is then added to the current folder. You can move objects between folders by using the cut, copy, paste, delete, and rename controls.

## Importing and Exporting Objects

You can move objects from one Zope system to another using *export* and *import*. You can export all types of Zope objects to an *export file*. This file can then be imported into any other Zope system.

You can think of exporting an object as cloning a piece of your Zope system into a file that you can then move around from machine to machine. You can take this file and graft the clone onto any other Zope server. Imagine you had some documents in a Zope folder. If you wanted to copy just those objects to your friend's Zope system, you could export the folder and send the export file by email to the friend, who could then import it.

Suppose you have a folder for homework that you want to export from your school Zope server and take it with you to work on at your home Zope server. You can create a folder in your Root folder called homeWork. Go to the folder that contains your homeWork folder. Select the homeWork folder by checking the check box next to it. Then click the Import/Export button. You should now be working in the Import/Export folder view, as shown in Figure 3.1.

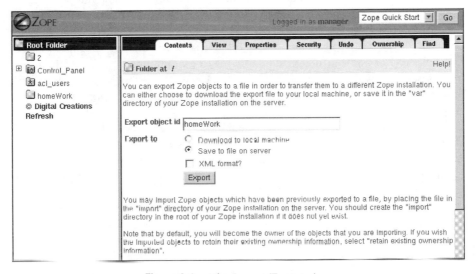

**Figure 3.1**    The Import/Export view.

This screen has two sections. The upper half is the export section and the lower half is the import section. To export an object from this screen, type the id of the object into the Export object id field. In our case, Zope already filled this field in for us because we selected the homeWork folder on the last screen.

The next option lets you choose between downloading the export file to your computer or leaving it on the server. If you check Download to local machine and click the Export button, your Web browser prompts you to download the export file. If you check Save to file on server, then Zope saves the file to the same machine on which Zope is running, and you must fetch the file from that location yourself. The export file is written to Zope's var directory on your server.

In general, it's handier to download the export file to your local machine. Sometimes it's more convenient to save the file to the server instead—for example, if you are on a slow link and the export file is very large, or if you are just trying to move the exported object to another Zope instance on the same computer.

The final export form element is the XML format check box. Checking this box exports the object in the eXtensible Markup Language (XML) format. Leaving this box unchecked exports the file in Zope's binary format. The XML format is much bigger to download, but it is humanly readable and XML parsable. For now, the only tool that understands this XML format is Zope, but in the future there might be other tools that can understand Zope's XML format. In general, you should leave this box unchecked unless you're curious about what the XML format looks like and you want to examine it by hand.

Click the Export button and save your homeWork.zexp export file.

Now, suppose that you've gone home and want to import the file into your home Zope server. First, you must copy the export file into the import directory of your Zope installation. This directory can be found on the computer where Zope is installed. This differs from computer to computer, so if you are not sure, check Zope's Control Panel or ask your system administrator to explain where to put the import file. Now, go to the Import/Export view of the folder where you want to perform the import. Enter the name of the export file in the Import file name form element and click Import to import those objects into Zope.

Zope gives you the option to either Take ownership of imported object or Retain existing ownership information. Ownership is discussed more in Chapter 6, "Users and Security." For now, just leave the Take Ownership button checked.

After you import the file you should have a new object in the Zope folder where you performed the import.

To bring your homework back to school, perform the same export and import procedure. Note that you cannot import an object into a folder that has an existing object with the same id. Therefore, when you bring your homework back to school, you'll need to import it into a folder that doesn't already have a homeWork folder in it. Then, you'll need to delete your old homeWork folder and copy the newly imported one into its place.

# Using Zope Documents

Documents hold text. In Web applications, you generally use documents to create Web pages. You can also use documents to hold text files, snippets of text, or HTML code, such as sidebars or headers. In addition to containing text, a document allows you to edit the text through the Web. Zope has several different types of documents. The most important is that of the DTML document.

Use DTML documents to create Web pages and sections of documents, such as sidebars that can be shared by Web pages. DTML documents can contain scripting commands in DTML (Zope's tag-based scripting language). The mix of HTML and DTML generates dynamic Web pages.

Other document types are available as Zope add-ons and allow you to manage other types of text. This chapter explores the most common Zope document—the DTML document. You can get other, third-party document types from Zope.org.

## Creating DTML Documents

Create a folder called Sales in the Root folder. Then, click the Sales folder and select DTML Document from the Add list you learned about in Chapter 2. This process takes you to the Add form for a DTML document. Specify the id SalesStaff and the title The Jungle Sales Staff and click Add. You have successfully created a DTML document.

## Editing DTML Documents

The easiest and quickest way to edit a DTML document is through the Web management interface. To select a document, click its name or icon, which brings up the form shown in Figure 3.2.

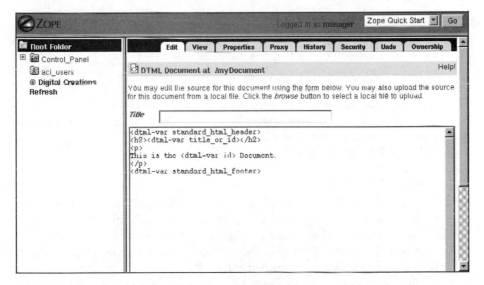

**Figure 3.2**    Editing a DTML document.

This view shows a text area in which you can edit the content of your document. If you click the Change button, you make effective any changes you made in the text area. If you were to scroll farther down on the page you would see buttons that allow you to control the size of the text area. They include the Taller, Shorter, Wider, and Narrower buttons. You can also upload a new file into the document with the File text box and the Upload File button.

Delete the default content that is automatically inside the current SalesStaff DTML document.

Add the following HTML content to the SalesStaff document:

```
<html>
<body>
<h2>Jungle Sales Staff</h2>

<ul>
  <li>Tarzan</li>
  <li>Cheetah</li>
  <li>Jane</li>
</ul>
</body>
</html>
```

After you have completed the changes to your document, click the Change button. Zope returns with a message telling you that your changes have taken effect. Now you can look at the document by clicking the View tab.

Congratulations! You've just used Zope to create an HTML page. You can edit your HTML online and view it immediately. In fact, you can create entire Zope sites with HTML documents and folders. This process just shows the surface of Zope's benefits, but it provides a good way to familiarize yourself with Zope. You can also write some dynamic content in Zope and let those who are interested purely in design, edit their own HTML Web pages in this way.

### Uploading an HTML File

Suppose you prefer not to edit your HTML files in a Web browser, or you have some existing HTML pages that you would like to bring into Zope. Zope allows you to upload your existing text files and convert them to DTML documents.

Select Add DTML Document from the Add menu. This takes you to the Add form for DTML documents. The last form element on the Add form is the Browse button. Click this button. Your browser then pops up a file selection dialog box. Select the text file on your computer that you want to upload to this document.

Type in an id for the new document and click Add. After clicking Add, you are taken back to the management screen where you your new document is.

### Remote Editing with FTP, WebDAV, and PUT

Zope enables you to edit documents directly in your Web browser, although this is not the only way documents can be edited in Zope. For simple documents, editing through the Web is a handy method. But for large, complex documents—or documents that have special formatting—it's useful to be able to use the editor you are most used to.

DTML documents can be edited with FTP, WebDAV, and the HTTP PUT protocol. Many HTML and text editors support these protocols for editing documents on remote servers. Each of these protocols has advantages and disadvantages:

- **FTP**—This is the File Transfer Protocol. FTP is used to transfer a file from one computer to another. Many text editors support FTP, so it is very useful.

- **WebDAV**—This is a new Internet protocol based on the Web's underlying protocol—HTTP. DAV stands for Distributed Authoring and Versioning. Because DAV is new, it might not be supported by as many text editors as FTP.

- **PUT**—This HTTP protocol supports a simple way to upload content to a server called PUT. PUT is supported by many HTML editors, such as Netscape Composer.

Using one of these methods, you can edit your content with a variety of tools. In the next couple sections, we show you a couple of simple tools that use FTP to edit Zope content.

### Uploading Documents and Files with WS_FTP

*WS_FTP* is a popular FTP client for Windows that you can use to upload documents and files into Zope with the FTP protocol. WS_FTP can be downloaded from the Ipswitch home page (`http://www.ipswitch.com/`).

Other popular Windows FTP clients exist, and many Web browsers, such as Netscape and Microsoft Internet Explorer, also come with FTP clients. This section applies to other FTP clients as well.

In Chapter 2, you determined the URL of your Zope system by looking at the start up log. To find out how to contact your Zope FTP server, you follow a similar process:

```
      - - -
        2000-00-07T23:00:53 INFO(0) ZServer Medusa (V1.18) started at
  Mon Aug  7 16:00:53 2000
                  Hostname: peanut
                  Port:8080


      - - -
        2000-08-07T23:00:53 INFO(0) ZServer FTP server started at
  Mon Aug  7 16:00:53 2000
                  Authorizer:None
                  Hostname: peanut
                  Port: 8021

      - - -
```

The startup log says that the Zope FTP server is listening to port 8021 on the machine named peanut. When you start WS_FTP, you need to know the machine name and port information so that you can connect to Zope via FTP. After typing in the machine name and port of your Zope server, hit the Connect button. WS_FTP now asks you for a username and password. Enter your management username and password for the Zope management interface.

If you type in your username and password correctly, WS_FTP shows you what your Zope site looks like through FTP. Folders and documents that correspond exactly to what your Root Zope folder looks like through the Web are shown in Figure 3.3.

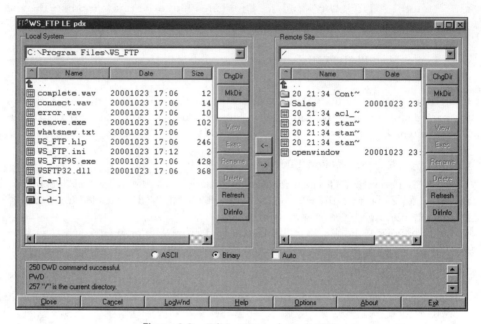

**Figure 3.3**    Editing Zope through FTP.

Transferring files to and from Zope is an easy task with WS_FTP. On the left side of the WS_FTP window is a file selection box that represents files on your local machine. The file selection box on the right side of the WS_FTP window represents objects in your Zope system. Transferring files from your computer to Zope, or back again, is as easy as selecting the file you want to transfer and clicking either the left arrow (download) or the right arrow (upload). WS_FTP has many cool features and customizations that you can use to make remote object management with Zope very easy.

### Editing Zope Objects with Emacs

Emacs is a very popular text editor. In fact, Emacs is more than just a text editor, it is a whole culture. Emacs comes in two flavors, GNU Emacs and XEmacs. Both of these can work directly over FTP to manipulate Zope documents and other textual content.

Emacs enable you to treat any remote FTP system like any other local file system, making remote management of Zope content an easy process. Therefore, you do not need to leave Emacs to use Zope.

Emacs provides a richer set of text-editing capabilities than most Web browser text areas. Emacs can be used to directly edit documents and manipulate objects through FTP; therefore, Emacs provides a nice Zope development environment.

By default when you start up Zope, Zope runs an FTP server—just as it runs an HTTP server. You can specify when you start Zope what port the FTP server should listen on, but by default this port is 8021.

To log into Zope, run Emacs. The file you use to open an FTP connection depends on which text editor you are running, XEmacs or Emacs:

- **XEmacs**—To visit a remote file in XEmacs, visit a file with this form:

`/user@server#port:/`

This opens a connection to the / folder of the FTP server running on `server` and listening on port `port`.

- **Emacs**—To visit a remote file in Emacs, visit a file by this form:

`/user@server port:/`

The literal space is inserted by holding down the Control key and the Q key, and then pressing the spacebar.

For the typical Zope installation with XEmacs, the filename to open up an FTP session with Zope is `/user@localhost#8021:/`.

Emacs asks you for a password to log into Zope's FTP server.

If you visit the / folder of an FTP server in Zope, Emacs lists the contents of the Root folder:

```
            drwxrwx—·   1 Zope      Zope              0 Dec 30   1998 Control_Panel
            drwxrwx—·   1 Zope      Zope              0 Dec 30   1998 QuickStart
            drwxrwx—·   1 Zope      Zope              0 Dec 30   1998 Sales
            -rw-rw——    1 Zope      Zope           1024 May  3   1999 index_html
            -rw-rw——    1 Zope      Zope           1381 May  3   1999
standard_error_message
            -rw-rw——    1 Zope      Zope             55 Dec 30   1998
standard_html_footer
            -rw-rw——    1 Zope      Zope             81 Dec 30   1998
standard_html_header
```

You can visit any of these files (which are really Zope objects) by selecting them in the usual Emacs way. Editing with Emacs is very useful, but for the most part, Emacs is a very complex program that is not very accessible to most people. Most Macintosh users, for example, would be very unfamiliar with a tool such as Emacs. A number of easier editors can be used that also use FTP and WebDAV. WebDAV is, in fact, designed to be used by more design-oriented tools, such as Adobe GoLive and Macromedia Dreamweaver.

### Editing DTML Documents with WebDAV

WebDAV is a newer Internet protocol compared to HTTP or FTP, so fewer clients support it. However, a lot of momentum is behind the WebDAV movement and more clients are being developed all the time. For more information on what programs support the WebDAV protocol, see the WebDAV home page (`http://www.webdav.org/`).

WebDAV is an extension to the HTTP protocol that provides rich features for many users concurrently authoring and editing content on Web sites. WebDAV offers features, such as locking, revision control, and tagging documents or objects with properties. Because WebDAV's goal of editing through the Web matches some of the goals of Zope, Zope has supported the WebDAV protocol for quite a while.

The WebDAV protocol is evolving quickly and new features are being added all the time. For Zope version 2.3, you can use any WebDAV client to edit your DTML documents by pointing the client at your document's URL and editing it. For most clients, however, this causes them to try to edit the result of the rendered document instead of the source. For documents that use Zope's DTML template language to render dynamic content, this can be a problem.

Until clients catch up to the latest WebDAV standard and understand the difference between the source of a document and its result, Zope 2.3 offers a special HTTP server you can enable with a z2.py command-line option. This server listens on a different port than your normal HTTP server and returns different, special source content for WebDAV requests that come in on that port. This is an advanced feature and is explained more in the Documentation section at Zope.org (`http://www.zope.org/ Documentation/`).

## Reviewing Changes to Documents

The Undo tab lets you undo one transaction at a time, but often it is useful to only undo the change to one object. Remember, a transaction can be a group of actions all taken at the same time. If a document was edited in a transaction that also included moving an object, you might just want to undo the change to the document, but not undo moving the file. To do that, you can go to that object's History view and look at the previous states of the object, as shown in Figure 3.4.

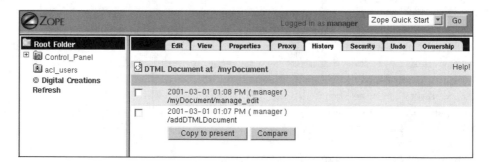

**Figure 3.4**   The History view.

Documents support the idea of comparing revisions, allowing you to track changes to your objects. For example, DTML methods and documents allow you to select two revisions and compare them to one another. You might want to use this to see what people have done to your object. For example, let's say you had a document that contained a list of all the animals in a zoo. If one of your coworkers goes and edits that list and saves it, you can use the history comparison feature to compare the most recent *new* version of the file with the next most recent version.

This comparison is displayed in a popular format called diff. The *diff* shows you the lines that have been added to the new document (with a plus sign), which lines have been subtracted from the old document (with a minus sign), and which lines have been replaced or changed (with an exclamation point).

## Viewing DTML Documents

The primary purpose of a DTML document is to hold useful content. This content's primary usage is to be viewed. DTML documents can be viewed several different ways:

- **Management interface**—From the management interface, you can click a document's View tab to view the contents of the document.
- **Calling directly through the web**—Documents can be called directly through the Web by going to their URL location with a Web browser.
- **Called by another object**—Other objects, especially other DTML objects, can display a document's contents.

### Calling Through the Web

Like all Zope objects, a DTML document's URL is based on its id. For example, if you have a DTML document in the Root folder called Bob, then its URL would be

```
http://localhost:8080/Bob
```

If Bob is in a subfolder called Uncles, its URL would be

```
http://localhost:8080/Uncles/Bob
```

There could also be other DTML documents in the Uncles folder called Rick, Danny, and Louis. You access them through the Web similarly:

```
http://localhost:8080/Uncles/Rick
http://localhost:8080/Uncles/Danny
http://localhost:8080/Uncles/Louis
```

Translating URLs to objects isn't a new idea—Web servers, such as Apache, do it all the time—they translate URLs to files and directories on a file system. Zope carries this simple idea to greater heights. In Zope, URLs are always simple to read because they map easily and simply onto the way objects are organized in Zope. This is why we said that your site's structure is key to your site's success.

Going directly to the URL of a DTML document is called *calling it through the web*. This causes the content of the DTML document to be evaluated and returned to your Web browser. In Chapter 4, "Dynamic Content with DTML," we see what it means for DTML to be evaluated—but for now, you can easily experiment with DTML and simple HTML content to get the idea.

### Calling from Another Object

Several times throughout this chapter you have seen the following code:

```
<dtml-var standard_html_header>

  <h1>This is some simple HTML</h1>

<dtml-var standard_html_footer>
```

Here we see that one DTML object, standard_html_header, is being called by the document that contains this code. In this case, the evaluated contents of the first document are inserted into the contents of this calling document. This is a very fundamental concept in Zope and is used throughout this book.

# Using Zope Files

Zope files contain raw data, just as the files on your computer do. Lots of information, such as software, audio, video, and documents are transported around the Internet and the world as files. You can use files to hold any kind of information that Zope doesn't specifically support, such as Flash files, applets, tarballs, and so forth.

Files do not consider their contents to be of any special format, textual or otherwise. Files are good for holding any kind of *binary content*, which is just raw computer information of some kind.

Every file object has a particular *content type*, which is a standard Internet MIME designation for file type. When you upload a file into Zope, Zope tries to guess the content type from the name of the file, but Zope doesn't always guess correctly.

## Uploading Files

Like DTML documents and methods, files allow you to upload a file from your computer when you create a new object. Click the Browse button to choose a file from your local computer when creating a new Zope file. Try choosing a file, such as a Word file (.doc) or a Portable Document Format file (.pdf). Note, when uploading a file with your browser, you might have to indicate the file type you're looking for in your browser's upload dialog box. After selecting a file to upload, click Add. Depending on the size of the file you want to upload, it might take a few minutes to add the file to Zope.

After adding the file, click the new file and look at its Properties view. Here you see that Zope has guessed the content type as shown in Figure 3.5.

If you add a Word document, the content type is application/msword. If you add a PDF file, the content type is application/pdf. If Zope does not recognize the file type, it chooses the default, generic content type of application/octet-stream.

You can change the contents of an existing file by going to the Upload view. Here you can replace the contents of the file with a new file. If you don't fill in an id and title in this form and you upload a file, Zope uses the filename as the id and the title of the object.

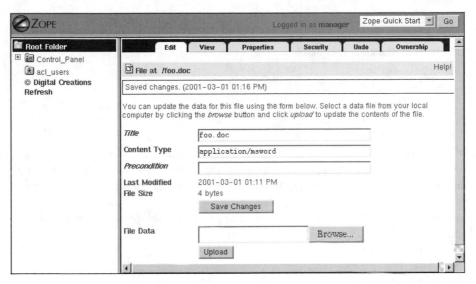

**Figure 3.5**    File Content Type property.

## Viewing Files

You can view a file by *going* to the View tab from the management interface. You can also view a file by visiting its URL. In fact, the View tab is just a way to get to a file's URL from the Zope management interface. For example, if you have a file in your Zope Root folder called employeeAgreement.pdf, then you can view that file in your Web browser by going to the URL `http://localhost:8080/employeeAgreement.pdf`. Depending on the type of file, your Web browser might display the file or download it.

# Using Zope Images

Images display graphics, such as GIF, JPEG, and PNG files. In Zope, images are similar to file objects, but include extra behavior for managing graphic content.

Image objects have the same management interface as file objects. Everything in the previous section about using file objects also applies to images.

## Viewing Images with HTML

The most common use for images in Zope is putting pictures on Web pages. To put a picture onto a Web page, you need to use the HTML IMG tag. Suppose you have an Image object in your Root folder called `logo` that contains an image of your organization's logo.

Using this image in your HTML is a straightforward process: You can reference it with an `IMG` tag as you would to include any type of image on a Web page:

```
<dtml-var standard_html_header>

  <img src="logo">

  <h1>Welcome!</h1>

<dtml-var standard_html_footer>
```

In this example, you reference the logo image by creating an HTML `IMG` tag, but usually it is not necessary to create your own `IMG` tags to display images. Image objects are capable of generating HTML tags. When you insert an image object in DTML, it generates an `IMG` tag.

Now, we want this logo to be seen on every page in the upper-left corner, so put a reference to it in the standard_html_header method:

```
<html>
  <body>
    <dtml-var logo>
```

Now, view the Root folder by clicking the View tab. If you look at the source of the Web page that Zope creates, you can see that the `<dtml-var logo>` DTML code was turned into an HTML `IMG` tag for you:

```
<html>
  <body>
    <img src="logo" width="50" height="30">
```

Using the DTML `var` tag to draw images makes things simple because Zope automatically figures out the height and width attributes of the `IMG` tag for you. If you don't like the way Zope constructs an `IMG` tag, it can be customized. See Appendix B, "API Reference," for more information on the image object and how it can control the `IMG` tag.

A number of third-party Zope products are shown in the visual section at Zope.org (`http://www.zope.org/Products/visual`).

## Viewing Images Through the Web

Images can be viewed directly by going to their URL in your Web browser. For example, let's say you want to view your company logo directly. The logo exists as an image object in your Root folder. It is called logo; you can easily view it by going directly to its URL (`http://localhost:8080/logo`).

Because Zope images work just like images stored in a normal Web server, you can access your Zope images from other Web servers. Suppose you have a Zope image where the URL is `http://imageserver:8080/Birds/Parakeet.jpg`. You can include this image in any Web page served from any Web server by using the image's absolute URL in your Web page:

```
<html>

<h1>Remote Image</h1>

<img src="http://imageserver:8080/Birds/Parakeet.jpg">

</html>
```

This example shows how you can use Zope data from outside Zope using standard Internet protocols. In Chapter 8, "Advanced Zope Scripting," we see how most Zope objects can provide services to the outside world.

## Using Object Properties

Properties are ways of associating information with objects in Zope. Many Zope objects, including folders and documents, support properties. Properties can label an object to identify its contents (many Zope content objects have a content type property). Another use for properties is to provide metadata for an object, such as its author, title, status, and so on.

Properties can be more complex than strings; they can also be numbers, lists, or other data structures. All properties are managed through the Properties view. Click a folder's Properties tab, and you are taken to the Properties Management view, as seen in Figure 3.6.

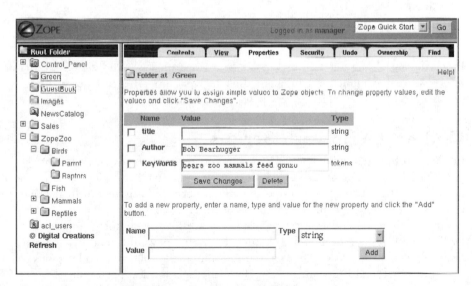

**Figure 3.6**    The Properties Management view.

A property consists of a name, a value, and a type. A property's type defines what kind of values it can have.

In Figure 3.6 you can see that the folder has two properties. One is named Author and the other is named KeyWords. The Author property is string, while the KeyWords property is tokens. A tokens property is like a sequence of words.

Zope supports a number of property types. Each type is suited to a specific task. The following list gives a brief overview of the kinds of properties you can create from the management interface:

- **string**—A string is an arbitrary length sequence of characters. Strings are the most basic and useful type of property in Zope.

- **int**—An int property is an integer, which can be any positive or negative number that is not a fraction. An int is guaranteed at least 32 bits long.

- **long**—A long property is like the int property, except that it has no range limitation.

- **float**—A float holds a floating point or decimal number. Monetary values, for example, often use floats.

- **lines**—A lines property is a sequence of strings.

- **tokens**—A tokens property is a list of words separated by spaces.

- **text**—A text property is like a string property, except that Zope normalizes the line-ending characters (different browsers use different line-ending conventions).

- **selection**—A selection property is special—it is used to render an HTML select input widget.

- **multiple selection**—A multiple selection property is special—it is used to render an HTML multiple select form input widget.

Properties are very useful tools for tagging your Zope objects with little bits of data or information. In conjunction with methods and scripts, properties make extending simple objects, such as folders, a very powerful technique.

## Coding Logic with Scripts

In traditional programming lingo, a *script* is a short piece of code written in a programming language. As of version 2.3, Zope now comes with two kinds of script objects: one that lets you write scripts in Python (http://www.python.org) and one that lets you write scripts in Perl (http://www.perl.org/).

Both Python and Perl are very popular and powerful programming languages. Python and Perl share many similar features: both offer powerful, rapid development, simple syntax, many add-on libraries, a strong community following, and copious amounts of free, online documentation. Both languages are also open source.

Because scripts are so powerful and flexible, their possible uses are endless. Scripts are primarily used to write what is called business logic. Business logic is different than presentation logic. *Presentation logic* is usually written in a presentation language, such as

DTML, and its purpose is to display information to a user. *Business logic* is usually written in a scripting language, and its purpose is to manipulate information that comes from content sources (such as documents or databases) or manipulate other objects. Often, presentation logic is based on top of business logic.

A simple example of using scripts is building an online Web form to help your users calculate the amount of compound interest on their debts. This kind of calculation involves the following procedure:

1. You need the following information:

   - Your current account balance (or debt)—called the *principal.*
   - The annual interest rate expressed as a decimal (such as 0.095)—called the *interest_rate.*
   - The number of times during the year interest is compounded (usually monthly)—which is called the *periods.*
   - The number of years from now you want to calculate—which is called the *years.*

2. Divide your interest_rate by periods (usually 12). We'll call this result i.

3. Take periods and multiply it by years. We'll call this result n.

4. Raise (1 + i) to the power n.

5. Multiply the result by your principal. This is the new balance (or debt).

For this example, you need two DTML methods named interestRateForm and interestRateDisplay to collect the information from the user and display it, respectively. You also need a Python-based script called calculateCompoundingInterest, which does the actual calculation. The first step is to create a Web form in interestRateForm that collects principal, interest_rate, periods, and years from your users. The following is an example interestRateForm DTML method:

```
<dtml-var standard_html_header>

<form action="interestRateDisplay" method="POST">
<p>Please enter the following information:</p>
Your current balance (or debt): <input name="principal:float"><br>
Your annual interest rate: <input name="interest_rate:float"><br>
Number of periods in a year: <input name="periods:int"><br>
Number of years: <input name="years:int"><br>
<input type="submit" value=" Calculate "><br>
</form>

<dtml-var standard_html_footer>
```

This form collects information and calls the interestRateDisplay method. Now, create a Python-based script called calculateCompoundingInterest that accepts four parameters, principal, interest_rate, periods, and years with the following Python code:

```
## Script (Python) "calculateCompoundInterest"
##parameters=principal, interest_rate, periods, years
##
"""
Calculate compounding interest.
"""
i = interest_rate / periods
n = periods * years
return ((1 + i) ** n) * principal
```

The preceding example returns the balance or debt compounded over the course of years. Next, create a interestRateDisplay DTML method that calls calculateCompoundingInterest and returns the following result:

```
<dtml-var standard_html_header>

<p>Your total balance (or debt) including compounded interest over
<dtml-var years> years is:</p>
<p><b><dtml-var expr= "calculateCompoundingInterest(principal,
                                             interest_rate,
                                             periods,
                                             years)" ></b></p>

<dtml-var standard_html_footer>
```

First, view the interestRateForm DTML method. Now, type in some information about your balance or debt and click Calculate. This causes interestRateForm to submit the collected information to interestRateDisplay, which calls the Python-based script calculateCompoundingInterest. The display method uses the value returned by the script in the resulting display.

As we said earlier, the possibilities for using scripts is almost endless. This example, however, gives you a good idea of the most common pattern for presentation objects and how they collect and display information and how they use business logic objects to make calculations.

# Using Methods

Methods are objects in Zope that hold special executable content. The name method is actually a bit of a misnomer, and its use in Zope is slowly being phased out for more common terms, such as script and template.

Zope comes with two kinds of methods, DTML methods and SQL methods. DTML methods are used to define presentation templates, which you can apply to content objects, such as DTML documents and files. A very common and popular way to use DTML methods is to define presentation layout separate from your content.

SQL methods are used to contain database queries that you can reuse throughout your Web application. SQL methods are explained in Chapter 10, "Relational Database Connectivity," where an example of creating a Web application by using a relational database is given.

All the various objects in Zope can be manipulated by calling methods on those objects. DTML methods can be used to write simple scripts, which call the assortment of methods that make up the Zope API. The API is documented in the Help system under API Documentation.

Before Zope 2.3, DTML methods were the only way to write scripts in Zope with your Web browser. Although DTML is useful for simple scripts, and for presenting information with templates, this approach had a lot of problems because DTML isn't as flexible as other programming languages.

Zope 2.3 introduces two new kinds of script objects, based on two very popular programming languages—Python (which Zope is written in) and Perl. You should use Python- and Perl-based scripts to write more complex scripts instead of a DTML method. While browsing through past Zope documentation, mail list archives, and other resources on Zope.org (http://www.zope.org), you might find a lot of references to complex DTML scripts. These scripts predate Python- and Perl-based scripts. In general, complex scripts should be written in either Python or Perl. Python- and Perl-based scripts are described in Chapter 8.

A simple example of using DTML methods is to create a DTML method in the Root folder called objectList:

```
<dtml-var standard_html_header>

<ul>
  <dtml-in objectValues>
    <li><dtml-var getId></li>
  </dtml-in>
</ul>

<dtml-var standard_html_footer>
```

When you view this method, it calls the objectValues method on the Root folder, and this shows you a simple HTML list of all the objects in the Root folder, as shown in Figure 3.7.

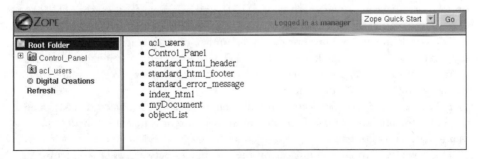

**Figure 3.7**   Results of the objectList DTML method.

All folders implement the objectValues method. The objectValues method is part of an interface that all folders implement called ObjectManager.

In addition to calling API methods on objects, DTML methods can also be used in a certain way to extend any Zope object. This is explained in more detail in Chapter 4, "Dynamic Content with DTML." In effect, this allows you to extend the Zope API by creating DTML methods.

You just saw the objectList method, which resides in the Root folder and makes a simple list of the contents in the Root folder. Because the method is in the Root folder, it is now usable by any other objects in or lower than the Root folder. This method extends the Zope API for these objects because it provides them with another callable method.

To demonstrate, let's create a subfolder called Primates and add three documents: Monkeys, Apes, and Humans. You can call the objectList method on the Primates folder by visiting the URL `Primates/objectList`. You can see how the effect of calling the objectList method on the Primates folder differs from the effect of calling it on the Root folder. The objectList method is defined in the Root folder, but here we are using it to display the contents of the Primates folder. This mechanism of reusing objects is called *acquisition* and is explained more in Chapter 4.

DTML methods mainly serve as presentation templates. DTML methods can act as templates tying reusable bits of content together into dynamic Web pages. The template features of DTML methods are discussed in further detail in Chapter 4.

## Comparing DTML Documents and Methods

DTML methods have the same user interface as DTML documents, which can be a bit confusing to the beginner. All the procedures that you learned in Chapter 2 for adding, editing, viewing, and uploading DTML documents are identical for DTML methods.

A source of frequent confusion for Zope beginners is the question of when to use a DTML document versus when to use a DTML method. On the surface, these two options seem identical. They both hold DTML and other content, execute DTML code, and have a similar user interface and a similar API. So what's the difference?

DTML documents are meant to hold document-like content. For example, the various chapters of a book could be held in a DTML document. A general rule is that if your content is mostly document-like and you want to present it on your site, then it should go into a DTML document.

DTML methods are meant to manipulate and display other objects. DTML methods don't usually hold a lot of content, unless the content is meant to change or manipulate other content.

Don't worry if you're still unclear on the differences between DTML documents and methods. Even the most experienced Zope programmers need to think a little before deciding what type of object to use, and this book hopefully clears up any confusion you might have. The following are some general rules to help you decide between DTML documents and methods:

- If it is content, use a DTML document.
- If it is simple logic, use a DTML method.
- If it is meant to be presented by other objects, use a DTML document.
- If it is meant to present other objects, use a DTML method.
- If it is complex behavior, use a Python- or Perl-based script.

As you've seen, DTML methods are a useful tool for presentation and quick scripting, but eventually you are going to want the power of a fully expressive programming language, and that's where scripts come in.

## Using Versions

Version objects help coordinate the work of many people on the same set of objects. While you are editing a document, someone else can be editing another document at the same time. In a large Zope site, hundreds or even thousands of people can be using Zope simultaneously. For the most part this works well, but problems can occur. For example, two people might edit the same document at the same time. When the first person finishes their changes, the changes are saved in Zope. When the second person finishes their changes, they overwrite the first person's changes. You can always work around this problem by using Undo and History, but it can still be a problem. To solve this problem, Zope has Version objects.

Another problem that you might encounter is that you might want to make some changes, but you might not want to make them public until you are done. For example, suppose you want to change the menu structure of your site. You don't want to work on these changes while folks are using your site because it might break the navigation system temporarily while you are working.

Versions are a way of making private changes in Zope. You can make changes to many different documents without other people seeing them. When you decide that you are done, you can choose to make your changes public, or discard them. You can work in a Version as long as you want. For example, it might take you a week to put the finishing touches on your new menu system. After you are done, you can make all your changes live at once by committing the Version.

Create a Version by choosing Version from the product Add list. You should be taken to an Add form. Give your Version an id of `MyChanges` and click the Add button. Now you have created a Version, but you are not yet using it. To use your Version, click it. You should be taken to the Join/Leave view of your Version, as shown in Figure 3.8.

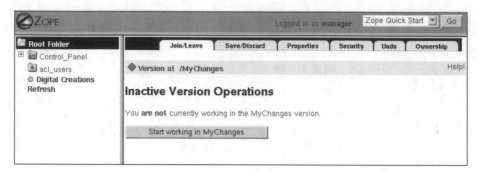

**Figure 3.8**   Joining a Version.

The Version is telling you that you are not currently using it. Click the Start working in MyChanges button. Now Zope should tell you that you are working in a Version. Now return to the Root folder. Notice that everywhere you go you see a small message at the top of the screen that says `You are currently working in Version /MyChanges`. This message lets you know that any changes you make at this point will not be public, but will be stored in your Version. For example, create a new DTML document named new. Notice how it has a small red diamond after its id. Now edit your standard_html_header method. Add a line to it like this:

```
<HTML>
  <HEAD>
    <TITLE><dtml-var title_or_id></TITLE>
  </HEAD>
  <BODY BGCOLOR="#FFFFFF">
  <H1>Changed in a Version</H1>
```

Any object that you create or edit while working in a Version is marked with a red diamond. Now return to your Version and click the Quit working in MyChanges button. Now try to return to the new document. Notice that the document you created while in your Version has now disappeared. Any other changes that you made in the Version are also gone. Notice how your standard_html_header method now has a small red diamond and a lock symbol after it. This indicates that this object has been changed in a Version. Changing an object in a Version locks it, so no one else can change it until you commit or discard the changes. Locking ensures that your Version changes don't overwrite changes that other people make while you're working in a Version. So, for example, if you want to make sure that only you are working on an object at a given time, you can change it in a Version. Although working in a Version protects you from unexpected changes, it also makes things inconvenient if you want to edit something that is locked by someone else. It is a good idea to limit your use of Versions to avoid locking other people out of making changes to objects.

Now return to your Version by clicking it and then clicking the Start working in MyChanges button. Notice how everything returns to the way it was when you left the Version. At this point, let's make your changes permanent. Go to the Save/Discard view as shown in Figure 3.9.

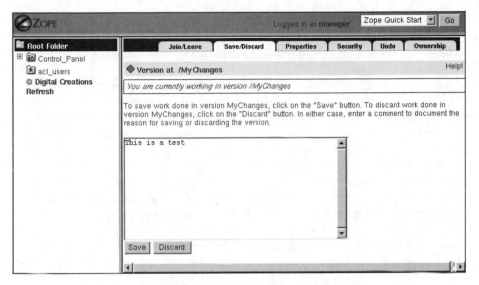

**Figure 3.9**    Committing Version changes.

Enter a comment, such as This is a test into the comment field, and click the Save button. Your changes are now public, and all objects that you changed in your Version are now unlocked. Notice that you are still working in your Version. Go to the Join/Leave view and click the Quit working in MyChanges button. Now verify that the document you created in your Version is visible. Your change to the standard_html_header should also be visible. Like anything else in Zope, you can choose to undo these changes if you want. Go to the Undo view. Notice that instead of many transactions (one for each change), you only have one transaction for all the changes you made in your Version. If you undo the transaction, all the changes you made in the Version are undone.

Versions are a powerful tool for group collaboration. You don't have to run both a live production server and a test server because Versions enable you to make experiments, evaluate them, and then make them public when you decide that all is well. You are not limited to working in a Version alone. Many people can work in the same Version. This way you can collaborate on Version's changes together, while keeping the changes hidden from the general public.

# Cache Manager

A *cache* is a temporary place to store information that you access frequently. The reason for using a cache is speed. Any kind of dynamic content, such as a DTML page or a Python script, must be evaluated each time it is called. For simple pages or quick scripts, this is usually not a problem. For very complex DTML pages or scripts that do a lot of computation or call remote servers, accessing that page or script could take more than a trivial amount of time. Both DTML and Python can get this complex, especially if you use a lot of looping (such as the `<dtml-in>` tag or the Python `for` loop), or if you call a lot of scripts that in turn call lots of scripts, and so on. Computations that take a lot of time are said to be expensive.

A cache can add a lot of speed to your site by calling an expensive page or script once and storing the result of that call so that it can be reused. The very first person to call that page gets the usual slow response time. However, after the value of the computation is stored in the cache, all subsequent users who call that page see a very quick response time. This is because the subsequent users are getting the *cached copy* of the result and are not actually going through the same expensive computation as the first user.

To give you an idea of how caches can improve your site speed, imagine the very first page of your site is very complex. Let's suppose this page has complex headers, footers, queries, several different database tables, and calls several special scripts that parse the results of the database queries in complex ways. Every time a user comes to `www.zopezoo.org`, Zope must render this very complex page. For the purposes of demonstration, let's suppose this page takes one half of a second, or 500 milliseconds, to compute.

Given that it takes one half of a second to render this fictional complex main page, your machine can only really serve 120 hits per minute. In reality, this number would probably be even lower than that because Zope has to do other things in addition to just serving up this main page. Now, imagine that you set this page up to be cached. Because none of the expensive computation needs to be done to show the cached copy of the page, many more users could see the main page. If it takes, for example, 10 milliseconds to show a cached page, then this page is being served 50 times faster to your Web site visitors. The actual performance of the cache and Zope depends a lot on your computer and your application, but this example gives you an idea of how caching can speed up your Web site quite a bit. However, some disadvantages to caching include the following:

- **Cache Lifetime**—If pages are cached for a long time, they might not reflect the most current information on your site. If you have information that changes very quickly, caching might hide the new information from your users because the cached copy contains the old information. How long a result remains cached is called the *cache lifetime* of the information.

- **Personal Information**—Many Web pages might be personalized for one particular user. Obviously, caching this information and showing it to another user would be bad because of privacy concerns and because the other user would not be getting information about himself, he'd be getting it about someone else. For this reason, caching is often never used for personalized information.

Zope allows you to get around these problems by setting up a *cache policy*. The cache policy allows you to control how content gets cached. Cache policies are controlled by cache manager objects.

## Adding a Cache Manager

Cache managers can be added just like any other Zope object. Currently, Zope comes with two kinds of cache managers:

- **HTTP Accelerated Cache Manager**—An HTTP Accelerated Cache Manager allows you to control an HTTP cache server that is external to Zope, for example, Squid (`http://www.squid-cache.org/`). HTTP Accelerated Cache Managers do not do the caching themselves, but rather set special HTTP headers that tell an external cache server what to cache. Setting up an external caching server, such as Squid, is beyond the scope of this book. See the Squid Web site for more details.

- **(RAM) Cache Manager**—A RAM Cache Manager is a Zope cache manager that caches the content of objects in your computer memory. This makes it very fast, but also causes Zope to consume more of your computer's memory. A RAM Cache Manager does not require any external resources, such as a Squid server, to work.

For the purposes of this example, create a RAM Cache Manager in the Root folder called CacheManager. This is going to be the cache manager object for your whole site.

Now, you can click CacheManager and see its configuration screen. A number of elements on this screen are given in the following list:

- **Title**—The title of the cache manager. This is optional.

- **REQUEST Variables**—This information is used to store the cached copy of a page. This is an advanced feature. For now, you can leave this set to AUTHEN-TICATED_USER.

- **Threshold Entries**—The number of objects the cache manager caches at one time.

- **Cleanup Interval**—The lifetime of cached results.

For now, leave all these entries as is, they are good, reasonable defaults. That's all it takes to set up a cache manager!

A couple more views on a cache manager that you may find useful are the Statistics view and the Associate view. The Statistics view shows you the number of cache hits and misses to tell you how effective your caching is.

The other view is the Associate view, which allows you to associate a specific type, or types, of Zope objects with a particular cache manager. For example, you might only want your cache manager to cache DTML documents. You can change these settings in the Associate view.

At this point, nothing is cached yet, you have just created a cache manager. The next section explains how you can cache the contents of actual documents.

## Caching a Document

Caching a document is very easy. First, before you can cache a document you must have a cache manager, such as the one you created in the preceding section.

To cache a document, create a new DTML document object in the Root folder called Weather. This object will contain some weather information. For example, let's say it contains:

```
<dtml-var standard_html_header>

  <p>Yesterday it rained.</p>

<dtml-var standard_html_footer>
```

Now, click the Weather DTML document and click its Cache view. This view lets you associate this document with a cache manager. If you pull down the select box at the top of the view, you'll see the cache manager you created in the preceding section called CacheManager. Select this as the cache manager for Weather.

Now, whenever anyone visits the Weather document, they get the cached copy instead. For a document as trivial as our Weather example, this is not much of a benefit. But imagine for a moment that Weather contained some database queries. For example:

```
<dtml-var standard_html_header>

  <p>Yesterday's weather was <dtml-var yesterdayQuery> </p>

  <p>The current temperature is <dtml-var currentTempQuery></p>

<dtml-var standard_html_footer>
```

Let's suppose that yesterdayQuery and currentTempQuery are SQL methods that query a database for yesterday's forecast and the current temperature, respectively (for more information on SQL methods, see Chapter 10, "Relational Database Connectivity"). Let's also suppose that the information in the database only changes once every hour.

Now, without caching, the Weather document would query the database every time it was viewed. If the Weather document was viewed hundreds of times in an hour, then all of those hundreds of queries would always contain the same information.

If you specify that the document should be cached, however, then the document only makes the query when the cache expires. The default cache time is 300 seconds (5 minutes), so setting this document up to be cached saves you 91% of your database queries by doing them only one twelfth as often. A trade-off with this method is that there is a chance the data might be five minutes out of date, but this is usually an acceptable compromise.

For more information about caching and using the more advanced options of caching, see the Zope Administrator's Guide (`http://www.zope.org/DocProjects/AdminGuide`).

## Virtual Hosting Objects

Zope comes with three objects that help you do virtual hosting: SiteRoot, Set Access Rule, and Virtual Host Monster. Virtual hosting is a way to serve many Web sites with one Zope server. Virtual hosting is an advanced administration function, which is beyond the scope of this book. See the Zope Administrator's Guide for more information on virtual hosting.

In this chapter, we have had an introduction to the basic types of Zope objects. In Chapter 4 we delve into some of the details of one of those object types when we begin to learn how to use DTML to control the presentation of your content.

4

# Dynamic Content
# with DTML

**D**OCUMENT TEMPLATE MARKUP LANGUAGE (DTML) is Zope's tag-based reporting language. DTML dynamically generates, controls, and formats content. DTML is commonly used to build modular and dynamic Web interfaces for your Web applications.

DTML is a server-side scripting language, such as SSI, PHP, ASP, and JSP. This means that DTML commands are executed by Zope at the server, and the result of that execution is sent to your Web browser. In contrast, client-side scripting languages, such as Javascript, are not processed by the server, but rather are sent to and executed by your Web browser.

You can use DTML scripting in two types of Zope objects, DTML documents, and DTML methods.

## Who Is DTML for?

DTML is designed for people familiar with HTML and basic Web scripting—not for application programmers. In fact, if you want to do programming with Zope you shouldn't use DTML. In Chapter 8, "Advanced Zope Scripting," we cover advanced programming using Python and Perl.

DTML is for presentation and should be managed by Web designers. Zope encourages you to keep your presentation and logic separate by providing different objects for presentation (DTML) and logic (Python, Perl, and others). A host of benefits result from keeping your presentation in DTML and your logic in other types of Zope objects. Some of those benefits include

- Keeping logic and presentation separate makes it easy to vary either component without disrupting the other.

- Often different people are in charge of maintaining logic and presentation. By using different objects for these tasks, you make it easier for people to collaborate without disrupting each other.

- It's easier to reuse existing presentation and logic components if they are not intermingled.

## What Is DTML Good for?

DTML is good for creating dynamic Web interfaces. It supports reusing content and layout, formatting heterogeneous data, and separating presentation from logic and data. For example, with DTML you can reuse shared Web page headers and footers:

```
<dtml-var standard_html_header>

<p>Hello world.</p>

<dtml-var standard_html_footer>
```

This Web page mixes HTML and DTML together. DTML commands are written as tags that begin with dtml. This example builds a Web page by inserting a standard header and footer into an HTML page. The resulting HTML page might look something like this:

```
<html>
<body bgcolor="#FFFFFF">

<p>Hello world.</p>

<hr>
<p>Last modified 2000/10/16 by AmosL</p>
</body>
</html>
```

As you can see, the standard header defined a white background color and the standard footer added a note at the bottom of the page telling you when the page was last modified and by whom.

In addition to reusing content, DTML enables you to easily and powerfully format all kinds of data. You can use DTML to call methods, query databases, introspect Zope objects, process forms, and more.

For example, when you query a database with a SQL method, it typically returns a list of results. Here's how you might use DTML to format each result from a database query in the same style:

```
<ul>
<dtml-in frogQuery>
  <li><dtml-var animal_name></li>
</dtml-in>
</ul>
```

The DTML in tag iterates over the results of the database query and formats each result. Suppose four results are returned by frogQuery. The following is what the resulting HTML might look like:

```
<ul>
  <li>Fire-bellied toad</li>
  <li>African clawed frog</li>
  <li>Lake Nabu reed frog</li>
  <li>Chilean four-eyed frog</li>
</ul>
```

The results of the database query are formatted as an HTML bulleted list.

Note that you don't have to tell DTML that you are querying a database, and you don't have to tell it where to find the arguments to call the database query. You just tell it what object to call, and it does the work of figuring out how to call the object and pass it appropriate arguments. If you replace the frogQuery SQL method with some other kind of object, such as a script, a ZCatalog, or even another DTML method, you don't have to change the way you format the results.

This ability to format all kinds of data makes DTML a powerful presentation tool and enables you to modify your business logic without changing your presentation.

# When Not to Use DTML

DTML is not a general-purpose programming language. For example, DTML does not enable you to create variables very easily. Although it may be possible to implement complex algorithms in DTML, it is painful and not recommended. If you want to implement programming logic, use Python or Perl (for more information on these subjects, see Chapter 8).

For example, let's suppose you were writing a simple Web page for a group of math students, and on that page you wanted to illustrate a simple calculation. You would not want to write the program that made this calculation in DTML. It could be done in DTML, but it would be difficult to understand. DTML would be perfect for describing the page that this calculation is inserted into, but it would be awful to do this calculation in DTML—whereas it might be very simple and trivial in Python or Perl.

String processing is another area where DTML is not the best choice. If you want to manipulate input from a user in a complex way using functions that manipulate string, you are better off doing it in Python or Perl—both of which have much more powerful string processing capabilities than DTML.

DTML is one tool among many available in Zope. If you find yourself scratching your head trying to figure out some complicated DTML construct, there's a good chance that things would work better if you broke your DTML script up into a collection of DTML- and Python- or Perl-based scripts.

# DTML Tag Syntax

DTML's syntax is similar to HTML. DTML is a tag-based mark-up language. In other words, DTML uses tags to do its work. A simple snippet of DTML follows:

```
<dtml-var standard_html_header>

<h1>Hello World!</h1>

<dtml-var standard_html_footer>
```

This DTML code contains two DTML var tags and some HTML. The h1 tags are HTML, not DTML. You typically mix DTML with other mark-up languages, such as HTML. Normally, DTML is used to generate HTML, but there's nothing keeping you from generating other types of text. As you'll see in Chapter 7, "Variables and Advanced DTML," you can also use DTML to generate mail messages and more.

DTML contains two kinds of tags, singleton and block tags. singleton tags consist of one tag enclosed by less than (<) and greater than (>) symbols. The var tag is an example of a singleton tag:

```
<dtml-var parrot>
```

There's no need to close the var tag.

Block tags consist of two tags—one that opens the block and one that closes the block—and content that goes between them:

```
<dtml-in mySequence>

  <!— this is an HTML comment inside the in tag block —>

</dtml-in>
```

The opening tag starts the block and the closing tag ends it. The closing tag has the same name as the opening tag with a slash preceding it. This is the same convention that HTML and XML use.

## Using DTML Tag Attributes

All DTML tags have attributes. An attribute provides information about how the tag is supposed to work. Some attributes are optional. For example, the var tag inserts the value of a variable. It has an optional missing attribute that specifies a default value in case the variable can't be found:

```
<dtml-var wingspan missing="unknown wingspan">
```

If the *wingspan* variable is not found then unknown wingspan is inserted instead.

Some attributes don't have values. For example, you can convert an inserted variable to uppercase with the upper attribute:

```
<dtml-var exclamation upper>
```

Notice that the upper attribute, unlike the missing attribute, doesn't need a value.

Different tags have different attributes. See Appendix A, "DTML Reference," for more information on the syntax of different DTML tags.

# Inserting Variables with DTML

Inserting a variable is the most basic task you can perform with DTML. You have already seen how DTML inserts a header and footer into a Web page with the var tag. Many DTML tags insert variables, and they all do it in a similar way. Let's look more closely at how Zope inserts variables.

Suppose you have a folder whose id is Feedbags and has the title Bob's Fancy Feedbags. Inside the folder, create a DTML method with an id of pricelist. Then change the contents of the DTML method to the following:

```
<dtml-var standard_html_header>

<h1>Price list for <dtml-var title></h1>

<p>Hemp Bag $2.50</p>
<p>Silk Bag $5.00</p>

<dtml-var standard_html_footer>
```

Now view the DTML method by clicking the View tab. You should see an HTML page whose source looks something like this:

```
<html>
<body>

<h1>Price list for Bob's Fancy Feedbags</h1>

<p>Hemp Bag $2.50</p>
<p>Silk Bag $5.00</p>

</body>
</html>
```

This is basically what you might expect. Zope inserts a header, a footer, and a title into the Web page. DTML gets the values for these variables from a number of different places. First, the var tag tries to find a variable in the current object. It then looks in the current object's containers, and then in the Web request (forms and cookies). If Zope cannot find a variable, then it raises an exception, and it stops executing the DTML.

Let's follow this DTML code step by step to see where the variables are found. First, Zope looks for *standard_html_header* in the current object, which is the pricelist DTML method. Next, Zope looks for the header in the current object's containers. The Feedbags folder also doesn't have any methods or properties or subobjects by that name. Next, Zope examines the Feedbags folder's container, and so on, until it gets to the Root folder. The Root folder does have a subobject named *standard_html_header.* The header object is a DTML method. So, Zope calls the header method and inserts the results.

Next, Zope looks for the *title* variable. Here, the search is a little shorter. First, it looks in the pricelist DTML method, which does not have a title, so Zope moves on and finds the Feedbags folder's title and inserts it.

Finally Zope looks for the *standard_html_footer* variable. It has to search all the way up to the Root folder to find it, just like it looked for *standard_html_header.*

This exercise might seem a bit tedious, but understanding how Zope looks up variables is very important. For example, some important implications of the way Zope looks up variables include how Zope objects can get content and behavior from their parents, and how content can be defined in one location reused by many objects.

## Processing Input from Forms

It's easy to do form processing with Zope. DTML looks for variables to insert in a number of locations, including information that comes from submitted HTML forms. You don't need any special objects. DTML documents and DTML methods will do.

Create two DTML documents, one with the id `infoForm` and the other with the id `infoAction`. Now edit the contents of the documents. The following example shows the contents of the infoForm document:

```
<dtml-var standard_html_header>

<p>Please send me information on your aardvark adoption
program.</p>

<form action="infoAction">
name: <input type="text" name="user_name"><br>
email: <input type="text" name="email"><br>
<input type="submit">
</form>

<dtml-var standard_html_footer>
```

Now view the document. It is a Web form that asks for information and sends it to the infoAction document when you submit the form.

Now edit the contents of the infoAction document to make it process this form:

```
<dtml-var standard_html_header>

<h1>Thanks <dtml-var user_name></h1>

<p>We received your request for information and will send you
email at <dtml-var email> describing our aardvark adoption
program as soon as it receives final governmental approval.
</p>

<dtml-var standard_html_footer>
```

This document displays a Thank You message, which includes name and email information gathered from the Web form.

Now go back to the infoForm document, view it, fill out the form, and submit it. If all goes well, you should see a Thank You message that includes your name and email address.

The infoAction document found the form information from the Web request that happened when you clicked the Submit button on the infoForm. As we mentioned in the previous section, DTML looks for variables in a couple of places, one of which is the Web request, so there's nothing special you need to do to enable your documents to process Web forms.

Let's perform an experiment. What happens if you try to view the infoAction document directly, as opposed to getting to it from the infoForm document. Click the infoAction document and then click the View tab, as shown in Figure 4.1.

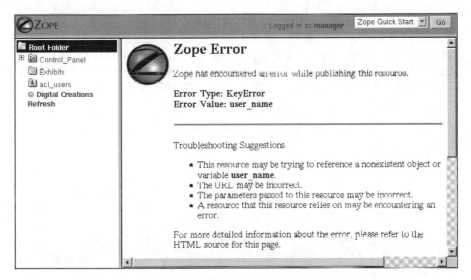

**Figure 4.1**    DTML error resulting from a failed variable lookup.

Zope couldn't find the *user_name* variable because it was not in the current object, its containers, or the Web request. This is an error that you're likely to see frequently as you learn Zope. Don't fear, it just means that you've tried to insert a variable that Zope can't find. In this example, you need to either insert a variable that Zope can find or use the `missing` attribute on the var tag as described earlier:

```
<h1>Thanks <dtml-var user_name missing="Anonymous User"></h1>
```

Understanding where Zope looks for variables can help you figure out how to fix this kind of problem. In this case, you have viewed a document that needs to be called from an HTML form, such as infoForm, to provide variables to be inserted in the output.

## Dynamically Acquiring Content

Zope looks for DTML variables in the current object's containers if it can't find the variable in the current object first. This behavior enables your objects to find and use content and behavior defined in their parents. Zope uses the term acquisition to refer to this dynamic use of content and behavior.

Now that you see how site structure fits into the way names are looked up, you can begin to understand that the placement of objects you are looking for is very important.

An example of acquisition that you've already seen is how Web pages use standard headers and footers. To acquire the standard header, just ask Zope to insert it with the var tag:

```
<dtml-var standard_html_header>
```

It doesn't matter where your DTML method or document is located. Zope searches upward until it finds the *standard_html_header* that is defined in the Root folder.

You can take advantage of how Zope looks up variables to customize your header in different parts of your site. Just create a new *standard_html_header* in a folder, and it overrides the global header for all Web pages in your folder and lower folders.

Create a folder in the Root folder with an id of Green. Enter the Green folder and create a DTML document with an id of welcome. Edit the welcome document to have these contents:

```
<dtml-var standard_html_header>

<p>Welcome</p>

<dtml-var standard_html_footer>
```

Now view the Welcome document. It should look like a simple Web page with the word Welcome, as shown in Figure 4.2.

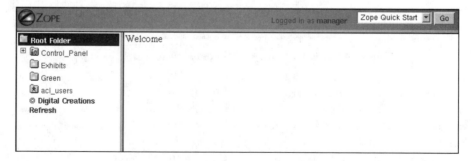

**Figure 4.2**    Welcome document.

Now let's customize the header for the Green folder. Create a DTML method in the Green folder with an id of *standard_html_header*. Then edit the contents of the header to the following:

```
<html>
<head>
  <style type="text/css">
  body {color: #00FF00;}
  p {font-family: sans-serif;}
  </style>
</head>
<body>
```

Notice that this is not a complete Web page. This is just a fragment of HTML that can be used as a header. This header uses Cascading Style Sheets (CSS) to make some changes to the look and feel of Web pages (`http://www.w3.org/Style/CSS`).

Now go back to the Welcome document and view it again, as shown in Figure 4.3.

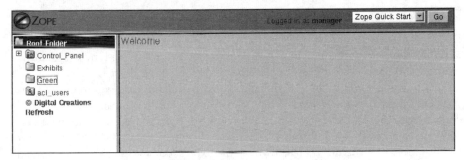

Figure 4.3    Welcome document with custom header.

The document now looks different. This is because it is now using the new header we introduced in the Green folder. This header can be used by all Web pages in the Green folder and its subfolders.

You can continue this process of overriding default content by creating another folder inside the Green folder and creating a *standard_html_header* DTML method there. Now Web pages in the subfolder use their local header rather than the Green folder's header. Using this pattern, you can quickly change the look and feel of different parts of your Web site. If you later decide that an area of the site needs a different header, just create one. You don't have to change the DTML in any of the Web pages; they'll automatically find the closest header and use it.

# Using Python Expressions from DTML

So far we've looked at simple DTML tags. The following is an example:

```
<dtml-var getHippo>
```

This code inserts the value of the variable named `getHippo`, whatever that might be. DTML automatically takes care of the details, such as finding the variable and calling it. We call this basic tag name syntax to differentiate it from expression syntax.

DTML expressions enable you to be more explicit about how to find and call variables. *Expressions* are tag attributes that contain snippets of code in the Python language. For example, instead of letting DTML find and call `getHippo`, we can use an expression to explicitly pass arguments:

```
<dtml-var expr="getHippo('with a large net')">
```

Here we've used a Python expression to explicitly call the `getHippo` method with the string argument `with a large net`. To find out more about Python's syntax, see the Python tutorial at the Python.org Web site (`http://www.python.org/doc/current/tut`). Many DTML tags can use expression attributes.

Expressions make DTML pretty powerful. For example, using Python expressions, you can easily test conditions:

```
<dtml-if expr="foo < bar">
  Foo is less than bar.
</dtml-if>
```

Without expressions, this simple task would have to be broken up into a separate method, and this would add a lot of overhead for something this trivial.

Before you get carried away with expressions, be mindful that expressions can make your DTML hard to understand. Code that is hard to understand is more likely to contain errors and is harder to maintain. Expressions can also lead to mixing logic in your presentation. If you find yourself staring blankly at an expression for more than five seconds, stop. Rewrite the DTML without the expression and use a script to do your logic. Just because you can do complex things with DTML doesn't mean you should.

## DTML Expression Gotchas

Using Python expressions can be tricky. One common mistake is to confuse expressions with basic tag syntax. For example:

```
<dtml-var objectValues>
```

and

```
<dtml-var expr="objectValues">
```

end up giving you two completely different results. The first example of the DTML var tag automatically renders variables. In other words, it tries to do the right thing to insert your variable, no matter what that variable might be. In general this means that if the variable is a method, it is called with appropriate arguments. This process is covered more thoroughly in Chapter 7.

In an expression, you have complete control over the variable rendering. In the case of our example, objectValues is a method. So,

```
<dtml-var objectValues>
```

calls the method. However,

```
<dtml-var expr="objectValues">
```

does not call the method, it just tries to insert it. The result is not a list of objects, but rather a string, such as `'<Python Method object at 8681298>'`. If you ever see results like this, you are probably returning a method rather than calling it.

To call a method from an expression, you must use standard Python calling syntax by using parenthesis:

```
<dtml-var expr="objectValues()">
```

The lesson is that if you use Python expressions, you must know what kind of variable you are inserting, and you must use the proper Python syntax to appropriately render the variable.

Before leaving the subject of variable expressions, we should mention that a deprecated form of the expression syntax exists. You can leave out the `expr=` part on a variable expression tag. But please don't do this. It is far too easy to confuse

```
<dtml-var aName>
```

with

```
<dtml-var "aName">
```

If this is done, you get two completely different results. These shortcuts were built into DTML long ago, but we do not encourage you to use them now unless you are prepared to accept the confusion and debugging problems that come from this subtle difference in syntax.

# The *var* Tag

The var tag inserts variables into DTML methods and documents. We've already seen many examples of how the var tag can be used to insert strings into Web pages.

As you've seen, the var tag looks up variables first in the current object, then in its containers, and finally, in the Web request.

The var tag can also use Python expressions to provide more control in locating and calling variables.

## *var* Tag Attributes

You can control the behavior of the var tag by using its attributes. The var tag has many attributes that help you in common formatting situations. The attributes are summarized in Appendix A. A sampling of the var tag attributes follows:

- **html_quote**—This attribute causes the inserted values to be HTML quoted. This means that <, >, and & are escaped.
- **missing**—This attribute enables you to specify a default value to use in case Zope can't find the variable. For example:

```
<dtml-var bananas missing="We have no bananas">
```

■ **fmt**—The fmt attribute enables you to control the format of the var tags output. Many formats are available, which are detailed in Appendix A.

One use of the fmt attribute is to format monetary values. For example, create a float property in your Root folder called `adult_rate`. This property represents the cost for one adult to visit the zoo. Give this property the value `2.2`.

You can display this cost in a DTML document or method like so:

```
One Adult pass: <dtml-var adult_rate fmt=dollars-and-cents>
```

This correctly prints "$2.20." It rounds more precise decimal numbers to the nearest penny.

### *var* Tag Entity Syntax

Zope provides a shortcut DTML syntax just for the simple var tag. Because the var tag is a `singleton`, it can be represented with an HTML entity, such as syntax:

```
&dtml-cockatiel;
```

This is equivalent to:

```
<dtml-var name="cockatiel" html_quote>
```

The main reason to use the entity syntax is to avoid putting DTML tags inside HTML tags. For example, instead of writing

```
<input type="text" value="<dtml-var name="defaultValue">">
```

you can use the entity syntax to make things more readable for you and your text editor:

```
<input type="text" value="&dtml-defaultValue;">
```

The var tag entity syntax is very limited. You can't use Python expressions or some tag attributes with it.

## The *if* Tag

One of DTML's important benefits is to enable you to customize your Web pages. Often customization means testing conditions are responding appropriately. The if tag enables you to evaluate a condition and carry out different actions based on the result.

What is a condition? A *condition* is either a true or false value. In general, all objects are considered true unless they are 0, None, an empty sequence, or an empty string. As with the var tag, you can use both name syntax and expression syntax. The following are some conditions expressed as DTML expressions:

■ **expr="1"**—Always true.

■ **expr="rhino"**—True if the rhino variable is true.

- **expr="x < 5"**—True if x is less than 5.
- **expr="objectValues('File')"**—True if calling the objectValues method with an argument of File returns a true value. This method is explained in more detail in the section, "Iterating Over Folder Contents."

The if tag is a block tag. The block inside the if tag is executed if the condition is true.

The following is how you might use a variable expression with the if tag to test a condition:

```
<p>How many monkeys are there?</p>

<dtml-if expr="monkeys > monkey_limit">
  <p>There are too many monkeys!</p>
</dtml-if>
```

In the preceding example, if the Python expression monkeys > monkey_limit is true, then you will see the first and the second paragraphs of HTML. If the condition is false, you will only see the first paragraph.

if tags can be nested to any depth, for example, you could have

```
<p>Are there too many blue monkeys?</p>

<dtml-if "monkeys.color == 'blue'">
  <dtml-if expr="monkeys > monkey_limit">
    <p>There are too many blue monkeys!</p>
  </dtml-if>
</dtml-if>
```

Nested if tags work by evaluating the first condition, and if that condition is true, then evaluating the second. In general, DTML if tags work very much like Python if statements.

## Name and Expression Syntax Differences

The name syntax checks for the existence of a name, as well as its value. For example:

```
<dtml-if monkey_house>
  <p>There <em>is</em> a monkey house Mom!</p>
</dtml-if>
```

If the *monkey_house* variable does not exist, then this condition is false. If there is a *monkey_house* variable, but it is false, then this condition is also false. The condition is only true if there is a *monkey_house* variable and it is not 0, None, an empty sequence, or an empty string.

The Python expression syntax does not check for variable existence. This is because the expression must be valid Python. For example:

```
<dtml-if expr="monkey_house">
  <p>There <em>is</em> a monkey house, Mom!</p>
</dtml-if>
```

This works as expected as long as *monkey_house* exists. If the *monkey_house* variable does not exist, Zope raises a KeyError exception when DTML tries to find the variable.

### *else* and *elif* Tags

The if tag only enables you to take an action if a condition is true. You might want to take a different action if the condition is false. This can be done with the DTML else tag. The if block can also contain an else singleton tag. For example:

```
<dtml-if expr="monkeys > monkey_limit">
  <p>There are too many monkeys!</p>
<dtml-else>
  <p>The monkeys are happy!</p>
</dtml-if>
```

The else tag splits the if tag block into two blocks, the first is executed if the condition is true, the second is executed if the condition is not true.

An if tag block can also contain an elif singleton tag. The elif tag specifies another condition, just like an additional if tag. This enables you to specify multiple conditions in one block:

```
<dtml-if expr="monkeys > monkey_limit">
  <p>There are too many monkeys!</p>
<dtml-elif expr="monkeys < minimum_monkeys">
  <p>There aren't enough monkeys!</p>
<dtml-else>
  <p>There are just enough monkeys.</p>
</dtml-if>
```

An if tag block can contain any number of elif tags, but only one else tag. The else tag must always come after the elif tags. elif tags can test for a condition using either the name or expression syntax.

## Using Cookies with the *if* Tag

Let's look at a more meaty if tag example. Often when you have visitors to your site, you want to give them a cookie to identify them with some kind of special value. Cookies are used frequently all over the Internet, and when they are implemented properly, they are quite useful.

Suppose we want to differentiate between new visitors and folks who have already been to our site. When a user visits the site, we can set a cookie. Then we can test for the cookie when displaying pages. If the user has already been to the site, they have the cookie. If they don't have the cookie yet, it means that they're new.

Suppose we're running a special. First time zoo visitors get in for half price. The following is a DTML fragment that tests for a cookie using the *hasVisitedZoo* variable and displays the price according to whether a user is new or a repeat visitor:

```
<dtml-if hasVisitedZoo>
  <p>Zoo admission <dtml-var adult_rate fmt="dollars-and-cents">.</p>
```

```
<dtml-else>
  <b>Zoo admission for first time visitors
      <dtml-var expr="adult_rate/2" fmt="dollars-and-cents"></p>
</dtml-if>
```

This fragment tests for the *hasVisitedZoo* variable. If the user has previously visited the zoo, it displays the normal price for admission. If the visitor is here for the first time, they get in for half price.

Just for completeness sake, the following is an implementation of the *hasVisitedZoo* method as a Python-based script:

```
## Script(Python) "hasVisitedZoo"
##parameters=REQUEST, RESPONSE
##
"""
Returns true if the user has previously visited
the zoo. Uses cookies to keep track of zoo visits.
"""
if REQUEST.has_key('zooVisitCookie'):
    return 1
else:
    RESPONSE.setCookie('zooVisitCookie', '1')
    return 0
```

In Chapter 8, we look more closely at how to script business logic with Python and Perl. For now, it is sufficient to see that the method looks for a cookie and returns a true or false value, depending on whether or not the cookie is found. Notice how Python uses if and else statements just like DTML uses if and else tags. DTML's if and else tags are based on Python's. In fact, Python also has an elif statement, just like DTML.

# The *in* Tag

The DTML in tag iterates over a sequence of objects, carrying out one block of execution for each item in the sequence. In programming, this is often called iteration or looping.

The in tag is a block tag like the if tag. The content of the in tag block is executed once for every iteration in the in tag loop. For example:

```
<dtml-in todo_list>
  <p><dtml-var description></p>
</dtml-in>
```

This example loops over a list of objects named todo_list. For each item, it inserts an HTML paragraph with a description of the to do item.

Iteration is very useful in many Web tasks. Consider a site that displays houses for sale. Users search your site for houses that match certain criteria. You want to format all of those results in a consistent way on the page. Therefore, you need to iterate over each result, one at a time, and render a similar block of HTML for each result.

In a way, the contents of an in tag block is a kind of template that is applied once for each item in a sequence.

## Iterating Over Folder Contents

Here's an example of how to iterate over the contents of a folder. This DTML loops over all the files in a folder and displays a link to each one. This example shows you how to display all the File objects in a folder, so to run this example, you need to upload some files into Zope as explained in Chapter 3, "Using Basic Zope Objects":

```
<dtml-var standard_html_header>
<ul>
<dtml-in expr="objectValues('File')">
  <li><a href="&dtml-absolute_url;"><dtml-var title_or_id></a></li>
</dtml-in>
</ul>
<dtml-var standard_html_footer>
```

The preceding code displayed the following file listing, as shown in Figure 4.4.

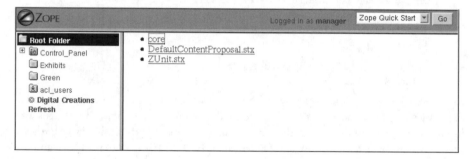

**Figure 4.4**   Iterating over a list of files.

Let's look at this DTML example step by step. First, the `var` tag is used to insert your common header into the document. Next, to indicate that you want the browser to draw an HTML bulleted list, you have the `ul` HTML tag.

Then, there is the `in` tag. This tag has an expression that is calling the Zope API method called `objectValues`. This method returns a sequence of objects in the current folder that match a given criteria. In this case, the objects must be files. This method call returns a list of files in the current folder.

The `in` tag loops over every item in this sequence. If four file objects are in the current folder, then the `in` tag executes the code in its block four times—once for each object in the sequence.

During each iteration, the `in` tag looks for variables in the current object first. In Chapter 7, we look more closely at how DTML looks up variables.

For example, this `in` tag iterates over a collection of file objects and uses the `var` tag to look up variables in each file:

```
<dtml-in expr="objectValues('File')">
  <li><a href="&dtml-absolute_url;"><dtml-var title_or_id></a></li>
</dtml-in>
```

The first var tag is an entity and the second is a normal DTML var tag. When the in tag loops over the first object, its *absolute_url* and *title_or_id* variables are inserted in the first bulleted list item:

```
<ul>
  <li><a href="http://localhost:8080/FirstFile">FirstFile</a></li>
```

During the second iteration, the second object's *absolute_url* and *title_or_id* variables are inserted in the output:

```
<ul>
  <li><a href="http://localhost:8080/FirstFile">FirstFile</a></li>
  <li><a href="http://localhost:8080/SecondFile">SecondFile</a></li>
```

This process continues until the in tag has iterated over every file in the current folder. After the in tag has iterated, you finally close your HTML bulleted list with a closing ul HTML tag and the *standard_html_footer* is inserted to close the document.

## *in* Tag Special Variables

The in tag provides you with some useful information that enables you to customize your HTML while you are iterating over a sequence. For example, you can make your file library easier to read by putting it in an HTML table and making every other table row an alternating color, as shown in Figure 4.5.

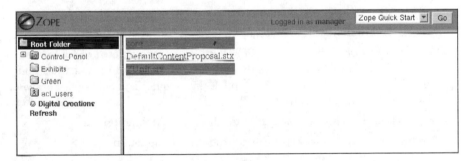

**Figure 4.5**   File listing with alternating row colors.

The in tag makes this easy. Change your file library method a bit to look like this:

```
<dtml-var standard_html_header>

<table>
<dtml-in expr="objectValues('File')">
  <dtml-if sequence-even>
    <tr bgcolor="grey">
  <dtml-else>
    <tr>
  </dtml-if>
```

*continues*

*continued*

```
    <td>
    <a href="&dtml-absolute_url;"><dtml-var title_or_id></a>
    </td></tr>
</dtml-in>
</table>

<dtml-var standard_html_footer>
```

In the preceding example, an `if` tag is used to test for a special variable called *sequence-even*. The `in` tag sets this variable to a true or false value each time through the loop. If the current iteration number is even, then the value is true. If the iteration number is odd, it is false.

The result of this test is that a `tr` tag (with either a gray or no background) is inserted into the document for every other object in the sequence. As you might expect, there is a `sequence-odd` that always has the opposite value of `sequence-even`.

The `in` tag defines many special variables for you. The following is a list of the most common and useful variables:

- *sequence-item*—This special variable is the current item in the iteration. In the case of the file library example, each time through the loop, the current file of the iteration is assigned to *sequence-item*. It is often useful to have a reference to the current object in the iteration.

- *sequence-index*—The current number of iterations completed so far, starting from 0. If this number is even, `sequence-even` is true and `sequence-odd` is false.

- *sequence-number*—The current number of iterations completed so far, starting from 1. This can be thought of as the cardinal position (first, second, third, and so on) of the current object in the loop. If this number is even, `sequence-even` is false and `sequence-odd` is true.

- *sequence-start*—This variable is true for the very first iteration.

- *sequence-end*—This variable is true for the very last iteration.

These special variables are detailed more thoroughly in Appendix A.

DTML is a powerful tool for creating dynamic content. It enables you to perform fairly complex calculations. In Chapter 7, you find out about many more DTML tags and powerful ways to use the tags you already have seen. Despite its power, you should resist the temptation to use DTML for complex scripting. In Chapter 8, you find out how to use Python and Perl for scripting business logic. But first, let's look at how to create some basic applications in Zope. That is the subject of Chapter 5, "Creating Basic Zope Applications."

# 5

# Creating Basic Zope Applications

I N CHAPTER 3, "USING BASIC ZOPE OBJECTS," and Chapter 4, "Dynamic Content with DTML," you learned about basic Zope objects and DTML. In this chapter you'll see how you can build simple, but powerful, Web applications using these tools. In later chapters of the book you'll discover more complex objects and more complex DTML (for example, Chapter 7, "Variables and Advanced DTML," and Chapter 8, "Advanced Zope Scripting.") However, the design techniques covered in this chapter are still relevant.

## Building Applications with Folders

Folders are the basic building blocks of Zope applications. Folders allow you to organize your Zope objects, and actively participate in your Web applications. Folders are given behavior by adding scripts to them.

For example, suppose you have an Invoices folder to hold invoices. You could create objects inside that folder named addInvoice and editInvoice to allow you to add and edit invoices. Now your Invoices folder becomes a small application.

Zope's simple and expressive URLs are used to work with the invoices application. As you've seen, you can display a Zope object by going to its URL in your browser. So, for example, the URL `http://localhost:8080/Invoices/addInvoice` calls the addInvoice object in the Invoices folder. This URL might take you to a screen that lets you add an invoice. Likewise, the URL `http://localhost:8080/Invoices/editInvoice?invoice_number=42` calls the editInvoice object in the Invoices folder and passes it the argument `invoice_number` with a value of 42. This URL could allow you to edit invoice number 42.

## Calling Objects on Folders with URLs

The invoices example demonstrates a powerful Zope feature. You can call an object in a folder by going to a URL that consists of the folder's URL followed by the id of the object. This facility is used throughout Zope and is a very general design pattern. In fact, you are not just restricted to calling objects in folders. You'll see later how you can call objects in all kinds of Zope objects by using the same URL technique.

For example, suppose you want to call an object named viewFolder in one of your folders. Perhaps you have many different viewFolder objects in different locations. Zope figures out which one you want by first looking in the folder that you are calling the object in. If it can't find the object there, it goes up one level and looks in the folder's containing folder. If the object can't be found there, it goes up another level. This process continues until Zope finds the object or gets to the Root folder. If Zope can't find the object in the Root folder it gives up and raises an exception.

You'll see this kind of dynamic behavior in many different places in Zope. This technique is called *acquisition*. A folder is said to *acquire* an object by searching for the object in its containers.

## The Special Folder Object—index_html

As you've seen, folders can acquire all kinds of objects. Zope uses one special object to display a folder. This object is named *index_html*.

The index_html object provides a default view of the folder. This is analogous to how an index.html file provides a default view for a directory in Apache and other Web servers.

For example, if you create an index_html object in your Invoices folder and view the folder by clicking the View tab or by visiting the URL `http://localhost:8080/Invoices/`, Zope calls the index_html object in the Invoices folder.

A folder can also acquire an index_html object from its parent folders—just as it can acquire any object. You can use this behavior to create a default view for a bunch of folders all in one place. If you want a different default view of a given folder, just create a custom index_html object in that folder. This way you can override the index_html object defined higher up.

# Building the Zope Zoo Web Site

In this section, you create a simple Web site for the Zope zoo. As the zoo Webmaster, it is your job to make the Web site easy to use and manage. Some things you'll need to ensure are the following:

- Zoo users must easily move around the site, just as if they were walking through a real zoo.
- All your shared Web layout tools, such as Cascading Style Sheets (CSS), must be in one easy-to-manage location.
- You must provide a simple file library of various documents that describe the animals.
- You need a site map so that users can quickly get an idea of the layout of the entire zoo.
- A guest book must be created so that zoo visitors can give you feedback and comments about your site.
- A What's New section must be added to the guest book so that you can see any recent comments that have been added.

## Navigating the Zoo

For your navigation system to work, your site needs some basic structure through which to navigate. Create some folders in your Zope system that represent the structure of your site. Let's use a zoo structure with the following layout, as shown in Figure 5.1.

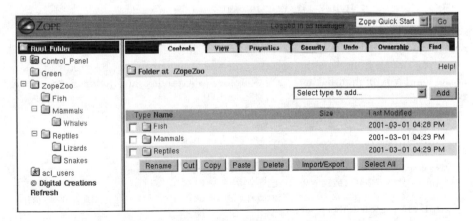

Figure 5.1    Zoo folder structure.

The main structure of the Zope zoo contains three top-level folders: Reptiles, Mammals, and Fish. To navigate your site, users should first go to your home page and click one of the top-level folders to enter that particular part of the zoo. They should also be able to use a very similar interface to keep going deeper into the site (for example, the Snakes section). Also, the user should be able to back out of a section and go up to the parent section.

You can accomplish this easily with Zope. In your ZopeZoo folder, create a DTML method called navigation using the following code:

```
<ul>
<dtml-in expr="objectValues('Folder')">
  <li><a href="&dtml-absolute_url;"><dtml-var title_or_id></a><br></li>
</dtml-in>
</ul>
```

The method you just created shows a list of links to the various subsections of the zoo. It's important to notice that this method can work on any zoo folder because it makes no assumptions about the folder. Also because we placed this method in the ZopeZoo folder, all the zoo folders can acquire it.

Now, you need to incorporate this method into the site. Put a reference to it in the standard_html_header object so that the navigation system is available on every page of the site. Your standard_html_header could look like this:

```
<html>
<head><title><dtml-var title></title></head>
<body>
<dtml-var navigation>
```

Next, we need to add a front page to the zoo site. Then, we can view the site and verify that the navigation works correctly.

## Adding a Front Page to the Zoo

Now, you need a front page that serves as the welcome screen for zoo visitors. Let's create a DTML method in the ZopeZoo folder called index_html with the following content:

```
<dtml-var standard_html_header>

  <h1>Welcome to the Zope Zoo</h1>

  <p>Here you will find all kinds of cool animals. You are in
  the <b><dtml-var getId></b> section.</p>

<dtml-var standard_html_footer>
```

Take a look at how your site appears by clicking the View tab in the Root folder, as shown in Figure 5.2.

**Figure 5.2**    Zope zoo front page.

You can start to see how things come together. At the top of your main page, you can see a list of links to the various subsections. These links are created by the navigation method, which is called by the standard_html_header method.

You can use the navigation links to travel through the various sections of the zoo. Use this navigation interface to find the Reptiles section.

Zope builds this page to display a folder by looking for the default folder view method ,index_html. It walks up the zoo site folder by folder until it finds the index_html method in the ZopeZoo folder. It then calls this method on the Reptiles folder. The index_html method calls the standard_html_header method, which in turn calls the navigation method. Finally, the index_html method displays a Welcome message and calls the standard_html_footer.

What if you want the Reptile page to display something besides the Welcome message? You can replace the index_html method in the Reptile section with a more appropriate display method and still take advantage of the zoo header and footer, including navigation.

In the Reptile folder create a DTML method named index_html. To give it content that is more appropriate to reptiles, perform the following.

```
<dtml-var standard_html_header>

<h1>The Reptile House</h1>

<p>Welcome to the Reptile House.</p>

<p>We are open from 6pm to midnight Monday through Friday.</p>

<dtml-var standard_html_footer>
```

Now take a look at the Reptile page by going to the Reptile folder and clicking the View tab.

Because the index_html method in the Reptile folder includes the standard headers and footers, the Reptile page still includes your navigation system.

Click the Snakes link on the Reptile page to see what the Snakes section looks like. The Snakes page looks like the Reptiles page because the Snakes folder acquires its index_html display method from the Reptiles folder.

## Improving Navigation

The navigation system for the zoo works pretty well, but it has one big problem. When you go deeper into the site, you need to use your browser's Back button to go back. No navigation links allow you to navigate up the folder hierarchy. Let's add a navigation link to allow you to go up the hierarchy. Change the navigation method in the Root folder:

```
<a href="..">Return to parent</a><br>

<ul>
<dtml-in expr="objectValues('Folder')">
  <li><a href="&dtml-absolute_url;"><dtml-var title_or_id></a><br></li>
</dtml-in>
</ul>
```

Now browse the zoo site to see how this new link works, as shown in Figure 5.3.

**Figure 5.3**   Improved zoo navigation controls.

As you can see, the Return to parent link allows you to go back up from a section of the site to its parent. However, some problems remain. When you are at the top level of the site, you still get a Return to parent link that leads nowhere. Let's fix this by changing the navigation method to hide the parent link when you're in the ZopeZoo folder:

```
<dtml-if expr="_.len(PARENTS) > 2">
  <a href="..">Return to parent</a><br>
</dtml-if>
```

```
<ul>
<dtml-in expr="objectValues('Folder')">
  <li><a href="&dtml-absolute_url;"><dtml-var title_or_id></a><br></li>
</dtml-in>
</ul>
```

Now the method tests to see if the current object has any parents before it displays a link to the parent. PARENTS is a list of the current object's parents, and len is a utility function that returns the length of a list. See Appendix A, "DTML Reference," for more information on DTML utility functions. Now view the site. Notice that now no parent link displays when you're viewing the main zoo page.

Some things still could be improved about the navigation system. For example, it's pretty hard to tell what section of the zoo you're in. You've changed the Reptile section, but the rest of the site looks pretty much the same—with the exception of having different navigation links. It would be nice to have each page tell you what part of the zoo you're in.

Let's change the navigation method again to display where you are by using the following code:

```
<dtml-if expr="_.len(PARENTS) > 2">
  <h2><dtml-var title_or_id> Section</h2>
  <a href="..">Return to parent</a><br>
</dtml-if>

<ul>
<dtml-in expr="objectValues('Folder')">
  <li><a href="&dtml-absolute_url;"><dtml-var title_or_id></a><br></li>
</dtml-in>
</ul>
```

Now view the site again (see Figure 5.4).

**Figure 5.4**    Zoo page with section information.

As you can see in Figure 5.4, the navigation method tells you what section you're in, along with links to go to different sections of the zoo.

## Factoring Out Style Sheets

Zoo pages are built by collections of methods that operate on folders. For example, the header method calls the navigation method to display navigation links on all pages. In addition to factoring out shared behavior, such as navigation controls, you can use different Zope objects to factor out shared content.

Suppose you would like to use Cascading Style Sheets (`http://www.w3.org/Style/CSS/`) to tailor the look and feel of the zoo site. One way to do this would be to include the CSS tags in the standard_html_header method. This way every page of the site would have the CSS information. This is a good way to reuse content, however, this is not a flexible solution because you might want a different look and feel in different parts of your site. Suppose you want the background of the Snakes page to be green, while the rest of the site should have a white background. You would have to override the standard_html_header in the Snakes folder and make it exactly the same as the normal header—with the exception of the style information. This is an inflexible solution because you can't vary the CSS information without changing the entire header.

You can create a more flexible way to define CSS information by factoring it out into a separate object that the header inserts. Create a DTML document in the ZopeZoo folder named style_sheet. Change the contents of the document to include some style information:

```
<style type="text/css">
h1{
  font-size: 24pt;
  font-family: sanserif;
}
p{
  color: #220000;
}
body{
  background: #FFFFDD;
}
</style>
```

This is a CSS style sheet that defines how to display h1, p, and body HTML tags. Now let's include this content into our Web site by inserting it into the standard_html_header method, as in the following:

```
<html>
<head>
<dtml-var style_sheet>
</head>
<body>
<dtml-var navigation>
```

Now, when you look at documents on your site, all of their paragraphs are dark red and the headers are in a sans-serif font.

To change the style information in a part of the zoo site, just create a new style_sheet document and drop it into a folder. All the pages in that folder and its subfolders use the new style sheet.

## Creating a File Library

File libraries are common on Web sites because many sites distribute files of some sort. The old fashioned way to create a file library is to upload your files, then create a Web page that contains links to those files. With Zope, you can dynamically create links to files. When you upload, change, or delete files, the file library links can change automatically.

Create a folder in the ZopeZoo folder called Files. This folder contains all of the file that you want to distribute to your Web visitors.

In the Files folder, create some empty file objects with names, such as DogGrooming or HomeScienceExperiments—just to give you some sample data to work with. Add some descriptive titles to these files.

DTML can help you save time in maintaining this library. Create an index_html DTML method in the Files folder to list all the files in the library:

```
<dtml-var standard_html_header>

<h1>File Library</h1>

<ul>
<dtml-in expr="objectValues('File')">
  <li><a href="&dtml-absolute_url;"><dtml-var title_or_id></a></li>
</dtml-in>
</ul>

<dtml-var standard_html_footer>
```

Now view the Files folder. You should see a list of links to the files in the Files folder, as shown in Figure 5.5.

If you add another file, Zope dynamically adjusts the file library page. You might also want to try changing the titles of the files, uploading new files, or deleting some of the files.

The file library, as it stands, is functional—but Spartan. The library doesn't let you know when a file was created, and it doesn't let you sort the files in any way. Let's make the library a little fancier.

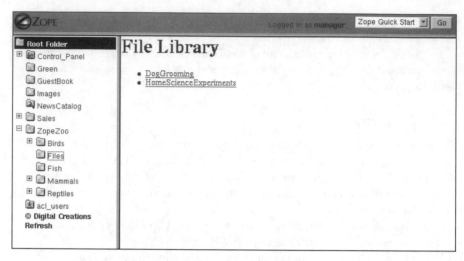

**Figure 5.5**   File library contents page.

Most Zope objects have a bobobase_modification_time method that returns the time the object was last modified. We can use this method in the file library's index_html method:

```
<dtml-var standard_html_header>

<h1>File Library</h1>

<table>
  <tr>
    <th>File</th>
    <th>Last Modified</th>
  </tr>

<dtml-in expr="objectValues('File')">
  <tr>
    <td><a href="&dtml-absolute_url;"><dtml-var title_or_id></a></td>
    <td><dtml-var bobobase_modification_time fmt="aCommon"></td>
  </tr>
</dtml-in>

</table>

<dtml-var standard_html_footer>
```

The new file library method uses an HTML table to display the files and their modification times.

Finally, let's add the ability to sort this list by filename or by modification date. Change the index_html method again:

```
<dtml-var standard_html_header>

<h1>File Library</h1>

<table>
  <tr>
    <th><a href="&dtml-URL0;?sort=name">File</a></th>
    <th><a href="&dtml-URL0;?sort=date">Last Modified</a></th>
  </tr>

<dtml-if expr="_.has_key('sort') and sort=='date'">
  <dtml-in expr="objectValues('File')"
          sort="bobobase_modification_time" reverse>
    <tr>
        <td><a href="&dtml-absolute_url;"><dtml-var title_or_id></a></td>
        <td><dtml-var bobobase_modification_time fmt="aCommon"><td>
    </tr>
  </dtml-in>
<dtml-else>
  <dtml-in expr="objectValues('File')" sort="id">
    <tr>
        <td><a href="&dtml-absolute_url;"><dtml-var title_or_id></a></td>
        <td><dtml-var bobobase_modification_time fmt="aCommon"><td>
    </tr>
  </dtml-in>
</dtml-if>

</table>

<dtml-var standard_html_footer>
```

Now, view the file library and click the File and Last Modified links to sort the files. This method works with two sorting loops. One uses the in tag to sort an object's id. The other does a reverse sort on an object's bobobase_modification_time method. The index_html method decides what loop to use by looking for the sort variable. If a sort variable exits and it has a value of date, then the files are sorted by modification time. Otherwise the files are sorted by id.

## Building a Guest Book

A guest book is a common and useful Web application that allows visitors to your site to leave messages. Figure 5.6 shows what the guest book you're going to write looks like.

Start by creating a folder called GuestBook in the Root folder. Give this folder the title The Zope Zoo Guest Book. The GuestBook folder holds the guest book entries and methods to view and add entries. The folder holds everything the guest book needs. After the guest book is done you will be able to copy and paste it elsewhere in your site to create new guest books.

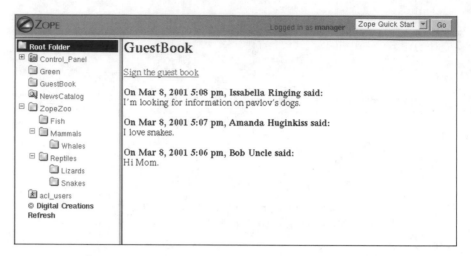

**Figure 5.6**  Zoo guest book.

You can use Zope to create a guest book in several different ways, but for this example, you'll use one of the simplest. The GuestBook folder holds a bunch of DTML documents, one document for each guest-book entry. When a new entry is added to the guest book, a new document is created in the GuestBook folder. To delete an unwanted entry, just go into the GuestBook folder and delete the unwanted document using the management interface.

Let's create a method that displays all the entries. Call this method index_html so that it is the default view of the GuestBook folder:

```
<dtml-var standard_html_header>

<h2><dtml-var title_or_id></h2>

<!-- Provide a link to add a new entry, this link goes to the
addEntryForm method -->

<p>
  <a href="addEntryForm">Sign the guest book</a>
</p>

<!-- Iterate over each DTML Document in the folder starting with
the newest documents first. -->

<dtml-in expr="objectValues('DTML Document')"
         sort="bobobase_modification_time" reverse>

<!-- Display the date, author and contents of each document -->

  <p>
```

```
    <b>On <dtml-var bobobase_modification_time fmt="aCommon">,
        <dtml-var guest_name html_quote null="Anonymous"> said:</b><br>

    <dtml-var sequence-item html_quote newline_to_br>

    <!— Make sure we use html_quote so the users can't sneak any
    HTML onto our page —>

</p>

</dtml-in>

<dtml-var standard_html_footer>
```

This method loops over all the documents in the folder and displays each one. Notice that this method assumes that each document has a guest_name property. If that property doesn't exist or is empty, then Zope uses Anonymous as the guest name. When you create a entry document you'll need to make sure to set this property.

Next, let's create a form for your site visitors to use to add new guest-book entries. In the index_html method shown earlier, we created a link to this form. In your GuestBook folder, create a new DTML method named addEntryForm:

```
<dtml-var standard_html_header>

<p>Type in your name and your comments and we'll add it to the
guest book.</p>

<form action="addEntryAction" method="POST">
<p> Your name:
    <input type="text" name="guest_name" value="Anonymous">
</p>
<p> Your comments: <br>
    <textarea name="comments" rows="10" cols="60"></textarea>
</p>

<p>
    <input type="submit" value="Send Comments">
</p>
</form>

<dtml-var standard_html_footer>
```

Now, when you click the Sign Guest Book link on the guest-book page you'll see a form allowing you to type in your comments. This form collects the user's name and comments, and submits this information to a method named addEntryAction.

Then, create an addEntryAction DTML method in the GuestBook folder to handle the form. This form creates a new entry document and returns a confirmation message:

```
<dtml-var standard_html_header>

<dtml-call expr="addEntry(guest_name, comments)">
```

*continues*

*continued*

```
<h1>Thanks for signing our guest book!</h1>

<p><a href="<dtml-var URL1>">Return</a>
to the guest book.</p>

<dtml-var standard_html_footer>
```

This method creates a new entry by calling the addEntry method, and a message returns to let the user know that their entry has been added.

The last remaining piece of the puzzle is to write the script that creates a document and sets its contents and properties. We'll do this in Python because it is much clearer than doing it in DTML. Create a Python-based script in the GuestBook folder called addEntry with parameters guest_name and comments:

```
## Script (Python) "addEntry"
##parameters=guest_name, comments
##
"""
Create a guest book entry.
"""
# create a unique document id
id='entry_%d' % len(context.objectIds())

# create the document
context.manage_addProduct['OFSP'].manage_addDTMLDocument(id,
                                          title="", file=comments)

# add a guest_name string property
doc=getattr(context, id)
doc.manage_addProperty('guest_name', guest_name, 'string')
```

This script uses Zope API calls to create a DTML document and to create a property on that document. This script performs the same sort of actions in a script that you could do manually; it creates a document, edits it, and sets a property.

The guest book is almost finished. To use the guest book, visit `http://localhost:8080/GuestBook/`.

One final thing is needed to make the guest book complete. More than likely your security policy does not allow anonymous site visitors to create documents. However, the guest-book application should be able to be used by anonymous visitors. In Chapter 6, "Users and Security," we explore this scenario in more detail. The solution is to grant special permission to the addEntry method so that it can do its work of creating a document. You can do this by setting the proxy role of the method to Manager. This means that when the method runs it works as though it was run by a Manager, regardless of who is actually running the method. To change the proxy roles, go to the Proxy view of the addEntry method, as shown in Figure 5.7.

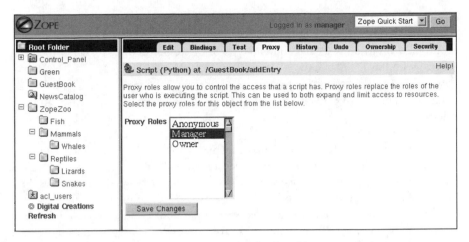

**Figure 5.7**    Setting proxy roles for the addEntry method.

Now select Manager from the list of proxy roles and click Change.

Congratulations, you've just completed a functional Web application. The guest book is complete and can be copied to different sites if you want.

## Extending the Guest Book to Generate XML

All Zope objects can create XML. It's fairly easy to create XML with DTML. XML is just a way of describing information. The power of XML is that it lets you easily exchange information across the network. The following is a simple way that you could represent your guest book in XML:

```
<guestbook>
  <entry>
    <comments>My comments</comments>
  </entry>
  <entry>
    <comments>I like your web page</comments>
  </entry>
  <entry>
    <comments>Please no blink tags</comments>
  </entry>
</guestbook>
```

This XML DTD might not be that complex but it's easy to generate. Create a DTML method named entries.xml in your GuestBook folder with the following contents:

```
<guestbook>
  <dtml-in expr="objectValues('DTML Document')">
  <entry>
    <comments><dtml-var document_src html_quote></comments>
  </entry>
  </dtml-in>
</guestbook>
```

As you can see, DTML is equally adept at creating XML as it is at creating HTML. Simply embed DTML tags among XML tags and you're set. The only tricky thing that you might want to do is set the content-type of the response to `text/xml`, which can be done with this DTML code:

```
<dtml-call expr="RESPONSE.setHeader('content-type', 'text/xml')">
```

The whole point of generating XML is to produce data in a format that can be understood by other systems. Therefore, you probably want to create XML in an existing format understood by the systems with which you want to communicate. In the case of the guest book, a reasonable format might be the RSS (Rich Site Summary) XML format. RSS is a format developed by Netscape for its `my.netscape.com` site, which has since gained popularity among other Weblogs and news sites. The Zope.org Web site uses DTML to build a dynamic RSS document.

Congratulations! You've XML-enabled your guest book in just a couple minutes. Pat yourself on the back. If you want extra credit, research RSS enough to figure out how to change entries.xml to generate RSS.

This chapter shows how simple Web applications can be made. Zope has many more features in addition to these, but these simple examples should get you started on creating well-managed, complex Web sites.

In the next chapter, we'll see how the Zope security system lets Zope work with many different users at the same time, and allows them to collaborate together on the same projects.

# II

# Creating Web Applications with Zope

# 6

# Users and Security

ALL WEB APPLICATIONS NEED TO MANAGE SECURITY. Managing security means controlling who can access your application, and determining what they can do. Security is not an afterthought that can be added to protect a working system. Instead, security should be an important design element that you consider as you build your Zope applications.

In this chapter you learn how to create and manage user accounts, and how to control user access to your application by creating security policies.

## Introducing Security

Security controls what the users of your site can do and how you and others can maintain your site. If you carefully consider security, you can provide powerful features to your users and allow large groups of people to safely work together to maintain your site. If you do not consider security, it will be difficult to safely give your users control—and managing your site will become a messy burden. Your site suffers not only from people doing harmful things that they shouldn't be able to do, but it is hard for you to provide value to your users and control to those who manage your site.

Zope weaves security into almost every aspect of Web-application building. Zope uses the same security system to control Zope management as you use to create users for your application. Zope makes no distinction between using and managing an application. This might seem confusing, but in fact, it allows you to leverage Zope's security framework for your application's needs.

## Logging In and Logging Out of Zope

As we saw in Chapter 2, "Using Zope," you log into Zope by going to a management URL in your Web browser and entering your username and password. We also pointed out in Chapter 2 that because of how most Web browsers work, you must quit your browser to log out of Zope.

If you attempt to access a protected resource for which you don't have access privileges, Zope prompts you to log in. This can happen even if you're already logged in. In general, you do not need to log in to Zope if you only want to use public resources.

## Authentication and Authorization

Security in the broadest sense controls two functions, authentication and authorization. *Authentication* means finding out who you are, and *authorization* means determining what you can do. Zope provides separate facilities to manage the process of identifying users and granting access to controlled actions.

When you access a protected resource (for example, by viewing a private Web page) Zope asks you to log in and it looks for your user account. This is the authentication process. Note that Zope only authenticates you if you ask for a protected resource. If you access only public resources, Zope continues to assume you are anonymous.

After you've been authenticated, Zope determines whether or not you have access to the protected resource. This process involves two intermediary layers between you and the protected resource—roles and permissions. Users have *roles* that describe what they can do, such as Author, Manager, and Editor. Zope objects have *permissions* that describe what can be done with them, such as View, Delete Objects, and Manage Properties.

Security policies map roles to permissions. In other words, policies say who can do what. For example, a security policy might associate the Manager role with the Delete Objects permission. This allows managers to delete objects. In this way Zope authorizes users to perform protected actions.

In the following sections, we'll look more closely at authentication and authorization and how to effectively set security policies. We start with users and user folders. Then, we cover controlling authorization with security policies.

# Authentication and Managing Users

A Zope user defines a user account. A Zope user has a name, a password, and (optionally) additional data about someone who uses Zope. To log into Zope, you must have a user account. Let's examine how to create and manage user accounts.

## Creating Users in User Folders

To create user accounts in Zope, you add users to user folders. In Chapter 2, you added a Manager user to your top-level user folder.

Let's create a new user so that your coworker can help you manage your Zope site. Go to the Root Zope folder. Click the user folder named acl_users. The user folder contains user objects that define Zope user accounts. Click the Add button to create a new user.

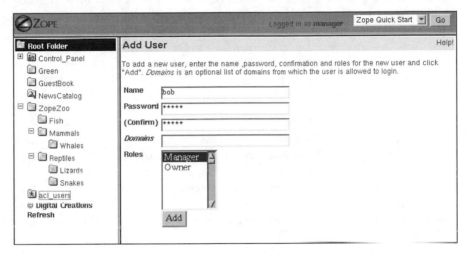

**Figure 6.1**     Adding a user to a user folder.

The form in Figure 6.1 lets you define the user. Type a username for your coworker in the Name field. For example, `Michel`. The username can contain letters, spaces, and numbers. The username is case sensitive.

Choose a password for your coworker and enter it in the Password and (Confirm) fields. We'll set things up so that your coworker can change their password later when they log in. You might want to use a password, such as Change Me, to help remind them to change their password.

The *Domains* field lets you restrict Internet domains from which the user can log in. This allows you to add another safety control to your account. For example, if you always want your coworker to log in from work, you could enter your work's domain. For example, type `myjob.com`, in the Domains field. You can specify multiple domains separated by spaces to allow the user to log in from multiple domains. If you decide that your coworker should be able to manage Zope from their home account too, you could set the domains to `myjob.com myhome.net`. You can also use IP numbers with asterisks to indicate a wild card instead of domain names to specify domains. (For example, 209.67.167.* matches all IP addresses that start with 209.67.167.)

If you specify a domain and leave the password for a user blank, then anyone from the permitted domains automatically gets the user's roles without having to log in. For example, on an intranet you might want all users from your company's domain to have the Manager role without logging in. You can do this by creating a user, leaving the password blank, specifying `myjob.com` as the domain, and Manager as the role.

The Roles select list indicates what roles the user should have. In general, users who are performing management tasks should be given the Manager role. In the case of your coworker, select the Manager role. The Owner role is not appropriate in most cases because a user is normally an owner of a specific object—not an owner in general. We look at ownership more later in this chapter in the section, "Advanced Security Issues: Ownership and Executable Content." We also see in the section "Working with Roles," how you can define your own roles, such as Editor and Reviewer.

To create the new user, click the Add button. You should see a new user object in the user folder.

## Editing Users

You can edit existing users by clicking them. This displays a form similar to the form you used to create a user. In fact, you can control all the same settings that we just discussed from this form. After your coworker logs in with the account you created for them, they should go to this management screen and change their password.

Like all Zope management functions, editing users is protected by the security policy. A user can change only their password, if they have the Manage Users permission, which managers have by default.

So, by default it's possible for a Manager defined in a given user folder to change other manager's accounts—if they both are defined in the same user folder. This might or might not be what you want. Later we look at ways to avoid this potential problem. Rest assured that it is not, however, possible for someone to find out your password from the management interface. Another Manager might have access to change your password, but the Manager cannot find out what your current password is without changing it.

In general, user folders work like normal Zope folders. You can create, edit, and delete contained objects. However, user folders are not as capable as normal folders. You cannot cut and paste users in a user folder, and you can't create anything besides a user in a user folder.

To delete an existing user from a user folder, select the user and click the Delete button. Remember, like all Zope actions, this can be undone if you make a mistake.

## Defining a User's Location

Zope can contain multiple user folders at different locations in the object hierarchy. A Zope user cannot access resources higher than the user folder they are defined in. Where your user account is defined determines what Zope resources you can access.

If your account is defined in a user folder in the Root folder, you have access to the Root folder. This is probably where the account you are using now is defined. You can, however, define users in any Zope folder.

Consider the case of a user folder at /BeautySchool/Hair/acl_users. Suppose the user Ralph Scissorhands is defined in this user folder. Ralph cannot log into Zope higher than the folder at /BeautySchool/Hair. Effectively Ralph's view of the Zope site is limited to things in the BeautySchool/Hair folder and lower. Regardless of the roles assigned to Ralph, he cannot access protected resources higher than his location.

Using this technique, it's easy to build simple security policies. One of the most common Zope management patterns is to place related objects in a folder together, and then create a user folder in that folder to define people who are responsible for those objects.

For example, suppose people in your organization wear uniforms. You are creating an intranet that provides information about your organization, including information about uniforms. You might create a uniforms folder somewhere in the intranet Zope site. In that folder you could put objects, such as pictures of uniforms and descriptions for how to wear and clean them. Then you could create a user folder in the uniforms folder and create an account for the head tailor. When a new style of uniform comes out the tailor doesn't have to ask the Webmaster to update the site, he or she can update their own section of the site without bothering anyone else. Additionally, the head tailor cannot log into any folder higher than the uniforms folder, which means the head tailor cannot manage any objects other than those in the uniforms folder.

This security pattern is called *delegation*, and is very common in Zope applications. By delegating different areas of your Zope site to different users, you can take the burden of site administration off of a small group of managers and spread that burden around to different specific groups of users. Later in the chapter we look at other security patterns (see "Security Usage Patterns").

## Working with Alternative User Folders

It might be that you don't want to manage your user account through the Web. This might be because you already have a user database, or perhaps you want to use other tools to maintain your account information. Zope allows you to use all sorts of authentication techniques with alternate user folders. You can find many alternate user folders on the Zope Web site at http://www.zope.org/Products/user_management. At the time of this writing, 19 contributed alternate user folders exist. A sampling of the more popular alternative user folders follows:

- **LoginManager**—This is a flexible and powerful user folder that allows you to plug in your own authorization methods. For example, you can use LoginManager to authenticate from a database.
- **etcUserFolder**—This user folder authenticates using standard UNIX /etc/ password style files.
- **LDAPAdapter**—This user folder allows you to authenticate from an LDAP server.
- **NTUserFolder**—This user folder authenticates from NT user accounts. It only works if you are running Zope under Windows NT or Windows 2000.

Some user folders provide alternate login and logout controls, such as log in Web forms, rather than browser HTTP authorization controls. Despite this variety, all user folders use the same general login procedure of prompting you for credentials when you access a protected resource.

Although most users are managed with user folders of one kind or another, Zope has a few special user accounts that are not managed via user folders.

## Special User Accounts

Zope provides three special user accounts that are not defined with user folders: the anonymous user, the emergency user, and the initial manager. The anonymous user is used frequently, while the emergency user and initial manager accounts are rarely used, but are important to know about.

### Zope Anonymous User

Zope has a built-in user account for guests—the anonymous user. If you don't have a user account on Zope, you are considered an *anonymous user*.

The anonymous user has security controls like any other, its role is Anonymous. By default, the Anonymous role can access only public resources, and can't change any Zope objects. You can tailor this policy, but most of the time the default anonymous security settings are adequate.

As we mentioned earlier in this chapter, see "Logging In and Logging Out of Zope," you must try to access a protected resource for Zope to authenticate you. The upshot is that even if you have a user account, Zope considers you anonymous until you have logged in.

### Zope Emergency User

Zope has a special user account for emergency use—known as the *emergency user*. We discussed the emergency user briefly in Chapter 2. The emergency user is not restricted by normal security settings. However, the emergency user cannot create any new objects with the exception of new user objects.

The emergency user is really useful only for two things: fixing messed up permissions and creating manager accounts. As we saw in Chapter 2, you can log in as the emergency user to create a Manager account when none exists. After you create a Manager account, you should log out as the emergency user and log back in as the Manager.

Another reason to use the emergency user account is that if you lock yourself out of Zope by removing permissions you need to manage Zope. In this case, log in as the emergency user and make sure that your Manager account has the View management screens and Change permissions permissions. Then log out and log back with your Manager account, and you should have enough access to fix anything else that is broken.

A common problem with the emergency user is trying to create a new object.

The error shown in Figure 6.2 lets you know that the emergency user cannot create new objects. The reason for this is a bit complex but becomes clear later in the chapter when we cover ownership (see "Advanced Security Issues: Ownership and Executable Content"). The short version of the story is that it would be unsafe for the emergency user to create objects because they would not be subject to the same security constraints as other objects.

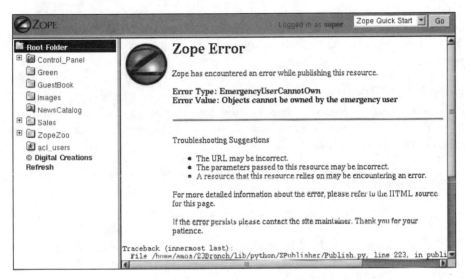

**Figure 6.2**    An error caused by trying to create a new object when logged in as the emergency user.

### Creating an Emergency User

Unlike normal user accounts that are defined through the Web, the emergency user account is defined in the file system. You can change the emergency user account by editing the access file in the Zope directory. Zope comes with a command-line utility, zpasswd.py to manage the emergency user account. Run zpasswd.py by passing it the access file path:

```
$ python zpasswd.py access

Username: superuser
Password:
Verify password:

Please choose a format from:
```

*continues*

*continued*

```
SHA - SHA-1 hashed password
CRYPT - UNIX-style crypt password
CLEARTEXT - no protection.

Encoding: SHA
Domain restrictions:
```

The zpasswd.py script steps you through the process of creating an emergency user account. Note that when you type in your password, it is not echoed to the screen. You can also run zpasswd.py with no arguments to get a list of command-line options.

## Zope Initial Manager

The initial Manager account is created by the Zope installer so that you can log into Zope the first time. When you first install Zope you should see a message such as this:

```
creating default inituser file
Note:
        The initial user name and password are 'admin'
        and 'IVX3kAwU'.

        You can change the name and password through the web
        interface or using the 'zpasswd.py' script.
```

This lets you know the initial Manager's name and password. You can use this information to log in to Zope for the first time as a Manager. Logged in as a Manager, you can create additional user accounts.

Initial users are defined in a similar way to the emergency user. Initial users are defined in a file on the file system call inituser. The zpasswd.py program can be used to edit this file in the same way it is used to edit the emergency user access file:

```
$ python zpasswd.py inituser

Username: bob
Password:
Verify password:

Please choose a format from:

SHA - SHA-1 hashed password
CRYPT - UNIX-style crypt password
CLEARTEXT - no protection.

Encoding: SHA
Domain restrictions:
```

This creates a new initial user called "bob" and sets his password. (Note: The password is not echoed back to you when you type it in.) When Zope starts, it checks this file for users and makes sure they can log into Zope. Normally, initial users are created by the

Zope Installer for you, and you shouldn't have to worry about changing them. If you want to create additional users, you do it through the Zope Web management interface.

So far we've covered how users and user folders control authentication. Next, we look at how to control authorization with security policies.

# Authorization and Managing Security

Zope security policies control authorization—they define who can do what. Security policies describe what roles have what permissions. Roles label classes of users, and permissions protect objects. Thus, security policies define what classes of users (roles) can take what kinds of actions (permissions) in a given part of the site.

Rather than stating the users that can take specific action on specific objects, Zope allows you to define the kinds of users that can take the kinds of action and in what areas of the site. This sort of generalizing makes your security policies simple and more powerful. Of course, you can make exceptions to your policy for specific users, actions, and objects.

In the following sections we examine roles, permissions, and security policies more closely with an eye to building simple and effective security policies.

## Working with Roles

Zope users have roles that define what kinds of actions they can take. Roles define classes of users, such as Manager, Anonymous, and Contributor.

Roles are similar to UNIX groups in that they abstract groups of users. Like UNIX groups, Zope users can have more than one role.

Roles make it easier for you to manage security. Instead of defining what every single user can do, you can set a couple of different security policies for different user roles.

Zope comes with three built-in roles:

- **Manager**—This role is used for users who perform standard Zope management functions, such as creating and editing Zope folders and documents.

- **Anonymous**—The Zope Anonymous user has this role. This role should be authorized to view public resources. In general this role should not be allowed to change Zope objects.

- **Owner**—This role is assigned automatically to users in the context of objects they create. We cover ownership later in this chapter.

For basic Zope sites you can get by with Manager and Anonymous. For more complex sites, you might want to create your own roles to classify your users into different groups.

## Defining Roles

To create a new role, go to the Security tab and scroll down to the bottom of the screen. Type the name of the new role in the User defined roles field, and click Add

Role. Role names should be short, one or two word descriptions of a type of user, such as Author, Site Architect, or Designer. You should pick role names that are relevant to your application.

You can verify that your role was created, noticing that a new role column now exists for your new role at the top of the screen. You can also delete a role by selecting the role from the Select list at the bottom of the security screen and clicking the Delete Role button. You can delete only your own custom roles. You cannot delete any of the "stock" roles that come with Zope.

You should notice that roles can be used at the level where they are defined and lower in the object hierarchy. So, if you want to create a role that is appropriate for your entire site, create it in the Root folder.

In general, roles should be applicable for large sections of your site. If you find yourself creating roles to limit access to parts of your site, chances are you can accomplish the same thing in a better way. For example, you could simply change the security settings for existing roles on the folder you want to protect. Or, you could define users deeper in the object hierarchy to limit their access. Later in this chapter we look at more examples of how to define security policies in the section "Defining Security Policies."

## Understanding Local Roles

Local roles are an advanced feature of Zope security. Users can be given extra roles when working with a certain object. If an object has local roles associated with a user, then that user gets those additional roles when working with that object.

For example, if a user owns an object, then they are usually given the additional local role of Owner when working with that object. A user might not have the capability to edit DTML methods in general, but for DTML methods they own, the user could have access to edit the DTML method through the Owner local role.

Local roles are a fairly advanced security control and are not needed very often. Zope's automatic control of the Owner local role is likely the only place you encounter local roles.

The main reason you might want to manually control local roles is to give a specific user special access to an object. In general, you should avoid setting security for specific users. It is easier to manage security settings that control groups of users instead of individuals.

## Understanding Permissions

Permissions define what actions can be taken with Zope objects. Just as roles abstract users, permissions abstract objects. For example, many Zope objects, including DTML methods and DTML documents, can be viewed. This action is protected by the View permission.

Some permissions are relevant only for one type of object. For example, the Change DTML Methods permission only protects DTML methods. Other permissions protect many types of objects, such as the FTP access permission.

You can find out what permissions are available on a given object by going to the Security management tab.

As you can see in Figure 6.3, a mail host has a limited palette of permissions available. Contrast this to the many permissions that you see when setting security on a folder.

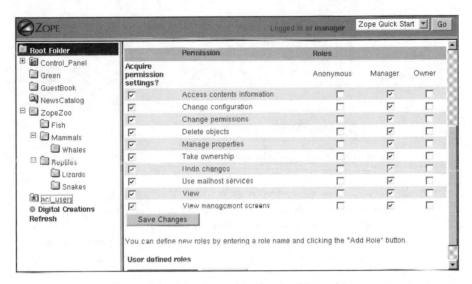

**Figure 6.3**    Security settings for a mail host object.

## Defining Security Policies

Security policies are where roles meet permissions. Security policies define who can do what in a given part of the site.

You can set security policies on almost any Zope object. To set a security policy, go to the Security tab. For example, click the Security tab of the Root folder.

A lot is going on in Figure 6.4. In the center of the screen is a grid of check boxes. The vertical columns of the grid represent roles, and the horizontal rows of the grid represent permissions. Checking the box at the intersection of a permission and a role, grants users with that role the ability to take actions protected by that permission.

Notice that Zope comes with a default security policy that allows managers to perform most tasks, and anonymous users to perform only a couple. You can tailor this policy to suit your needs by changing the security settings in the Root folder.

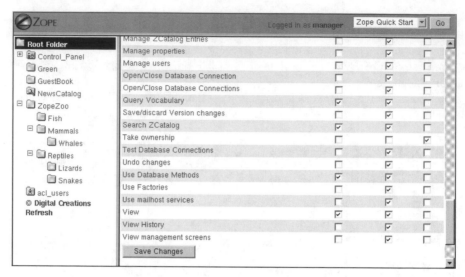

**Figure 6.4** Security policies for the Root folder.

For example, you can make your site private by disallowing anonymous users the ability to view any Web pages. To do this, deny all anonymous users View access by unchecking the View permission where it intersects the Anonymous role. You can make your entire site private by making this security policy change in the Root folder. If you want to make one part of your site private, you can make this change in the folder you want to make private.

This example points out a very important point about security policies: Security policies control security only for a given part of the site. The only global security policy is the one in the Root folder.

## Security Policy Acquisition

How do different security policies interact? We've seen that you can create security policies on different objects, but what determines which policies control which objects? The answer is that objects use their own policy—if they have one. Additionally, they inherit their parents' security policies through a process called acquisition.

*Acquisition* is a mechanism in Zope for sharing information among objects contained in a folder and its subfolders. The Zope security system uses acquisition to share security policies so that access can be controlled from high-level folders.

You can control security policy acquisition from the Security tab. Notice that a column of check boxes is to the left of the screen and it is labeled Acquire permission settings. Every check box in this column is checked by default. This means that security policy acquires its parent's setting for each permission-to-role setting, in addition to any settings specified on this screen. Keep in mind that for the Root folder, which has no parent to acquire from, this left-most check box column does not exist.

So, for example, suppose you want to make this folder private. As we saw before, this merely requires denying the Anonymous role the View permission. But, as you can see on this screen, the Anonymous role doesn't have the View permission, and yet this folder is not private. Why is this? The answer is that the Acquire permission settings option is checked for the View permission. This means that the current settings are augmented by the security policies of this folder's parents. Somewhere higher than this folder the Anonymous role must be assigned to the View permission. You can verify this by examining the security policies of this folder's parents. To make the folder private, we must uncheck the Acquire permission settings option. This ensures that only the settings explicitly in this security policy are in effect.

As you can see, security policy acquisition can get tricky. In general, you should always acquire security settings unless you have a specific reason not to. This makes managing your security settings much easier because much of the work can be done from the Root folder.

Next, we consider some examples of how to create effective security policies using the tools that you've learned about so far in this chapter.

# Security Usage Patterns

The basic concepts of Zope security are simple: roles and permissions combine to create security policies, and users actions are controlled by these policies. However these simple tools can be put together in many different ways. This can make managing security complex. Let's look at some basic patterns for managing security that provide good examples of how to create an effective and easy-to-manage security architecture.

## Security Rules of Thumb

This section covers a few simple guidelines for Zope security management. The security patterns that follow offer more specific recipes, but these guidelines give you some guidance when you face uncharted territory:

1. Define users at their highest level of control, but no higher.

2. Group objects that should be managed by the same people together in folders.

3. Keep it simple.

Rules one and two are closely related. Both are part of a more general rule for Zope site architecture. In general, you should refactor your site to locate related resources and users near each other. Granted, it's never possible to force resources and users into a strict hierarchy. However, a well-considered arrangement of resources and users into folders and subfolders helps tremendously.

Regardless of your site architecture, try to keep things simple. The more you complicate your security settings, the harder it will be to understand, manage, and keep it effective. For example, limit the number of new roles you create, and try to use security policy acquisition to limit the number of places you have to explicitly define security settings. If you find that your security policies, users, and roles are growing into a complex thicket, you should rethink what you're doing. There's probably a simpler way.

## Global and Local Policies

The most basic Zope security pattern is to define a global security policy in the Root folder and acquire this policy everywhere. Then, as needed, you can add additional policies deeper in the object hierarchy to augment the global policy. Try to limit the number of places that you override the global policy. If you find that you have to make changes in a number of places, consider consolidating the objects in those separate locations into the same folder so that you can make the security settings in one place.

You should choose to acquire permission settings in your subpolicies unless your subpolicy is more restrictive than the global policy. In this case, you should uncheck this option for the permission that you want to restrict.

This simple pattern takes care of many of your security needs. Its advantages are that it is easy to manage and easy to understand. These characteristics are extremely important for any security architecture.

## Delegating Control to Local Managers

This security pattern is central to Zope, and is part of what gives Zope its unique flavor. Zope encourages you to collect like resources in folders together and then to create user accounts in these folders to manage the content.

Let's say you want to delegate the management of the Sales folder over to the new sales Web manager—Steve. First, you don't want Steve messing with anything other than the Sales folder, so you don't need to add him to the acl_users folder in the Root folder. Instead, create a new User folder in the Sales folder.

Now you can add Steve to the User folder in Sales and give him the role Manager. Steve can now log directly into the Sales folder to manage his area by pointing his browser to `http://www.zopezoo.org/Sales/manage`.

Notice in Figure 6.5 that the navigation tree on the left shows that Sales is the Root folder. The local Manager defined in this folder never has the ability to log into any folders higher than Sales, so Sales is shown as the top folder.

This pattern is very powerful because it can be applied recursively. For example, Steve can create a subfolder for multilevel marketing sales. Then, he can create a user folder in the multilevel marketing Sales folder to delegate control of this folder to the multilevel marketing sales manager, and so on. This is a recipe for huge Web sites managed by thousands of people.

The beauty of this pattern is that higher-level managers need not concern themselves too much with what their underlings do. If they choose, managers can pay close attention, but they can safely ignore the details because they know that their delegates cannot make any changes outside their area of control. They also know that their security settings are acquired.

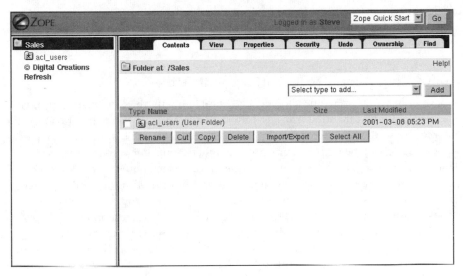

**Figure 6.5**    Managing the Sales folder.

## Different Levels of Access with Roles

The local manager pattern is powerful and scalable, but it takes a rather coarse view of security. Either you have access or you don't. Sometimes you need to have more fine-grained control. Many times, you have resources that need to be used by more than one type of person. Roles provide you with a solution to this problem. Roles allow you to define classes of users and set security policies for them.

Before creating new roles, make sure that you really need them. Suppose that you have a Web site that publishes articles. The public reads articles and managers edit and publish articles. However, a third class of user can author articles, but not publish or edit them.

One solution would be to create an authors folder where author accounts are created and given the Manager role. This folder would be private so that it could be viewed only by Managers. Articles could be written in this folder and then Managers could move the articles out of this folder to publish them. This is a reasonable solution, but it requires that authors work in only one part of the site and it requires extra work by Managers to move articles out of the authors folder. Also, consider the problems that result when an author wants to update an article that has been moved out of the authors folder.

A better solution is to add an Author role. Adding a role helps us because it allows access controls not based on location. So, in our example, by adding an author role we make it possible for articles to be written, edited, and published anywhere in the site. We can set a global security policy that gives authors the ability to create and write articles, but doesn't grant them permissions to publish or edit articles.

Roles allow you to control access based on who a user is, not just where they are defined.

## Controlling Access to Locations with Roles

Roles can help you overcome another subtle problem with the local manager pattern. The problem is that the local manager pattern requires a strict hierarchy of control. No provision exists to allow two different groups of people to access the same resources without one group being the Manager of the other group. Put another way, users defined in one part of the site cannot manage resources in another part of the site.

Let's look at an example to illustrate the second limitation of the local manager pattern. Suppose you run a large site for a pharmaceutical company. You have two classes of users—scientists and salespeople. In general, the scientists and the salespeople manage different Web resources. However, suppose that some things both types of people need to manage, such as advertisements that have to contain complex scientific warnings. If we define our scientists in the Science folder and the salespeople in the Sales folder, where should we put the AdsWithComplexWarnings folder? Unless the Science folder is inside the Sales folder, or vice versa, there is no place that we can put the AdsWithComplexWarnings folder so that both scientists and salespeople can manage it. It is not a good political or practical solution to have the salespeople manage the scientists or vice versa. What can be done?

The solution is to use roles. You should create two roles at a level higher than both the Science and Sales folders, say Scientist and SalesPerson. Then, instead of defining the scientists and salespeople in their own folders, define them higher in the object hierarchy so that they have access to the AdsWithComplexWarnings folder.

When you create users at this higher level, you should not give them the Manager role, but instead give them Scientist or SalesPerson as appropriate. Then you should set the security policies. In the Science folder the Scientist role should have the equivalent of Manager control. In the Sales folder, the SalesPerson role should have the same permissions as Manager. Finally, in the AdsWithComplexWarnings folder you should give both Scientist and SalesPerson roles adequate permissions. In this way, roles are used not to provide different levels of access, but to provide access to different locations based on who you are.

Another common situation when you might want to employ this pattern is when you cannot define your managers locally. For example, you might be using an alternate user folder that requires all users to be defined in the Root folder. In this case, you would want to make extensive use of roles to limit access to different locations based on roles.

This wraps up our discussion of security patterns. By now you should have a reasonable grasp of how to use user folders, roles, and security policies to shape a reasonable security architecture for your application. Next, we cover two advanced security issues: how to perform security checks and securing executable content.

# Performing Security Checks

Most of the time you don't have to perform any security checks. If a user attempts to perform a secured operation, Zope prompts them to log in. If the user doesn't have adequate permissions to access a protected resource, Zope denies them access. However, sometimes you might want to manually perform security checks. The main reason to do this is to limit the choices you offer a user to those for which they are authorized. This doesn't prevent a sneaky user from trying to access secured actions, but it does reduce user frustration by not giving the user the option to try something that does not work.

The most common security query asks whether the current user has a given permission. For example, suppose your application allows some users to upload files. This action might be protected by the Add Documents, Images, and Files standard Zope permission. You can test to see if the current user has this permission in DTML:

```
<dtml-if expr="_.SecurityCheckPermission(
               'Add Documents, Images, and Files', this())">

  <form action="upload">
  ...
  </form>

</dtml-if>
```

The SecurityCheckPermission function takes two arguments, a permission name, and an object. In this case, we pass `this()` as the object, which is a reference to the current object. By passing the current object, we make sure that local roles are taken into account when testing whether the current user has a given permission.

You can find out about the current user by accessing the user in DTML. The current user is a Zope object like any other, and you can perform actions on it using methods defined in the API documentation.

Suppose you want to display the current username on a Web page to personalize the page. You can do this easily in DTML:

```
<dtml-var expr="_.SecurityGetUser().getUserName()">
```

You can retrieve the currently logged in user with the SecurityGetUser DTML function. This DTML fragment tests the current user by calling the getUserName method on the current user object. If the user is not logged in, you get the name of the anonymous user, which is Anonymous User.

Next, we look at another advanced issue that affects security of DTML and scripts.

# Advanced Security Issues: Ownership and Executable Content

You've now covered all the basics of Zope security. What remains are the advanced concepts of ownership and executable content. Zope uses *ownership* to associate objects with users who create them, and *executable content* refers to objects, such as scripts and DTML methods and documents, which execute user code.

For small sites with trusted users, you can safely ignore these advanced issues. However, for large sites where you allow untrusted users to create and manage Zope objects, it's important to understand ownership and securing executable content.

## The Problem: Trojan Horse Attacks

The basic scenario that motivates both ownership and executable content controls is a Trojan horse attack. A *Trojan horse* is an attack on a system that operates by tricking a user into taking a potentially harmful action. A typical Trojan horse masquerades as a benign program that causes harm when you unwittingly run it.

All Web-based platforms, including Zope and many others, are subject to this style of attack. All that is required is to trick someone into visiting a URL that performs a harmful action.

This kind of attack is very hard to protect against. You can trick someone into clicking a link fairly easily, or you can use more advanced techniques, such as Javascript, to cause a user to visit a malicious URL.

Zope offers some protection from this kind of Trojan horse. Zope helps protect your site from server-side Trojan attacks by limiting the power of Web resources based on who authored them. If an untrusted user authors a Web page, then the power of the Web pages to do harm to unsuspecting visitors is limited. For example, suppose an untrusted user creates a DTML document or Python script that deletes all the pages in your site. If they attempt to view the page, it fails because they do not have adequate permissions. If a Manager views the page, it also fails, even though the Manager does have adequate permissions to perform the dangerous action.

Zope uses ownership information and executable content controls to provide this limited protection.

## Managing Ownership

When a user creates a Zope object, they own that object. An object that has no owner is referred to as unowned. Ownership information is stored in the object itself. This is similar to how UNIX keeps track of the owner of a file.

You find out how an object is owned by viewing the Ownership management tab, as shown in Figure 6.6.

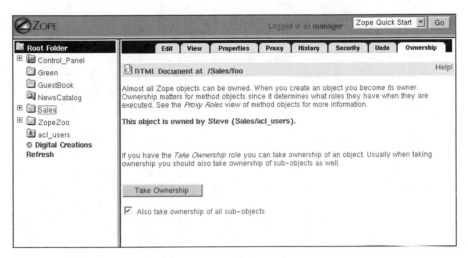

**Figure 6.6**    Managing ownership settings.

This screen tells you if the object is owned and, if so, by whom. If the object is owned by someone else, and you have the Take ownership permission, you can take over the ownership of an object. You also have the option of taking ownership of all subobjects by checking the Take ownership of all subobjects box. Taking ownership is mostly useful if the owner account has been deleted, or if objects have been turned over to you for continued management.

As we mentioned earlier, ownership affects security policies because a user has the local role Owner on objects they own. However, ownership also affects security because it controls the roles executable content.

## Roles of Executable Content

Through the Web you can edit scripts on some kinds of Zope objects. These objects include DTML documents, DTML methods, SQL methods, Python-based scripts, and Perl-based scripts. These objects are said to be *executable* because they run scripts that are edited through the Web.

When you visit an executable object by going to its URL or calling it from DTML or a script, Zope runs the object's script. The script is restricted by the roles of the object's owner and your roles. In other words, an executable object can perform only those actions that both the owner and the viewer are authorized for. This keeps an unprivileged user from writing a harmful script and then tricking a powerful user into executing the script. You can't fool someone else into performing an action that you are not authorized to perform yourself. This is how Zope uses ownership to protect against server-side Trojan horse attacks.

## Proxy Roles

Sometimes Zope's system of limiting access to executable objects isn't exactly what you want. Sometimes you might want to clamp down security on an executable object—despite whoever might own or execute it as a form of extra security. Other times you might want to provide an executable object with extra access to allow an unprivileged viewer to perform protected actions. Proxy roles provide you with a way to tailor the roles of an executable object.

Suppose you want to create a mail form that allows anonymous users to send email to the Webmaster of your site. Sending email is protected by the Use mailhost services permission. Anonymous users don't normally have this permission and for good reason. You don't want just anyone to be able to anonymously send email with your Zope server.

The problem with this arrangement is that your DTML method that sends email fails for anonymous users. How can you get around this problem? The answer is to set the Proxy roles on the DTML method that sends email so that when it executes it has the Manager role. Visit the Proxy management tab on your DTML method, as shown in Figure 6.7.

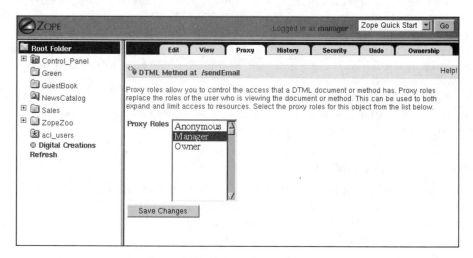

Figure 6.7    Proxy role management.

Select Manager and click the Change button. This sets the Proxy roles of the mail sending method to Manager. Note that you must have the Manager role yourself to set it as a Proxy role. Now when anyone—anonymous or not—runs your mail sending method, it executes with the Manager role, and thus has authorization to send email.

Proxy roles define a fixed set of the permissions of executable content. Thus, you can also use them to restrict security. For example, if you set the Proxy roles of a script to the Anonymous role, then the script never executes any other roles besides Anonymous—despite the roles of the owner and viewer.

Use Proxy roles with care because they can be used to skirt the default security restrictions.

Security consists of two processes—authentication and authorization. User folders control authentication, and security policies control authorization. Zope security is intimately tied with the concept of location. Users have location, security policies have location, even roles can have location. Creating an effective security architecture requires attention to location. When in doubt refer to the security usage patterns discussed in this chapter.

In the next chapter we switch gears and explore advanced DTML. DTML can be a very powerful tool for presentation and scripting. You'll find out about many new tags, and we take a look at some DTML-specific security controls that were not covered in this chapter.

# 7

# Variables and Advanced DTML

DTML IS THE KIND OF LANGUAGE THAT "does what you mean." That is good when it does what you actually want it to do, but when it does something you don't want it to do, it's bad. This chapter tells you how to make DTML do what you *really* mean.

DTML has a reputation for complexity. DTML is really simple if all you want to do is simple layout, like you've seen so far. However, if you want to use DTML for more advanced tasks, you have to understand where DTML variable names come from.

The following example illustrates a very tricky error that almost all newbies encounter. Imagine you have a DTML document called zooName. This document contains an HTML form, such as the following:

```
<dtml-var standard_html_header>

  <dtml-if zooName>

    <p><dtml-var zooName></p>

  <dtml-else>

    <form action="<dtml-var URL>" method="GET">
      <input name="zooName">
      <input type="submit" value="What is zooName?">
    </form>

  </dtml-if>

<dtml-var standard_html_footer>
```

This looks simple enough. The idea is that this is an HTML page that calls itself. The page calls itself because the HTML action is the URL variable, which becomes the URL of the DTML document.

If there is a *zooName* variable, then the page prints it. If no *zooName* variable exists, the page shows a form that asks for it. When you click Submit, the data you enter makes the if evaluate true, and this code should print what was entered in the form.

Unfortunately, this is one of those instances where DTML does not do what you mean because the name of the DTML document that contains this DTML is also named zooName. DTML doesn't use the variable out of the request, it uses itself, which causes it to call itself and call itself—ad infinitum—until you get an excessive recursion error. So, instead of doing what you really meant, DTML sends you an error. This is what confuses beginners. In the next couple of sections, we show you how to fix this example so that DTML does what you mean.

## How Variables Are Looked Up

The DTML error in the zooName document can be fixed two ways. The first way is to rename the document to something, such as zopeNameFormOrReply. However, if you take this approach, you must always remember this special exception (naming the document and the variable the same thing) and never do it, never understanding why the error happens. The second way to fix the error is to understand how names are looked up and be explicit about where you want the name to come from in the namespace.

The DTML namespace is a collection of objects arranged in a stack. A *stack* is a list of objects that can be manipulated by *pushing* and *popping* objects onto and off of the stack.

When a DTML document or method is executed, Zope creates a DTML namespace to resolve DTML variable names. Understanding the workings of the DTML namespace is important so that you can accurately predict how DTML will locate variables. Some of the trickiest problems you run into with DTML can be resolved by understanding the DTML namespace.

When Zope looks for names in the DTML namespace stack, it first looks at the very top object in the stack. If the name can't be found there, then Zope looks in the next item down. DTML works its way down the stack, checking each object in turn, until it finds the name that it is looking for.

If Zope gets all the way down to the bottom of the stack and can't find what it is looking for, then an error is generated. For example, try looking for the non-existent name unicorn:

```
<dtml-var unicorn>
```

As long as no variable is named *unicorn*, viewing this DTML returns an error, as shown in Figure 7.1.

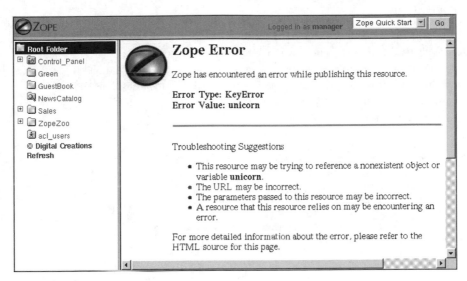

Figure 7.1    DTML error message indicating that it cannot find a variable.

However, the DTML stack does not exclusively have all of the names because DTML doesn't start with an empty stack. Before you even begin executing DTML in Zope, it is possible that many objects are pushed onto the namespace stack.

# DTML Namespaces

DTML namespaces are built dynamically for every request in Zope. When you call a DTML method or DTML document through the Web, the DTML namespace starts with the same first two stack elements—the client object and the request, as shown in Figure 7.2

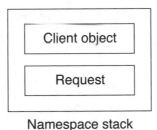

Namespace stack

Figure 7.2    Initial DTML namespace stack.

The client object is the first object on the top of the DTML namespace stack. What the client object is varies, depending on whether or not you are executing a DTML method or a DTML document. In our preceding example, the client object is named zooName, which is why it breaks. The form input that we really wanted comes from the Web request, but the client is looked at first.

The request namespace is always on the bottom of the DTML namespace stack, and therefore, it is the last namespace to be looked in for names. This means that we must be explicit in our example about what namespace we want:

```
<dtml-var standard_html_header>

  <dtml-with REQUEST only>
    <dtml-if zooName>
      <p><dtml-var zooName></p>
    <dtml-else>
      <form action="<dtml-var URL>" method="GET">
        <input name="zooName">
        <input type="submit" value="What is zooName?">
      </form>
    </dtml-if>
  </dtml-with>

<dtml-var standard_html_footer>
```

Here, the with tag says to look in the REQUEST namespace, and *only* the REQUEST namespace, for the name zooName.

## DTML Client Object

The client object in DTML varies, depending on whether or not you are executing a DTML method or a DTML document. In the case of a document, the client object is always the document itself, or in other words, a DTML document is its own client object.

A DTML method, however, can have different kinds of client objects, depending on how it is called. For example, if you had a DTML method that displayed all the contents of a folder, then the client object would be the folder that is being displayed. This client object can change, depending on which folder the method in question is displaying. For example, consider the following DTML method named list in the Root folder:

```
<dtml-var standard_html_header>

<ul>
<dtml-in objectValues>
  <li><dtml-var title_or_id></li>
</dtml-in>
</ul>

<dtml-var standard_html_footer>
```

What this method displays depends upon how it is used. If you apply this method to the Reptiles folder with the URL http://localhost:8080/Reptiles/list, then you get something that looks like Figure 7.3.

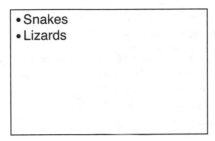

- Snakes
- Lizards

**Figure 7.3**  Applying the list method to the Reptiles folder.

However, if you were to apply the method to the Birds folder with the URL `http://localhost:8080/Birds/list`, then you would get something different—the two items in the list would be Parrot and Raptors.

Same DTML method, different results. In the first example, the client object of the list method was the Reptiles folder. In the second example, the client object was the Birds folder. When Zope looked up the *objectValues* variable in the first case, it called the objectValues method of the Reptiles folder. In the second case, it called the objectValues method of the Birds folder.

In other words, the client object is where variables, such as methods and properties, are looked up first.

As you saw in Chapter 4, "Dynamic Content with DTML," if Zope cannot find a variable in the client object, it searches through the object's containers. Zope uses acquisition to automatically inherit variables from the client object's containers. So, when Zope walks up the object hierarchy looking for variables, it always starts at the client object and works its way up from there.

## DTML Request Object

The request object is on the very bottom of the DTML namespace stack. The request contains all the information specific to the current Web request.

Just as the client object uses acquisition to look in a number of places for variables, the request object also looks up variables in a number of places. When the request looks for a variable, it consults these sources in order:

1. **The CGI environment.** The Common Gateway Interface or CGI interface defines a standard set of environment variables to be used by dynamic Web scripts (`http://www.w3.org/CGI/`). These variables are provided by Zope in the REQUEST namespace.

2. **Form data.** If the current request is a form action, then any form input data that was submitted with the request can be found in the REQUEST object.

3. **Cookies.** If the client of the current request has any cookies, these can be found in the current REQUEST object.

4. **Additional variables.** The REQUEST namespace provides you with lots of other useful information, such as the URL of the current object and all its parents.

The REQUEST namespace is very useful in Zope because it is the primary way that clients (in this case, Web browsers) communicate with Zope by providing form data, cookies, and other information about themselves. For more information about the REQUEST object, see Appendix B, "API Reference."

A very simple and enlightening example is to print the REQUEST out in an HTML page:

```
<dtml-var standard_html_header>

<dtml-var REQUEST>

<dtml-var standard_html_footer>
```

Try this yourself. You should get something that looks like Figure 7.4.

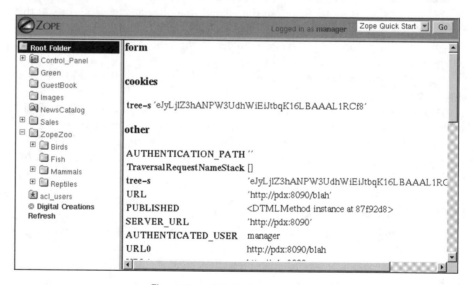

**Figure 7.4**   Displaying the request.

Because the request comes after the client object, if names exist in both the request and the client object, DTML always finds them first in the client object. This can be a problem. Let's look at some ways to get around this problem by controlling more directly how DTML looks up variables.

## Rendering Variables

When you insert a variable using the var tag, Zope first looks up the variable using the DTML namespace. Zope then renders it and inserts the results. *Rendering* means turning an object or value into a string suitable for inserting the output. Zope renders simple variables by using Python's standard method for coercing objects into strings. For complex objects, such as DTML methods and SQL methods, Zope calls the object—instead of just trying to turn it into a string. This enables you to insert DTML methods into other DTML methods.

In general, Zope renders variables in the way you would expect. It's only when you start doing more advanced tricks that you become aware of the rendering process. Later in this chapter we look at some examples of how to control rendering using the getitem DTML utility function (see "DTML Namespace Utility Functions").

# Modifying the DTML Namespace

Now that you have seen that the DTML namespace is a stack, you might be wondering how, or even why, new objects get pushed onto it.

Some DTML tags modify the DTML namespace while they are executing. A tag might push some objects onto the namespace stack during the course of execution. These tags include the in tag, the with tag, and the let tag.

### *in* Tag Namespace Modifications

When the in tag iterates over a sequence, it pushes the current item in the sequence onto the top of the namespace stack:

```
<dtml-var getId> <!— This is the id of the client object —>

<dtml-in objectValues>

  <dtml-var getId> <!— this is the id of the current item in the
                   objectValues sequence —>
</dtml-in>
```

You've seen this many times throughout the examples in this book. While the in tag is iterating over a sequence, each item is pushed onto the namespace stack for the duration of the contents of the in tag block. When the block is finished executing, the current item in the sequence is popped off the DTML namespace stack and the next item in the sequence is pushed on.

### The *with* Tag

The with tag pushes an object that you specify onto the top of the namespace stack for the duration of the with block. This enables you to specify where variables should be looked up first. When the with block closes, the object is popped off the namespace stack.

Consider a folder that contains a bunch of methods and properties that you are interested in. You could access those names with Python expressions such as this:

```
<dtml-var standard_html_header>

<dtml-var expr="Reptiles.getReptileInfo()">
<dtml-var expr="Reptiles.reptileHouseMaintainer">

<dtml-in expr="Reptiles.getReptiles()">
  <dtml-var species>
</dtml-in>

<dtml-var standard_html_footer>
```

Notice that a lot of complexity is added to the code just to get things out of the Reptiles folder. Using the with tag, you can make this example much easier to read:

```
<dtml-var standard_html_header>

<dtml-with Reptiles>

  <dtml-var getReptileInfo>
  <dtml-var reptileHouseMaintainer>

  <dtml-in getReptiles>
    <dtml-var species>
  </dtml-in>

</dtml-with>

<dtml-var standard_html_footer>
```

Another reason you might want to use the with tag is to put the request, or some part of the request, on top of the namespace stack. For example, suppose you have a form that includes an input named id. If you try to process this form by looking up the id variable like so:

```
<dtml-var id>
```

you will not get your form's id variable, but the client object's id. One solution is to push the Web request's form on to the top of the DTML namespace stack using the with tag:

```
<dtml-with expr="REQUEST.form">
  <dtml-var id>
</dtml-with>
```

This ensures that you get the form's id first. See Appendix B for complete API documentation of the request object.

If you submit your form without supplying a value for the id input, the form on top of the namespace stack does you no good because the form doesn't contain an id variable. You still get the client object's id because DTML searches the client object after failing to find the id variable in the form. The with tag has an attribute that enables you to trim the DTML namespace to include only the object you specify:

```
<dtml-with expr="REQUEST.form" only>
  <dtml-if id>
    <dtml-var id>
  <dtml-else>
    <p>The form didn't contain an "id" variable.</p>
  </dtml-if>
</dtml-with>
```

Using the `only` attribute enables you to be sure about where your variables are being looked up.

### The *let* Tag

The `let` tag enables you to push a new namespace onto the namespace stack. This namespace is defined by the tag attributes to the `let` tag:

```
<dtml-let person="'Bob'" relation="'uncle'">
  <p><dtml-var person>'s your <dtml-var relation>.</p>
</dtml-let>
```

This would display:

```
<p>Bob's your uncle.</p>
```

The `let` tag accomplishes many of the same goals as the `with` tag. The main advantage of the `let` tag is that you can use it to define multiple variables to be used in a block. The `let` tag creates one or more new variables and their values. It also pushes a namespace object containing those variables and their values on to the top of the DTML namespace stack. In general, the `with` tag is more useful to push existing objects on to the namespace stack, although the `let` tag is better suited for defining new variables for a block.

When you find yourself writing complex DTML that requires things like new variables, there's a good chance that you could do the same thing better with Python or Perl. Advanced scripting is covered in Chapter 8, "Advanced Zope Scripting."

The DTML namespace is a complex place, and this complexity evolved over a long period of time. Although it helps to understand where names come from, it is much more helpful to always be specific about where you are looking for a name. The `with` and `let` tags enable you to control the namespace to look exactly in the right place for the name you are looking for.

# DTML Namespace Utility Functions

Like all things in Zope, the DTML namespace is an object, and it can be accessed directly in DTML with the _ (underscore) object. The _ namespace is often referred to as *the under namespace*.

The under namespace provides you with many useful methods for certain programming tasks. Let's look at a few of them.

Say you wanted to print your name three times. This can be done with the `in` tag, but how do you explicitly tell the `in` tag to loop three times? Just pass it a sequence with three items:

```
<dtml-var standard_html_header>

<ul>
<dtml-in expr="_.range(3)">
  <li><dtml-var sequence-item>: My name is Bob.</li>
</dtml-in>
</ul>

<dtml-var standard_html_footer>
```

The `_.range(3)` Python expression returns a sequence of the first three integers: 0, 1, and 2. The *range* function is a standard Python built-in function, and many of Python's built-in functions can be accessed through the _ namespace, including

- `range([start,], stop, [step])`—Returns a list of integers from `start` to `stop` counting `step` integers at a time. `start` defaults to 0 and `step` defaults to 1. For example:
  - `_.range(3,9,2)`—gives `[3,5,7,9]`.
- `len(sequence)`—`len` returns the size of sequence as an integer.

Many of these names come from the Python language, which contains a set of special functions called *built-ins*. The Python philosophy is to have a small, set number of built-in names. The Zope philosophy can be thought of as having a large, complex array of built-in names.

The under namespace can also be used to explicitly control variable look up. That is a very common usage of this syntax. You've seen that the `in` tag defines a number of special variables, such as *sequence-item* and *sequence-key* that you can use inside a loop to help you display and control it. What if you wanted to use one of these variables inside a Python expression?

```
<dtml-var standard_html_header>

<h1>The squares of the first three integers:</h1>
<ul>
<dtml-in expr="_.range(3)">
  <li>The square of <dtml-var sequence-item> is:
    <dtml-var expr="sequence-item * sequence-item">
  </li>
</dtml-in>
</ul>

<dtml-var standard_html_footer>
```

Try this, does it work? No! Why not? The problem lies in this `var` tag:

```
<dtml-var expr="sequence-item * sequence-item">
```

Remember, everything inside a Python expression attribute must be a valid Python expression. In DTML, *sequence-item* is the name of a variable, but in Python this means "The object *sequence* minus the object *item*." This is not what you want.

What you really want is to look up the variable *sequence-item*. The way to do this in a DTML expression is to use the `getitem` utility function to explicitly look up a variable:

```
The square of <dtml-var sequence-item> is:
<dtml-var expr="_.getitem('sequence-item')*
_.getitem('sequence-item')">
```

The getitem function takes the variable name *(sequence-item)* to look up as its first argument. Now, the DTML method correctly displays the sum of the first three integers. The `getitem` method takes an optional second argument, which specifies whether or not to render the variable. Recall that rendering a DTML variable means turning it into a string. By default, the getitem function does not render a variable.

The following is how to insert a rendered variable named *myDoc*:

```
<dtml-var expr="_.getitem('myDoc', 1)">
```

This example is in some ways rather pointless because it's the functional equivalent to:

```
<dtml-var myDoc>
```

However, suppose you had a form in which a user got to select the document they wanted to see from a list of choices. Suppose the form had an input named selectedDoc, which contained the name of the document. You could then display the rendered document like so:

```
<dtml-var expr="_.getitem(selectedDoc, 1)">
```

Notice in the preceding example that *selectedDoc* is not in quotes. We don't want to insert the variable named *selectedDoc*. We want to insert the variable *named by* *selectedDoc*. For example, the value of *selectedDoc* might be *chapterOne*. Using indirect variable insertion, you can insert the *chapterOne* variable. This way you can insert a variable whose name you don't know when you are authoring the DTML.

If you are a Python programmer and you begin using the more complex aspects of DTML, consider doing a lot of your work in Python scripts that you call from DTML. This is explained more in Chapter 8. Using Python sidesteps many of the issues in DTML.

# DTML Security

Zope can be used by many different kinds of users. For example, the Zope site, Zope.org (`http://www.zope.org/`), has over 11,000 community members at the time of this writing. Each member can log into Zope, add objects and news items, and manage their own personal area.

Because DTML is a programming language, it is very flexible about working with objects and their properties. If no security systems constrained DTML, then a user could potentially create malicious or privacy-invading DTML code.

DTML is restricted by standard Zope security settings. So, if you don't have permission to access an object by going to its URL, you also don't have permission to access it through DTML. You can't use DTML to trick the Zope security system.

For example, suppose you have a DTML document named Diary, which is private. Anonymous users can't access your Diary through the Web. If an Anonymous user views DTML and tries to access your Diary, they are denied:

```
<dtml-var Diary>
```

DTML verifies that the current user is authorized to access all DTML variables. If the user does not have authorization, then the security system raises an *Unauthorized* error, and the user is asked to present more privileged authentication credentials.

In Chapter 6, "Users and Security," you can read about security rules for executable content. The roles of a DTML document or method can be tailored to allow it to access restricted variables—regardless of the viewer's roles.

## Safe Scripting Limits

DTML does not enable you to gobble up memory or execute infinite loops and recursions; the restrictions on looping and memory are pretty tight, which makes DTML the wrong language for complex, expensive programming logic. For example, you cannot create huge lists with the `_.range` utility function. You also have no way to access the file system directly in DTML.

Keep in mind, however, that these safety limits are simple and can be outsmarted by determined users. Generally, it is not a good idea to let anyone you don't trust write DTML code on your site.

# Advanced DTML Tags

In the rest of this chapter, we look at the many advanced DTML tags. These tags are summarized in Appendix A, "DTML Reference." DTML has tags to do all kind of things. In fact, you can download many interesting contributed DTML tags from the Zope.org Web site. For example, Ty Sarna's `Calendar` tag gives you the ability to easily format date-oriented objects as a calendar.

This section covers what could be referred to as Zope *miscellaneous* tags. These tags don't really fit into any broad categories except for one group of tags, the *exception handling* DTML tags, which are discussed at the end of this chapter in the section, "Exception Handling Tags."

## The *call* Tag

The `var` tag calls methods, but it also inserts the return value. Using the `call` tag, you can call methods without inserting their return value into the output. This is useful if you are more interested in the effect of calling a method rather than its return value.

For example, when you want to change the value of the property `animalName`, you are more interested in the effect of calling the `manage_changeProperties` method than the return value the method gives you. Here's an example:

```
<dtml-if expr="REQUEST.has_key('animalName')">
  <dtml-call expr="manage_changeProperties(animalName=REQUEST['animalName'])">
  <h1>The property 'animalName' has changed</h1>
<dtml-else>
  <h1>No properties were changed</h1>
</dtml-if>
```

In this example, the page changes a property, depending on whether a certain name exists. The result of the `manage_changeProperties` method is not important and does not need to be shown to the user.

Another common usage of the `call` tag is calling methods that affect client behavior, such as the `RESPONSE.redirect` method. In this example, you make the client redirect to a different page, change the page that gets redirected, and change the value for the *target* variable defined in the `let` tag:

```
<dtml-var standard_html_header>

<dtml-let target="'http://example.com/new_location.html'">

  <h1>This page has moved, you will now be redirected to the
  correct location.  If your browser does not redirect, click <a
  href="<dtml-var target>"><dtml-var target></a>.</h1>

  <dtml-call expr="RESPONSE.redirect(target)">

</dtml-let>

<dtml-var standard_html_footer>
```

In short, the `call` tag works exactly like the `var` tag with the exception that it doesn't insert the results of calling the variable.

## The *comment* Tag

DTML can be documented with comments using the comment tag:

```
<dtml-var standard_html_header>

<dtml-comment>

  This is a DTML comment and will be removed from the DTML code
  before it is returned to the client.  This is useful for
  documenting DTML code.  Unlike HTML comments, DTML comments
  are NEVER sent to the client.

</dtml-comment>
```

*continues*

*continued*

```
<!—
```

```
This is an HTML comment, this is NOT DTML and will be treated
as HTML and like any other HTML code will get sent to the
client.  Although it is customary for an HTML browser to hide
these comments from the end user, they still get sent to the
client and can be easily seen by 'Viewing the Source' of a
document.
```

```
—>
```

```
<dtml-var standard_html_footer>
```

The comment block is removed from DTML output.

In addition to documenting DTML, you can use the `comment` tag to temporarily comment out other DTML tags. Later you can remove the `comment` tags to re-enable the DTML.

## The *tree* Tag

The `tree` tag enables you to easily build dynamic trees in HTML to display hierarchical data. A *tree* is a graphical representation of data that starts with a "root" object that has objects underneath it often referred to as "branches." Branches can have their own branches, just like a real tree. This concept should be familiar to anyone who has used a file manager program, such as Microsoft Windows Explorer, to navigate a file system. And, in fact, the left navigation view of the Zope management interface is created using the `tree` tag.

For example, Figure 7.5 shows a tree that represents a collection of folders and subfolders.

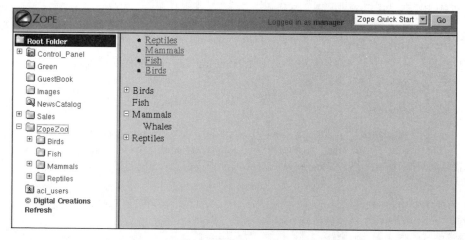

**Figure 7.5**   HTML tree generated by the `tree` tag.

The DTML that generated this tree display follows:

```
<dtml-var standard_html_header>

<dtml-tree>

  <dtml-var getId>

</dtml-tree>

<dtml-var standard_html_footer>
```

The `tree` tag queries objects to find their subobjects and takes care of displaying the results as a tree. The `tree` tag block works as a template to display nodes of the tree.

Because the basic protocol of the Web (HTTP) is stateless, you need to somehow remember what state the tree is in every time you look at a page. To do this, Zope stores the state of the tree in a cookie. Because this tree state is stored in a cookie, only one tree can appear on a Web page at a time, otherwise they would confusingly use the same cookie.

You can tailor the behavior of the `tree` tag quite a bit with `tree` tag attributes and special variables. A sampling of `tree` tag attributes follows:

- **branches**—The name of the method used to find subobjects. This method defaults to *tpValues*, which is a method defined by a number of standard Zope objects.

- **leaves**—The name of a method used to display objects that do not have subobject branches.

- **nowrap**—Either 0 or 1. If 0, then branch text wraps to fit in available space. Otherwise, text might be truncated. The default value is 0.

- **sort**—Sorts branches before text insertion is performed. The attribute value is the name of the attribute on which items should be sorted.

- **assume_children**—Either 0 or 1. If 1, then all objects are assumed to have subobjects, and therefore always have a plus sign in front of them when they are collapsed. Only when an item is expanded are subobjects looked for. This could be a good option when the retrieval of subobjects is a costly process. The default value is 0.

- **single**—Either 0 or 1. If 1, then only one branch of the tree can be expanded. Any expanded branches collapse when a new branch is expanded. The default value is 0.

- **skip_unauthorized**—Either 0 or 1. If 1, then no errors are raised trying to display subobjects for which the user does not have sufficient access. The protected subobjects are not displayed. The default value is 0.

Suppose you want to use the `tree` tag to create a dynamic site map. You don't want every page to show up in the site map. Let's say that you put a property on folders and documents that you want to show up in the site map.

Let's first define a script with the id of publicObjects that returns public objects:

```
## Script (Python) "publicObjects"
##
"""
Returns sub-folders and documents that have a
true 'siteMap' property.
"""
results=[]
for object in context.objectValues(['Folder', 'DTML Document']):
    if object.hasProperty('siteMap') and object.siteMap:
        results.append(object)
return results
```

Now we can create a DTML method that uses the tree tag and our scripts to draw a site map:

```
<dtml-var standard_html_header>

<h1>Site Map</h1>

<p><a href="&dtml-URL0;?expand_all=1">Expand All</a> ¦
   <a href="&dtml-URL0;?collapse_all=1">Collapse All</a>
</p>

<dtml-tree branches="publicObjects" skip_unauthorized="1">
  <a href="&dtml-absolute_url;"><dtml-var title_or_id></a>
</dtml-tree>

<dtml-var standard_html_footer>
```

This DTML method draws a link to all public resources and displays them in a tree. Figure 7.6 shows what the resulting site map looks like.

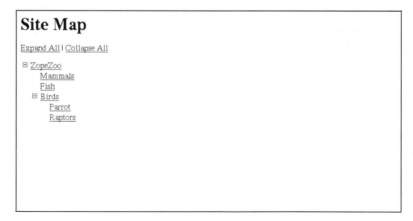

**Figure 7.6**   Dynamic site map using the tree tag.

For a summary of the tree tag arguments and special variables, see Appendix A.

## The *return* Tag

In general, DTML creates textual output. You can, however, make DTML return other values besides text. Using the `return` tag, you can make a DTML method return an arbitrary value, just like a Python- or Perl-based script.

An example follows:

```
<p>This text is ignored.</p>

<dtml-return expr="42">
```

This DTML method returns the number 42.

Another upshot of using the `return` tag is that DTML execution stops after the `return` tag.

If you find yourself using the `return` tag, you almost certainly should be using a script instead. The `return` tag was developed before scripts were, and it is largely useless now that you can easily write scripts in Python and Perl.

## The *sendmail* Tag

The `sendmail` tag formats and sends email messages. You can use the `sendmail` tag to connect to an existing MailHost, or you can manually specify your SMTP host.

The following is an example of how to send an email message with the `sendmail` tag:

```
<dtml-sendmail>
To: <dtml-var recipient>
Subject: Make Money Fast!!!!

Take advantage of our exciting offer now! Using our exclusive method
you can build unimaginable wealth very quickly. Act now!
</dtml-sendmail>
```

Notice that an extra blank line separates the mail headers from the body of the message.

A common use of the `sendmail` tag is to send an email message generated by a feedback form. The `sendmail` tag can contain any DTML tags you want, so it's easy to tailor your message with form data.

## The *mime* Tag

The `mime` tag allows you to format data using *Multipurpose Internet Mail Extensions* (MIME). MIME is an Internet standard for encoding data in email messages. By using the `mime` tag, you can use Zope to send emails with attachments.

Suppose you want to upload your resume to Zope and then have Zope email this file to a list of potential employers.

The following is the upload form:

```
<dtml-var standard_html_header>

<p>Send your resume to potential employers</p>
```

*continues*

*continued*

```
        <form method=post action="sendresume" ENCTYPE="multipart/form-data">
        <p>Resume file: <input type="file" name="resume_file"></p>
        <p>Send to:</p>
        <p>
        <input type="checkbox" name="send_to:list" value="jobs@yahoo.com">
Yahoo<br>
        <input type="checkbox" name="send_to:list" value="jobs@microsoft.com">
Microsoft<br>
        <input type="checkbox" name="send_to:list" value="jobs@mcdonalds.com">
Mc Donalds</p>

        <input type=submit value="Send Resume">
        </form>

        <dtml-var standard_html_footer>
```

Create another DTML method called `sendresume` to process the form and send the resume file:

```
<dtml-var standard_html_header>

<dtml-if send_to>

  <dtml-in send_to>

    <dtml-sendmail smtphost="my.mailserver.com">
    To: <dtml-var sequence-item>
    Subject: Resume
    <dtml-mime type=text/plain encode=7bit>

    Hi, please take a look at my resume.

    <dtml-boundary type=application/octet-stream disposition=attachment
    encode=base64><dtml-var expr="resume_file.read()"></dtml-mime>
    </dtml-sendmail>

  </dtml-in>

  <p>Your resume was sent.</p>

<dtml-else>

  <p>You didn't select any recipients.</p>

</dtml-if>

<dtml-var standard_html_footer>
```

This method iterates over the *sendto* variable and sends one email for each item.

Notice that no blank line is between the `To:` header and the starting `mime` tag. If a blank line is inserted between them, then the message is not interpreted as a *multipart* message by the receiving mail reader.

Also, notice that there is no newline between the `boundary` tag and the `var` tag or between the end of the `var` tag and the closing `mime` tag. This is important, if you break the tags up with newlines, then they will be encoded and included in the MIME part, which is probably not what you're after.

As per the MIME spec, `mime` tags can be nested within `mime` tags arbitrarily.

## The *unless* Tag

The `unless` tag executes a block of code unless the given condition is true. The `unless` tag is the opposite of the `if` tag. The DTML code

```
<dtml-if expr="not butter">
  I can't believe it's not butter.
</dtml-if>
```

is equivalent to:

```
<dtml-unless expr="butter">
  I can't believe it's not butter.
</dtml-unless>
```

What is the purpose of the `unless` tag? It is simply a convenience tag. The `unless` tag is more limited than the `if` tag because it cannot contain an `else` or `elif` tag.

Like the `if` tag, calling the `unless` tag by name does existence checking, so:

```
<dtml-unless the_easter_bunny>
  The Easter Bunny does not exist or is not true.
</dtml-unless>
```

checks for the existence of `the_easter_bunny` as well as its truth. However, the following example only checks for the truth of `the_easter_bunny`:

```
<dtml-unless expr="the_easter_bunny">
  The Easter Bunny is not true.
</dtml-unless>
```

This example raises an exception if `the_easter_bunny` does not exist.

Anything that can be done by the `unless` tag can be done by the `if` tag. Thus, its use is totally optional and a matter of style.

## Batch Processing with the *in* Tag

Often you want to present a large list of information, but only show it to the user one screen at a time. For example, if a user queried your database and got 120 results, you probably only want to show them to the user in a small batch—say 10 or 20 results per page. Breaking up large lists into parts is called *batching*. Batching has a number of benefits.

- The user only needs to download a reasonably sized document rather than a potentially huge document. This makes pages load faster because they are smaller.
- Because smaller batches of results are being used, often less memory is consumed by Zope.
- *Next* and *Previous* navigation interfaces make scanning large batches relatively easy.

The in tag provides several variables to facilitate batch processing. The following example shows how to display 100 items in batches of 10 at a time:

```
<dtml-var standard_html_header>

  <dtml-in expr="_.range(100)" size=10 start=query_start>

    <dtml-if sequence-start>

      <dtml-if previous-sequence>
        <a href="<dtml-var URL><dtml-var sequence-query
           >query_start=<dtml-var previous-sequence-start-number>">
           (Previous <dtml-var previous-sequence-size> results)
        </a>
      </dtml-if>

      <h1>These words are displayed at the top of a batch:</h1>
      <ul>

    </dtml-if>

      <li>Iteration number: <dtml-var sequence-item></li>

    <dtml-if sequence-end>

      </ul>
      <h4>These words are displayed at the bottom of a batch.</h4>

      <dtml-if next-sequence>
        <a href="<dtml-var URL><dtml-var sequence-query
           >query_start=<dtml-var
           next-sequence-start-number>">
        (Next <dtml-var next-sequence-size> results)
        </a>

      </dtml-if>

    </dtml-if>

  </dtml-in>

<dtml-var standard_html_footer>
```

Let's take a look at the DTML to get an idea of what's going on. First, we have an `in` tag that iterates over 100 numbers that are generated by the `range` utility function. The size attribute tells the `in` tag to display only 10 items at a time. The start attribute tells the `in` tag what item number to display first.

Inside the `in` tag are two main `if` tags. The first one tests special variable *sequence-start*. This variable is only true on the first pass through the `in` block. So, the contents of this `if` tag are executed only once at the beginning of the loop. The second `if` tag tests for the special variable *sequence-end*. This variable is only true on the last pass through the `in` tag. So, the second `if` block is executed only once at the end. The paragraph between the `if` tags is executed each time through the loop.

Inside each `if` tag is another `if` tag that checks for the special variables *previous-sequence* and *next-sequence*. The variables are true when the current batch has previous or further batches, respectively. In other words, *previous-sequence* is true for all batches, except the first, and *next-sequence* is true for all batches, except the last. So, the DTML tests to see if additional batches are available, and if so, it draws navigation links.

The batch navigation consists of links back to the document with a *query_start* variable set, which indicates where the `in` tag should start when displaying the batch. To better get a feel for how this works, click the previous and next links a few times and watch how the URLs for the navigation links change.

Finally, some statistics about the previous and next batches are displayed using the *next-sequence-size* and *previous-sequence-size* special variables. All of this ends up generating the following HTML code:

```
<html><head><title>Zope</title></head><body bgcolor="#FFFFFF">

  <h1>These words are displayed at the top of a batch:</h1>
  <ul>
    <li>Iteration number: 0</li>
    <li>Iteration number: 1</li>
    <li>Iteration number: 2</li>
    <li>Iteration number: 3</li>
    <li>Iteration number: 4</li>
    <li>Iteration number: 5</li>
    <li>Iteration number: 6</li>
    <li>Iteration number: 7</li>
    <li>Iteration number: 8</li>
    <li>Iteration number: 9</li>
  </ul>
  <h4>These words are displayed at the bottom of a batch.</h4>

    <a href="http://pdx:8090/batch?query_start=11">
    (Next 10 results)
    </a>

</body></html>
```

Batch processing can be complex. A good way to work with batches is to use the Searchable Interface object to create a batching search report for you. You can then modify the DTML to fit your needs.

## Exception Handling Tags

Zope has extensive exception handling facilities. You can get access to these facilities with the `raise` and `try` tags. For more information on exceptions and how they are raised and handled, see a book on Python or read the online Python tutorial (`http://www.python.org/doc/current/tut/node10.html`).

### The *raise* Tag

You can raise exceptions with the `raise` tag. One reason to raise exceptions is to signal an error. For example, you could check for a problem with the `if` tag, and in case something was wrong, you could report the error with the `raise` tag.

The `raise` tag has a type attribute for specifying an error type. The error type is a short descriptive name for the error. In addition, there are some standard error types, such as Unauthorized and Redirect that are returned as HTTP errors. Unauthorized errors cause a login prompt to be displayed on the user's browser. You can raise HTTP errors to make Zope send an HTTP error. For example:

```
<dtml-raise type="404">Not Found</dtml-raise>
```

This raises an HTTP 404 (Not Found) error. Zope responds by sending the HTTP 404 error back to the client's browser.

The `raise` tag is a block tag. The block enclosed by the `raise` tag is rendered to create an error message. If the rendered text contains any HTML markup, then Zope displays the text as an error message on the browser; otherwise, a generic error message is displayed.

The following is a `raise` tag example:

```
<dtml-if expr="balance >= debit_amount">

  <dtml-call expr="debitAccount(account, debit_amount)">

  <p><dtml-var debit_amount> has been deducted from your
  account <dtml-var account>.</p>

<dtml-else>

  <dtml-raise type="Insufficient funds">

    <p>There is not enough money in account <dtml-account>
    to cover the requested debit amount.</p>

  </dtml-raise>

</dtml-if>
```

An important side effect to raising an exception is that exceptions cause the current transaction to be rolled back. This means any changes made by a Web request are ignored. So, in addition to reporting errors, exceptions allow you to back out of changes if a problem crops up.

### The *try* Tag

If an exception is raised either manually with the `raise` tag, or as the result of some error that Zope encounters, you can catch it with the `try` tag.

Exceptions are unexpected errors that Zope encounters during the execution of a DTML document or method. After an exception is detected, the normal execution of the DTML stops. Consider the following example:

```
Cost per unit: <dtml-var
                    expr="_.float(total_cost/total_units)"
                    fmt=dollars-and-cents>
```

This DTML works fine if `total_units` is not zero. However, if `total_units` is zero, a ZeroDivisionError exception is raised indicating an illegal operation. So, rather than rendering the DTML, an error message is returned.

You can use the `try` tag to handle these kind of problems. With the `try` tag you can anticipate and handle errors yourself, rather than getting a Zope error message whenever an exception occurs.

The `try` tag has two functions. First, if an exception is raised, the `try` tag gains control of execution and handles the exception appropriately, and thus, avoids returning a Zope error message. Second, the `try` tag allows the rendering of any subsequent DTML to continue.

Within the `try` tag are one or more `except` tags that identify and handle different exceptions. When an exception is raised, each `except` tag is checked in turn to see if it matches the exception's type. The first `except` tag to match handles the exception. If no exceptions are given in an `except` tag, then the `except` tag matches all exceptions.

Here's how to use the `try` tag to avoid errors that could occur in the last example:

```
<dtml-try>

  Cost per unit: <dtml-var
                      expr="_.float(total_cost/total_units)"
                      fmt="dollars-and-cents">

<dtml-except ZeroDivisionError>

  Cost per unit: N/A

</dtml-try>
```

If a ZeroDivisionError is raised, control goes to the `except` tag, and `Cost per unit: N/A` is rendered. After the `except` tag block finishes, execution of DTML continues after the try block.

DTML's except tags work with Python's class-based exceptions. In addition to matching exceptions by name, the except tag matches any subclass of the named exception. For example, if ArithmeticError is named in an except tag, the tag can handle all ArithmeticError subclasses, including ZeroDivisionError. See a Python reference, such as the online Python Library Reference (`http://www.python.org/doc/current/lib/module-exceptions.html`), for a list of Python exceptions and their subclasses. An except tag can catch multiple exceptions by listing them all in the same tag. Inside the body of an except tag you can access information about the handled exception through several special variables.

- *error_type*—The type of the handled exception.
- *error_value*—The value of the handled exception.
- *error_tb*—The traceback of the handled exception.

You can use these variables to provide error messages to users or to take different actions, such as sending email to the Webmaster or logging errors, depending on the type of error.

### The try Tag Optional Else Block

The try tag has an optional else block that is rendered if an exception didn't occur. The following is an example of how to use the else tag within the try tag:

```
<dtml-try>

  <dtml-call feedAlligators>

<dtml-except NotEnoughFood WrongKindOfFood>

  <p>Make sure you have enough alligator food first.</p>

<dtml-except NotHungry>

  <p>The alligators aren't hungry yet.</p>

<dtml-except>

  <p>There was some problem trying to feed the alligators.<p>
  <p>Error type: <dtml-var error_type></p>
  <p>Error value: <dtml-var error_value></p>

<dtml-else>

  <p>The alligators were successfully fed.</p>

</dtml-try>
```

The first except block to match the type of error raised is rendered. If an except block has no name, then it matches all raised errors. The optional else block is rendered when no exception occurs in the try block. Exceptions in the else block are not handled by the preceding except blocks.

### *The* try *Tag* Optional Finally *Block*

You can also use the try tag in a slightly different way. Instead of handling exceptions, the try tag can be used not to trap exceptions, but to clean up after them.

The finally tag inside the try tag specifies a cleanup block to be rendered even when an exception occurs.

The finally block is only useful if you need to clean up something that will not be cleaned up by the transaction abort code. The finally block will always be called, whether there is an exception or not, and whether a return tag is used. If you use a return tag in the try block, any output of the finally block is discarded. The following is an example of how you might use the finally tag:

```
<dtml-call acquireLock>
<dtml-try>
    <dtml-call useLockedResource>
<dtml-finally>
    <!— this always gets done even if an exception is raised —>
    <dtml-call releaseLock>
</dtml-try>
```

In this example, you first acquire a lock on a resource, then try to perform some action on the locked resource. If an exception is raised, you don't handle it, but you make sure to release the lock before passing control off to an exception handler. If all goes well and no exception is raised, you still release the lock at the end of the try block by executing the finally block.

The try/finally form of the try tag is seldom used in Zope. This kind of complex programming control is often better done in Python or Perl.

DTML provides some very powerful functionality for designing Web applications. In this chapter, we looked at the more advanced DTML tags and some of their options. A more complete reference can be found in Appendix A.

Chapter 8 teaches you to put presentations together with logic by introducing Zope scripting in Python and Perl. With these tools, any kind of Web application system can be developed.

# 8

# Advanced Zope
# Scripting

Zope MANAGES YOUR PRESENTATION, LOGIC, AND DATA with objects. So far, you've seen how Zope can manage presentation and data with files and images using DTML. This chapter shows you how to add script objects that enable you to write scripts through your Web browser in Python (http://www.python.org) and Perl (http://www.perl.org).

What is *logic* and how does it differ from presentation? *Logic* provides the actions that change objects, send messages, test conditions, and respond to events. Whereas, *presentation* formats and displays information and reports. Typically, you use DTML to handle presentation and Zope scripting with Python and Perl to handle logic.

## Zope Scripts

Zope script objects are objects that encapsulate a small chunk of code written in a programming language. Currently, Zope provides Python-based scripts, which are written in the Python language, and Perl-based scripts, which are written in the Perl language. Script objects are new as of Zope 2.3, and they are the preferred way to write programming logic in Zope.

So far, you have heavily used DTML methods and documents to create simple Web applications in Zope. DTML enables you to perform simple scripting operations, such as string manipulation. For the most part, however, DTML methods should be used for presentation. DTML methods are explained in Chapter 4, "Dynamic Content with DTML," and Chapter 7, "Variables and Advanced DTML."

The following is an overview of Zope's scripts:

- **Python-based scripts**—You can use Python, a general purpose scripting language, to control Zope objects and perform other tasks. These scripts give you general purpose programming facilities within Zope.

- **Perl-based scripts**—You can use Perl, a powerful text-processing language, to script Zope objects and access Perl libraries. Perl scripts offer benefits similar to Python-based scripts, but Perl might be more appealing for folks who know Perl, but not Python—or who want to use Perl libraries for which no Python equivalents exist.

You can add these scripts to your Zope application just like any other object.

# Calling Scripts

Zope scripts are called from the Web or from other scripts or objects. Almost any type of script can be called by any other type of object. You can call a Python-based script from a DTML method or a built-in method from a Perl-based script. In fact, scripts can call scripts that call other scripts, and so on. As you saw in Chapter 4, you can replace a script transparently with a script implemented in another language. For example, if you're using Perl to perform a task, but later decide that it would be better done in Python, you can usually replace the script with a Python-based script with the same id.

When you call a script, the way that you call it gives the script a context in which to execute. A script's context is important. For example, when you call a script, you usually want to single out some object that is central to the script's task. You would call the script in the context of the object on which you want it to carry out its task. It is simpler just to say that you are calling the script *on* the object.

## Calling Scripts from the Web

You can call a script directly from the Web by visiting its URL. You can call a single script on different objects by using different URLs. This works because by using different URLs, you can give your scripts different contexts, and scripts can operate differently—depending on their context. This is a powerful feature that enables you to apply logic to objects, such as documents or folders, without having to embed the actual code within the object.

To call a script on an object from the Web, simply visit the URL of the object followed by the name of the script. This places the script in the context of your object. For example, suppose you have a collection of objects and scripts as shown in Figure 8.1.

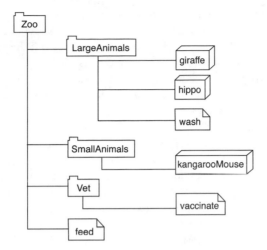

**Figure 8.1**   A collection of objects and scripts.

To call the feed script on the `hippo` object, you visit the URL `Zoo/LargeAnimals/` `hippo/feed`. To call the feed script on the `kangarooMouse` object, you visit the URL `Zoo/SmallAnimals/kangarooMouse/feed`. These URLs place the feed script in the context of the `hippo` and `kangarooMouse` objects, respectively.

Zope uses a URL as a map to find the object and the script you want to call.

Zope breaks apart the URL and compares it to the object hierarchy, working backward until it finds a match for each part. This process is called *URL traversal*. For example, when you give Zope the URL `Zoo/LargeAnimals/hippo/feed`, it starts at the Root folder and looks for an object named `Zoo`. It then moves to the Zoo folder and looks for an object named `LargeAnimals`. It moves to the LargeAnimals folder and looks for an object named `hippo`. It moves to the `hippo` object and looks for an object named `feed`. The feed script can't be found in the `hippo` object, so it is located in the Zoo folder by a process called *acquisition*.

Acquisition does two things. First, it tries to find the object in the current object's containers. If that doesn't work, it backs up along the URL path and tries again. In this example, Zope first looks for the `feed` object in `hippo`, then it goes to the first container, LargeAnimals, and then to the next container, Zoo, where feed is finally found.

Now Zope has reached the end of the URL. It calls the last object found, `feed`. The feed script operates on its context, which is the second to last object found, the `hippo` object. This is how the feed script is called on the `hippo` object.

Likewise, you can call the `wash` method on the `hippo` with the URL `Zoo/LargeAnimals/hippo/wash`. In this case, Zope acquires the `wash` method from the LargeAnimals folder.

More complex arrangements are possible. Suppose you want to call the vaccinate script on the `hippo` object. What URL can you use? If you visit the URL `Zoo/LargeAnimals/hippo/vaccinate`, Zope will not be able to find the vaccinate script because it isn't in any of the `hippo` object's containers.

The solution is to give the path to the script as part of the URL. This way, when Zope uses acquisition to find the script, it finds the right script as it backtracks along the URL. The URL to vaccinate the hippo is `Zoo/Vet/LargeAnimals/hippo/vaccinate`. Likewise, if you want to call the vaccinate script on the `kargarooMouse` object, you should use the URL `Zoo/Vet/SmallAnimals/kargarooMouse/vaccinate`.

Let's follow along as Zope traverses the URL `Zoo/Vet/LargeAnimals/hippo/vaccinate`. Zope starts in the Root folder and looks for an object named `Zoo`. It then moves to the Zoo folder and looks for an object named `Vet`. It moves to the Vet folder and looks for an object named `LargeAnimals`. The Vet folder doesn't contain an object with that name, but it can acquire the LargeAnimals folder from its container, Zoo folder. So it moves to the LargeAnimals folder and looks for an object named `hippo`. It then moves to the `hippo` object and looks for an object named `vaccinate`. Because the `hippo` object does not contain a `vaccinate` object, and neither do any of it's containers, Zope backtracks along the URL path trying to find a `vaccinate` object. First, it backs up to the LargeAnimals folder where vaccinate still can't be found. It then backs up to the Vet folder. Here it finds a vaccinate script in the Vet folder. Because Zope has now come to the end of the URL, it calls the vaccinate script in the context of the `hippo` object.

When Zope looks for a subobject during URL traversal, it first looks for the subobject in the current object. If it can't find it in the current object, it looks in the current object's containers. If it still can't find the subobject, it backs up along the URL path and searches again. It continues this process until it either finds the object or raises an error if it can't be found.

This is a very useful mechanism, and it allows you to be quite expressive when you compose URLs. The path that you tell Zope to take on its way to an object determines how it uses acquisition to look up the object's scripts.

## Calling Scripts from Other Objects

You can call scripts from other objects. For example, it is common to call scripts from DTML methods.

As you saw in Chapter 7, you can call Zope scripts from DTML with the `call` tag. For example:

```
<dtml-call updateInfo>
```

DTML calls the updateInfo script. You don't have to specify whether the script is implemented in Perl, Python, or any other language. (You can also call other DTML objects and SQL methods this way.)

If the updateInfo script requires parameters, you must either choose a name for the DTML namespace binding, (see the section, "Binding Variables," later in the chapter) so that the parameters will be looked up in the namespace, or you must pass the parameters in an expression, such as this:

```
<dtml-call expr="updateInfo(color='brown', pattern='spotted')">
```

Calling scripts from Python and Perl works the same way, except that you must always pass script parameters when you call a script from Python or Perl. For example, the following is how you might call the updateInfo script from Python:

```
context.updateInfo(color='brown',
                   pattern='spotted')
```

You could do the same thing from Perl using standard Perl semantics for calling scripts:

```
$self->updateInfo(color => 'brown',
                  pattern => 'spotted');
```

Each scripting language has a different way of writing a script call, but you don't have to know what language is used in the script you are calling. Effectively, Zope objects can have scripts implemented in several different languages. However, when you call a script, you don't have to know how it's implemented, you just need to pass the appropriate parameters.

Zope locates the scripts you call using acquisition the same way it does when calling scripts from the Web. Returning to our hippo feed example in the previous section, let's see how to vaccinate a hippo from Python and Perl. Figure 8.2 shows a slightly updated object hierarchy that contains two scripts, vaccinateHippo.py and vaccinateHippo.pl.

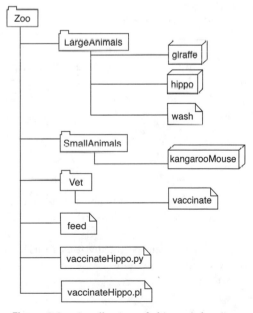

**Figure 8.2**  A collection of objects and scripts.

Suppose `vaccinateHippo.py` is a Python script. The following is how you call the vaccinate script on the `hippo` object from Python:

```
context.Vet.LargeAnimals.hippo.vaccinate()
```

In other words, you simply access the object using the same acquisition path as you would use if calling it from the Web. Likewise, in Perl you would say:

```
$self->Vet->LargeAnimals->hippo->vaccinate();
```

Using scripts from other scripts is very similar to calling scripts from the Web. The semantics differ slightly, but the same acquisition rules apply. Later in this chapter, you see more examples of how scripts work in both Perl ("Using Perl-Based Scripts") and Python ("Using Python-Based Scripts").

## Passing Parameters to Scripts

All scripts can be passed parameters. A *parameter* gives a script more information about what to do. When you call a script from the Web, Zope tries to find the script's parameters in the Web request and passes them to your script. For example, if you have a script with parameters dolphin and REQUEST, Zope looks for dolphin in the Web request, and passes the request itself as the REQUEST parameter. In practical terms, this means that it is easy to do form processing in your script. For example, consider the following form:

```
<form action="actionScript">
Name <input type="text" name="name"><br>
Age <input type="text" name="age:int"><br>
<input type="submit">
</form>
```

You can easily process this form with a script named actionScript, which includes name and age in its parameter list:

```
## Script (Python) "actionScript"
##parameters=name, age
##
"Process form"
context.processName(name)
context.processAge(age)
return context.responseMessage()
```

The form does not need to be processed manually to extract values from it. Form elements are passed as strings, or as lists of strings in the case of check boxes, and as multiple-select input.

In addition to *form* variables, you can specify any *request* variables as script parameters. For example, to get access to the request and response objects, just include REQUEST and RESPONSE in your list of parameters. Request variables are detailed more fully in Appendix B, "API Reference."

One thing to note is that the *context* variable refers to the object on which your script is called. This works similarly in Perl scripts, for example:

```
my $self = shift;
$self->processName($name);
$self->processAge($age);
return $context->responseMessage();
```

A subtle problem exists in the Python version of the example. You are probably expecting an integer rather than a string for age. You could manually convert the string to an integer by using the Python int built-in:

```
age=int(age) # convert a string to an integer
```

However, this manual conversion can be inconvenient. Zope provides a way for you to specify form input types in the form instead of in the processing script. Instead of converting the *age* variable to an integer in the processing script, you can indicate that it is an integer with the following form:

```
Age <input type="text" name="age:int">
```

The :int appended to the form input name tells Zope to automatically convert the form input to an integer. If the user of your form types something that can't be converted to an integer (such as "22 going on 23"), then Zope raises an exception as shown in Figure 8.3.

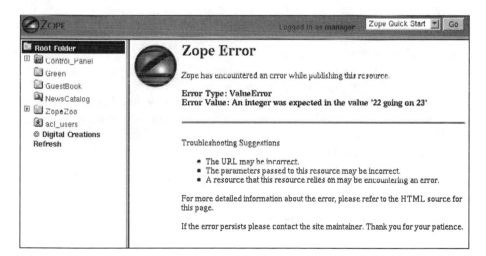

**Figure 8.3**   Parameter conversion error.

It is handy to have Zope catch conversion errors, but you might not like Zope's error messages. You should avoid using Zope's converters if you want to provide your own error messages.

Zope can perform many parameter conversions. The following is a list of Zope's basic parameter converters.

- **boolean**—Converts a variable to true or false. Variables that are 0, None, an empty string, or an empty sequence are false—all others are true.
- **int**—Converts a variable to an integer.
- **long**—Converts a variable to a long integer.
- **float**—Converts a variable to a floating point number.
- **text**—Converts a variable to a string with normalized line breaks. Different browsers on various platforms encode line endings differently, so this script makes sure the line endings are consistent, regardless of how they were encoded by the browser.
- **list**—Converts a variable to a Python list.
- **tuple**—Converts a variable to a Python tuple. A tuple is like a list, but cannot be modified.
- **tokens**—Converts a string to a list by breaking it on white spaces.
- **lines**—Converts a string to a list by breaking it on new lines.
- **date**—Converts a string to a `DateTime` object. The formats accepted are fairly flexible, for example `10/16/2000` and `12:01:13 pm`.
- **required**—Raises an exception if the variable is not present.

These converters all work in more or less the same way to coerce a *string form* variable into a specific type. You might recognize these converters from Chapter 3, "Using Basic Zope Objects," where we discussed properties. These converters are used by Zope's property facility to convert properties to the correct type.

The *list* and *tuple* converters can be used in combination with other converters. This enables you to apply additional converters to each element of the list or tuple. Consider this form:

```
<form action="processTimes">

<p>I would prefer not to be disturbed at the following
times:</p>

<input type="checkbox" name="disturb_times:list:date"
value="12:00 AM"> Midnight<br>

<input type="checkbox" name="disturb_times:list:date"
value="01:00 AM"> 1:00 AM<br>

<input type="checkbox" name="disturb_times:list:date"
value="02:00 AM"> 2:00 AM<br>

<input type="checkbox" name="disturb_times:list:date"
value="03:00 AM"> 3:00 AM<br>
```

```
<input type="checkbox" name="disturb_times:list:date"
value="04:00 AM"> 4:00 AM<br>

<input type="submit">
</form>
```

By using the *list* and *date* converters together, Zope converts each selected time to a date, and then combines all selected dates into a list named disturb_times.

A more complex type of form conversion is to convert a series of inputs into records. *Records* are structures that have attributes. By using records, you can combine a number of form inputs into one variable with attributes. The available record converters are

- **record**—Converts a variable to a record attribute.

- **records**—Converts a variable to a record attribute in a list of records.

- **default**—Provides a default value for a record attribute if the variable is empty.

- **ignore_empty**—Skips a record attribute if the variable is empty.

The following examples show how these converters are used:

```
<form action="processPerson">

First Name <input type="text" name="person.fname:record"><br>
Last Name <input type="text" name="person.lname:record"><br>
Age <input type="text" name="person.age:record:int"><br>

<input type="submit">
</form>
```

The following form calls the processPerson script with one parameter, person. The *person* variable has fname, lname, and age attributes. The following is an example of how you might use the *person* variable in your processPerson script:

```
## Script (Python) "processPerson"
##parameters=person
##
" process a person record "
full_name="%s %s" % (person.fname, person.lname)
if person.age < 21:
    return "Sorry, %s. You are not old enough to adopt an aardvark." % full_name
return "Thanks, %s. Your aardvark is on its way." % full_name
```

The *records* converter works like the *record* converter, except that it produces a list of records instead of just one. The following is an example form:

```
<form action="processPeople">

<p>Please, enter information about one or more of your next of
kin.</p>
```

*continues*

*continued*

```
<p>First Name <input type="text" name="people.fname:records">
Last Name <input type="text" name="people.lname:records"></p>

<p>First Name <input type="text" name="people.fname:records">
Last Name <input type="text" name="people.lname:records"></p>

<p>First Name <input type="text" name="people.fname:records">
Last Name <input type="text" name="people.lname:records"></p>

<input type="submit">
</form>
```

We'll call this form the processPeople script with a variable called *people*, which is a list of records. Each record will have *fname* and *lname* attributes.

Another useful parameter conversion uses *form* variables to rewrite the action of the form. This enables you to submit a form to different scripts, depending on how the form is filled out. This is most useful in the case of a form with multiple submit buttons. Zope's action converters are as follows:

- **action**—Changes the action of the form. This is most useful in the case where you have multiple submit buttons on one form. Each button can be assigned to a script that gets called when that button is clicked to submit the form.

- **default_action**—Changes the action script of the form when no other method converter is found.

The following is an example form that uses action converters:

```
<form action="">

<p>Select one or more employees</p>

<input type="checkbox" name="employees:list" value="Larry"> Larry<br>
<input type="checkbox" name="employees:list" value="Simon"> Simon<br>
<input type="checkbox" name="employees:list" value="Rene"> Rene<br>

<input type="submit" name="fireEmployees:action"
value="Fire!"><br>

<input type="submit" name="promoteEmployees:action"
value="Promote!">

</form>
```

This form calls either the `fireEmployees` or the `promoteEmployees` script, depending on which of the two submit buttons is used. Notice also how it builds a list of employees with the list converter. Form converters can be very useful when designing Zope applications.

# Script Security

All scripts that can be edited through the Web are subject to Zope's standard security policies. The only scripts that are not subject to these security restrictions are scripts that must be edited through the file system. These unrestricted scripts include Python and Perl *external methods*.

Chapter 6, "Users and Security," covers security in more detail. You should consult the "Roles of Executable Objects" and "Proxy Roles" sections for more information on how scripts are restricted by Zope security constraints.

# The Zope API

One of the main reasons to script in Zope is to get convenient access to the Zope *Application Programmer Interface* (API). The Zope API describes built-in actions that can be called on Zope objects. You can examine the Zope API in the Help system, as shown in Figure 8.4.

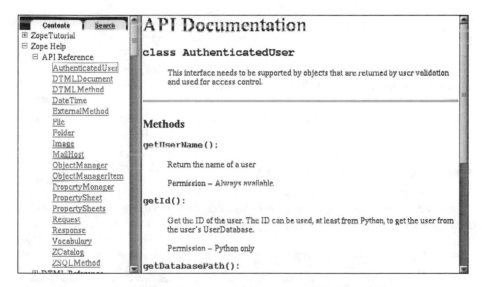

**Figure 8.4**   Zope API documentation.

Suppose you want a script that takes an uploaded file from a form and creates a Zope File object in a folder. To do this, you need to know a number of Zope API actions. It's easy enough to read files in Python or Perl, but after you have the file, you need to know what actions to call to create a new File object in a folder.

You might like to script many other things using the Zope API. Any management task that you can perform through the Web can be scripted using the Zope API. This includes creating, modifying, and deleting Zope objects. You can even perform maintenance tasks, such as restarting Zope and packing the Zope database.

The Zope API is documented in Appendix B as well as in the Zope online help. The API documentation shows you what classes inherit from what other classes. For example, Folder inherits from ObjectManager. This means that Folder objects have all the actions listed in the ObjectManager section of the API reference.

# Using Python-Based Scripts

Earlier in this chapter, you saw some examples of scripts. Now let's take a look at scripts in more detail.

## The Python Language

Python (`http://www.python.org/`)is a high-level, object-oriented, scripting language. Most of Zope is written in Python. Many folks like Python because of its clarity, simplicity, and ability to scale to large projects.

Many resources are available for learning Python. The Python.org Web site has a lot of Python documentation, including a tutorial by Python's creator, Guido van Rossum (`http://www.python.org/doc/current/tut/tut.html`).

Python comes with a rich set of modules and packages. You can find out more about the Python standard library at the Python.org Web site (`http://www.python.org/doc/current/lib/lib.html`).

Another highly respected source for reference material is a book by David Beazley, *Python Essential Reference*, Second Edition published by New Riders Publishing.

## Creating Python-Based Scripts

To create a Python-based script, choose Script (Python) from the Product Add list. Name the script `hello`, and click the Add and Edit button. You should now see the Edit view of your script, as shown in Figure 8.5.

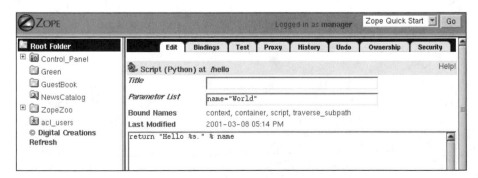

**Figure 8.5** Script editing view.

This screen allows you to control the parameters and body of your script. You can enter your script's parameters in the *Parameter List* field. Type the body of your script in the text area at the bottom of the screen.

Enter `name="World"` into the Parameter List field, and type

```
return "Hello %s." % name
```

in the body of the script. The preceding example is equivalent to the following example in standard Python syntax:

```
def hello(name="World"):
    return "Hello %s" % name
```

You can now test this script by going to the Test tab, as shown in Figure 8.6.

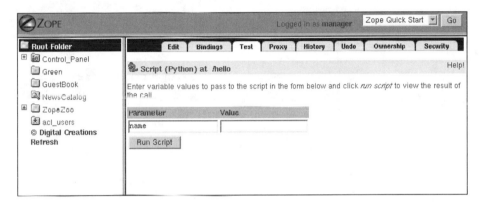

**Figure 8.6**   Testing a script.

Leave the name field blank and click the Run Script button. Zope should return `Hello World`. Now go back and try entering your name in the value field and click the Run Script button. Zope should now say hello to you.

Because scripts are called on Zope objects, you can get access to Zope objects through the *context* variable. For example, the following script returns the number of objects contained by a given Zope object:

```
## Script (Python) "numberOfObjects
##
return len(context.objectIds())
```

The script calls `context.objectIds()` to find out the number of contained objects. When you call this script on a given Zope object, the *context* variable is bound to the `context` object. So, if you called this script by visiting the URL `FolderA/FolderB/numberOfObjects`, the context parameter would refer to the `FolderB` object.

When writing your logic in Python, you typically want to query Zope objects, call other scripts, and return reports. For example, suppose you want to implement a simple workflow system in which various Zope objects are tagged with properties that indicate their status. You might want to produce reports that summarize what objects are in what state. You can use Python to query objects and test their properties. For example, the following is a script named objectsForStatus with one parameter status:

```
## Script (Python) "objectsForStatus"
##parameters=status
##
"""
Returns all subobjects that have a given status
property.
"""
results=[]
for object in context.objectValues():
    if object.getProperty('status') == status:
        results.append(object)
return results
```

This script loops through an object's subobjects and returns all the subobjects that have a status property with a given value.

You could use the following script from DTML to email reports. For example:

```
<dtml-sendmail>
To: <dtml-var ResponsiblePerson>
Subject: Pending Objects

These objects are pending and need attention.

<dtml-in expr="objectsForStatus('Pending')">
<dtml-var title_or_id> (<dtml-var absolute_url>)
</dtml-in>
</dtml-sendmail>
```

This example shows how you can use DTML for presentation or report formatting, while Python handles the logic. This is a very important pattern that you'll see over and over in Zope.

## String Processing

One common use for scripts is to do string processing. Python has a number of standard modules for string processing. You cannot do regular expression processing from Python-based scripts, but you do have access to the string module. You have access to the string module from DTML as well, but it is much easier to use from Python. Suppose you want to change all the occurrences of a given word in a DTML document. Here's a script, replaceWord, that accepts two arguments, word and replacement. This script changes all the occurrences of a given word in a DTML document:

```
## Script (Python) "replaceWord"
##parameters=word, replacement
##
"""
Replaces all the occurrences of a word with a
```

```
replacement word in the source text of a DTML
Document. Call this script on a DTML Document to use
it.

Note: you'll need permission to edit a document to
call this script on the document.
"""
import string
text=context.document_src()
text=string.replace(text, word, replacement)
context.manage_edit(text, context.title)
```

You can call this script from the Web on a DTML document to change the source of the document. For example, the URL Swamp/replaceWord?word=Alligator&replacement =Crocodile calls the replaceWord script on a document named Swamp and replaces all occurrences of the word Alligator with Crocodile.

The string module that you can access through scripts does not have all the features available in the standard Python string module. These limitations are imposed for security reasons. See Appendix A, "DTML Reference," for more information on the string module.

You might be tempted to use Python scripts to search for objects that contain a given word in their text or as a property. You can do this, but Zope has a much better facility for this kind of work: the *Catalog*. See Chapter 9, "Searching and Categorizing Content," for more information on searching with catalogs.

## Doing Math

Another common use of scripts is to perform mathematical calculations, which would be unwieldy in DTML. The math and random modules give you access from Python to many math functions. These modules are standard Python services as described on the Python.org Web site.

- **math**—Mathematical functions, such as sin and cos
  (http://www.python.org/doc/current/lib/module-math.html).

- **random**—Pseudo-random number generation functions
  (http://www.python.org/doc/current/lib/module-random.html).

One interesting function of the random module is the choice function, which returns a random selection from a sequence of objects. The following is an example of how to use this function in a script called randomImage:

```
## Script (Python) "randomImage"
##
"""
When called on a Folder that contains Image objects this
script returns a random image.
"""
import random
return random.choice(context.objectValues('Image'))
```

Suppose you had a folder named Images that contained a number of images. You could display a random image from the folder in DTML like so:

```
<dtml-with Images>
  <dtml-var randomImage>
</dtml-with>
```

This DTML calls the randomImage script on the Images folder. The result is an HTML IMG tag that references a random image in the Images folder.

## Binding Variables

A set of special variables is created whenever a Python-based script is called. These variables—defined on the Bindings view—are used by your script to access other Zope objects and scripts.

By default, the names of these binding variables are set to reasonable values and you should not need to change them. They are explained here so that you know how each special variable works and how you can use these variables in your scripts.

- *Context*—The *Context* binding defaults to the name *context*. This variable refers to the object on which the script is called.

- *Container*—The *Container* binding defaults to the name *container*. This variable refers to the folder in which the script is defined.

- *Script*—The *Script* binding defaults to the name *script*. This variable refers to the script object itself.

- *Namespace*—The *Namespace* binding is left blank by default. This is an advanced variable that you will not need for any of the examples in this book. If your script is called from a DTML method, and you have chosen a name for this binding, then the named variable contains the DTML namespace explained in Chapter 7. Also, if this binding is set, the script searches for its parameters in the DTML namespace when called from DTML without explicitly passing any arguments.

- *Subpath*—The *Subpath* binding defaults to the name *traverse_subpath*. This is an advanced variable that you will not need for any of the examples in this book. If your script is traversed, meaning that other path elements follow it in a URL, then those path elements are placed in a list, from left to right, in this variable.

If you edit your scripts through FTP, you'll notice that these bindings are listed in comments at the top of your script files. For example:

```
## Script (Python) "example"
##bind container=container
##bind context=context
##bind namespace=
##bind script=script
##bind subpath=traverse_subpath
##parameters=name, age
##title=
##
return "Hello %s you are %d years old." % (name, age)
```

You can change your script's bindings by changing these comments and then uploading your script.

## Print Statement Support

Python-based scripts have a special facility to help you print information. Normally, printed data is sent to standard output and is displayed on the console. This is not practical for a server application, such as Zope, because most of the time you do not have access to the server's console. Scripts enable you to use print anyway and to retrieve what you printed with the special variable *printed*. For example:

```
## Script (Python) "printExample"
##
for word in ('Zope', 'on', 'a', 'rope'):
    print word
return printed
```

This script returns:

```
Zope
on
a
rope
```

The reason a line break is in between each word is because Python adds a new line after every string that is printed.

You might want to use the print statement to perform simple debugging in your scripts. For more complex output control, you probably should manage things yourself by accumulating data, modifying it, and returning it manually rather than relying on the print statement.

## Security Restrictions

Scripts are restricted to limit their ability to do harm. What could be harmful? In general, scripts keep you from accessing private Zope objects, making harmful changes to Zope objects, hurting the Zope process itself, and accessing the server on which Zope is running. These restrictions are implemented through a collection of limits on what your scripts can do.

- **Loop limits**—Scripts cannot create infinite loops. If your script loops a very large number of times, Zope raises an error. This restriction covers all kinds of loops, including for and while loops. The reason for this restriction is to limit your ability to hang Zope by creating an infinite loop.

- **Import limits**—Scripts cannot import arbitrary packages and modules. You are limited to importing the Products.PythonScripts.standard utility module, the AccessControl module, modules available through DTML (string, random, and math), and modules which have been specifically made available to scripts by product authors. See Appendix A for more information on these modules. If you want to be able to import any Python module, use an external method, as described in the section, "Using External Methods," later in the chapter.

- **Access limits**—You are restricted by standard Zope security policies when accessing objects. In other words, the user executing the script is checked for authorization when accessing objects. As with all executable objects, you can modify the effective roles a user has when calling a script using proxy roles (see Chapter 6 for more information). In addition, you cannot access objects whose names begin with underscore because Zope considers these objects to be private.

- **Writing limits**—In general, you cannot change Zope object attributes using scripts. You should call scripts on Zope objects to change them rather than directly changing instance attributes.

Despite these limits, a determined user could use large amounts of CPU time and memory using Python-based scripts. Malicious scripts could constitute a kind of "denial-of-service" attack by using a lot of resources. These are difficult problems to solve, and DTML suffers from the same potential for abuse. As with DTML, you probably shouldn't grant untrusted people access to scripts.

## Built-in Functions

Python-based scripts give you a slightly different menu of built-ins than you find in normal Python. Most of the changes are designed to keep you from performing unsafe actions. For example, the open function is not available, which keeps you from being able to access the file system. To partially make up for some missing built-ins, a few extra functions are available.

The following is a list of restricted built-ins, which work the same as standard Python built-ins: None, abs, apply, callable, chr, cmp, complex, delattr, divmod, filter, float, getattr, hash, hex, int, isinstance, issubclass, list, len, long, map, max, min, oct, ord, repr, round, setattr, str, tuple. For more information on what these built-ins do, see the online Python documentation (http://www.python.org/doc/).

The range and pow functions are available and work the same way they do in standard Python; however, they are limited to keep them from generating very large numbers and sequences. This limitation helps protect against denial-of-service attacks as described previously.

In addition, these DTML utility functions are available: DateTime, test, namespace, and render. See Appendix A for more information on these functions.

Finally, to make up for the lack of a type function, the same_type function compares the type of two or more objects, returning true if they are of the same type. So instead of saying:

```
if type(foo) == type([]):
    return "foo is a list"
```

to check if foo is a list, you instead use the same_type function to check this:

```
if same_type(foo, []):
    return "foo is a list"
```

Now let's take a look at external methods, which provide more power and less restrictions than Python-based scripts.

# Using External Methods

Sometimes the security constraints imposed by scripts get in your way. For example, you might want to read files from a disk, access the network, or use some advanced libraries for things, such as regular expressions or image processing. In these cases, you want to use external methods.

To create and edit external methods, you need access to the file system. This makes editing these scripts more cumbersome because you can't edit them right in your Web browser. However, requiring access to the server's file system provides an important security control. If a user has access to a server's file system, they already have the ability to harm Zope. So, by requiring that unrestricted scripts be edited on the file system, Zope ensures that only people who are entrusted have access.

Unrestricted scripts are created and edited in files on the Zope server in the Extensions directory. This directory is located in the top-level Zope directory. Alternately, you can create and edit unrestricted scripts in an Extensions directory inside an installed Zope product directory.

Create a file named Example.py in the Zope Extensions directory on your server. In the Example.py file, enter the following code:

```
def hello(name="World"):
    return "Hello %s." % name
```

You've created a Python function in a Python module. Now let's use this function in the external method.

You manage external methods the same way you manage restricted scripts with the exception that you cannot edit the script itself through the Web. Instead of editing code, you must tell Zope where to find your code on the file system. You do this by specifying the name of your Python file and the name of the function within the module.

To create an external method, choose External Method from the product Add list. You are taken to an Add form where you must provide an id. Type "hello" into the Id field and "hello" in the Function Name field, and "Example" in the Module Name field, and click the Add button. You should now see a new External Method object in your folder. Click it. You should be taken to the Properties view of your new External Method object, as shown in Figure 8.7.

Now, test your new script by going to the Text view. You should see a greeting. You can pass different names to the script by specifying them in the URL. For example, `hello?name=Spanish+Inquisition`.

This example is exactly the same as the hello world example you saw for using scripts. In fact, for simple string processing tasks such as this, restricted scripts offer a better solution because they are easier to work with.

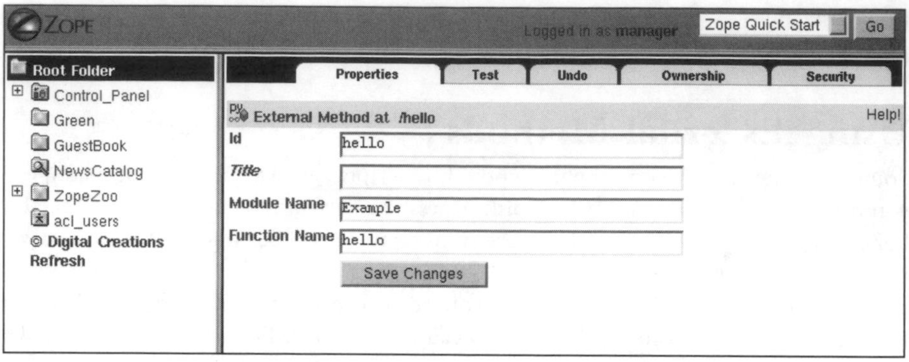

**Figure 8.7**   External method Properties view.

The main reason to use an unrestricted script is to access the file system or network, or to use Python packages that are not available to restricted scripts.

The following is an example external method that uses the *Python Imaging Library* (PIL) to create a thumbnail version of an existing Image object in a folder. Enter the following code in a file named Thumbnail.py in the Extensions directory:

```
def makeThumbnail(self, original_id, size=128):
    """
    Makes a thumbnail image given an image Id when called on a Zope
    folder.

    The thumbnail is a Zope image object that is a small JPG
    representation of the original image. The thumbnail has a
    'original_id' property set to the id of the full size image
    object.
    """

    from PIL import Image
    from cStringIO import StringIO
    import os.path

    # create a thumbnail image file
    original_image=getattr(self, original_id)
    original_file=StringIO(original_image.data)
    image=Image.open(original_file)
    image=image.convert('RGB')
    image.thumbnail((size,size))
    thumbnail_file=StringIO()
    image.save(thumbnail_file, "JPEG")
    thumbnail_file.seek(0)

    # create an id for the thumbnail
    path, ext=os.path.splitext(original_id)
    thumbnail_id=path + '.thumb.jpg'
```

```
# if there's and old thumbnail, delete it
if thumbnail_id in self.objectIds():
    self.manage_delObjects(thumbnail_id)

# create the Zope image object
self.manage_addProduct['OFSP'].manage_addImage(thumbnail_id,
                                       thumbnail_file,
                                       'thumbnail image')
thumbnail_image=getattr(self, thumbnail_id)

# set the 'originial_id' property
thumbnail_image.manage_addProperty('original_id', original_id, 'string')
```

You must have PIL installed for this example to work. See the PythonWorks Web site for more information on PIL (`http://www.pythonworks.com/products/pil`). To use the following code, create an external method named makeThumbnail that uses the makeThumbnail function in the Thumbnail module.

Now you have a method that creates a thumbnail image. You can call it on a folder with a URL, such as `ImageFolder/makeThumbnail?original id=Horse.gif`. This would create a thumbnail image named Horse.thumb.jpg.

You can use a script to loop through all the images in a folder and create thumbnail images for them. Create a script named makeThumbnails:

```
## Script (Python) "makeThumbnails"
##
for image_id in context.objectIds('Image'):
    context.makeThumbnail(image_id)
```

This loops through all the images in a folder and creates a thumbnail for each one.

Now call this script on a folder that has images in it. It creates a thumbnail image for each contained image. Try calling the makeThumbnails script on the folder again, and you'll notice it created thumbnails of your thumbnails. This is no good. You need to change the makeThumbnails script to recognize existing thumbnail images and not make thumbnails of them. Because all thumbnail images have an original_id property, you can check for that property as a way of distinguishing between thumbnails and normal images:

```
## Script (Python) "makeThumbnails"
##
for image in context.objectValues('Image'):
    if not image.hasProperty('original_id'):
        context.makeThumbnail(image.getId())
```

Delete all the thumbnail images in your folder and try calling your updated makeThumbnails script on the folder. It seems to work correctly now.

Now with a little DTML, you can glue your script and external method together. Create a DTML method called displayThumbnails:

```
<dtml-var standard_html_header>

<dtml-if updateThumbnails>
```

*continues*

*continued*

```
    <dtml-call makeThumbnails>
</dtml-if>

<h2>Thumbnails</h2>

<dtml-in expr="objectValues('Image')">
  <dtml-if original_id>
    <p>
      <a href="&dtml-original_id;"><dtml-var sequence-item></a><br>
      <dtml-var original_id>
    </p>
  </dtml-if>
</dtml-in>

<form>
<input type="submit" name="updateThumbnails" value="Update Thumbnails">
</form>

<dtml-var standard_html_footer>
```

When you call this DTML method on a folder, it loops through all the images in the folder, displays all the thumbnail images, and links them to the originals—as shown in Figure 8.8.

# Thumbnails

platy3.gif

platypus.jpg

platypus1.gif

Update Thumbnails

**Figure 8.8**  Displaying thumbnail images.

This DTML method also includes a form that enables you to update the thumbnail images. If you add, delete, or change the images in your folder, you can use this form to update your thumbnails.

The previous example shows how to use scripts, external methods, and DTML together. Python takes care of the logic, while the DTML handles presentation. Your external methods handle external packages while your scripts do simple processing of Zope objects.

## Processing XML with External Methods

You can use external methods to do darn near anything. One interesting thing that you can do is communicate using XML. You can generate and process XML with external methods.

Zope already understands some kinds of XML messages, such as XML-RPC and WebDAV. As you create Web applications that communicate with other systems, you might want to have the ability to receive XML messages. You can receive XML a number of ways: You can read XML files from the file system or over the network, or you can define scripts that take XML arguments, which can be called by remote systems.

After you have received an XML message, you must process the XML to find out what it means and how to act on it. Let's take a quick look at how you might parse XML manually using Python. Suppose you want to connect your Web application to a Jabber chat server (`http://www.jabber.com/`). You might want to allow users to message you and receive dynamic responses based on the status of your Web application. For example, suppose you want to allow users to check the status of animals using instant messaging. Your application should respond to XML instant messages like this:

```
<message to="cage_monitor@zopezoo.org" from="user@host.com">
  <body>monkey food status</body>
</message>
```

You could scan the body of the message for commands, call a script, and return responses like this:

```
<message to="user@host.com" from="cage_monitor@zopezoo.org">
  <body>Monkeys were last fed at 3:15</body>
</message>
```

The following is a sketch of how you could implement this XML messaging facility in your Web application using an external method:

```
# Uses Python 2.x standard xml processing packages.  See
# http://www.python.org/doc/current/lib/module-xml.sax.html for
# information about Python's SAX (Simple API for XML) support If
# you are using Python 1.5.2 you can get the PyXML package. See
# http://pyxml.sourceforge.net for more information about PyXML.

from xml.sax import parseString
from xml.sax.handler import ContentHandler
```

*continues*

*continued*

```
class MessageHandler(ContentHandler):
    """
    SAX message handler class

    Extracts a message's to, from, and body
    """

    inbody=0
    body=""

    def startElement(self, name, attrs):
        if name=="message":
            self.recipient=attrs['to']
            self.sender=attrs['from']
        elif name=="body":
            self.inbody=1

    def endElement(self, name):
        if name=="body":
            self.inbody=0

    def characters(self, content):
        if self.inbody:
            self.body=self.body + content

def receiveMessage(self, message):
    """
    Called by a Jabber server
    """
    handler=MessageHandler()
    parseString(message, handler)

    # call a script that returns a response string
    # given a message body string
    response_body=self.getResponse(handler.body)

    # create a response XML message
    response_message="""
      <message to="%s" from="%s">
        <body>%s</body>
      </message>""" % (handler.sender, handler.recipient, response_body)

    # return it to the server
    return response_message
```

The receiveMessage external method uses Python's *Simple API for XML* (SAX) package
to parse the XML message. The MessageHandler class receives callbacks as Python
parses the message. The handler saves information it is interested in. The external
method uses the handler class by creating an instance of it and passing it to the

parseString function. It then figures out a response message by calling getResponse with the message body. The getResponse script (which is not shown here) presumably scans the body for commands, queries the Web applications state, and returns some response. The receiveMessage method then creates an XML message using response and the sender information and returns it.

The remote server would use this external method by calling the receiveMessage method using the standard HTTP POST command. Voila, you've implemented a custom XML chat server that runs over HTTP.

### External Method Gotchas

Although you are essentially unrestricted in what you can do in an external method, some things are still hard to do.

Although your Python code can do as it pleases, if you want to work with the Zope framework, you need to respect its rules. Although programming with the Zope framework is too advanced a topic to cover here, you should be aware of a few things.

Problems can occur if you hand instances of your own classes to Zope and expect them to work like Zope objects. For example, you cannot define a class in an external method script file and assign it as an attribute of a Zope object. This causes problems with Zope's persistence machinery. You also cannot easily hand instances of your own classes over to DTML or scripts. The issue here is that your instances will not have Zope security information. You can define and use your own classes and instances to your heart's delight, just don't expect Zope to use them directly. Limit yourself to returning simple Python structures, such as strings, dictionaries, and lists of Zope objects.

## Using Perl-Based Scripts

Perl-based scripts enable you to script Zope in Perl. If you love Perl and don't want to learn Python to use Zope, these scripts are for you. By using Perl-based scripts, you can use all your favorite Perl modules and treat Zope like a collection of Perl objects.

### The Perl Language

Perl (http://www.perl.com/) is a high-level scripting language like Python. From a broad perspective, Perl and Python are very similar languages—they have similar primitive data constructs and employ similar programming constructs.

Perl is a popular language for Internet scripting. In the early days of CGI scripting, Perl and CGI were practically synonymous. Perl continues to be the dominant Internet scripting language.

Perl has a very rich collection of modules for tackling almost any computing task. *Comprehensive Perl Archive Network* (CPAN) is the authoritative guide to Perl resources (http://search.cpan.org/).

Perl-based Zope scripts are available for download from ActiveState (`http://downloads.activestate.com/Zope-Perl/`). Perl scripts require you to have Perl and a few other packages installed. How to install these things is beyond the scope of this book. See the documentation that comes with Perl-based scripts from the earlier URL. More information is also provided by Andy McKay and is available on Zope.org (`http://www.zope.org/Members/andym/wiki/FrontPage`).

## Creating Perl-Based Scripts

Perl-based scripts are quite similar to Python-based scripts. Both have access to Zope objects and are called in similar ways. The following is the Perl hello world program:

```
my $name=shift;
return "Hello $name.";
```

Let's take a look at a more complex example script by Monty Taylor. It uses the `LWP::UserAgent` package to retrieve the URL of the daily Dilbert comic from the network. Create a Perl-based script named get_dilbert_url with the following code:

```
use LWP::UserAgent;

my $ua = LWP::UserAgent->new;

# retrieve the Dilbert page
my $request = HTTP::Request->new('GET','http://www.dilbert.com');
my $response = $ua->request($request);

# look for the image URL in the HTML
my $content = $response->content;
$content =~ m,(/comics/dilbert/archive/images/[^"]*),s;

# return the URL
return $content
```

You can display the daily Dilbert comic by calling the following script from DTML by calling the script inside an HTML `IMG` tag:

```
<img src="&dtml-get_dilbert_url;">
```

However, a problem exists with this code. Each time you display the cartoon, Zope has to make a network connection. This is inefficient and wasteful. It is much better to figure out and access the Dilbert URL only once a day.

The following script, cached_dilbert_url, improves the situation by keeping track of when it last fetched the Dilbert URL with a dilbert_url_date property:

```
my $context=shift;
my $date=$context->getProperty('dilbert_url_date');

if ($date==null or $now-$date > 1){
    my $url=$context->get_dilbert_url();
    $context->manage_changeProperties(
      dilbert_url => $url
```

```
        dilbert_url_time => $now
    );
}
return $context->getProperty('dilbert_url');
```

This script uses two properties, dilbert_url and dilbert_url_date. If the URL gets too old, a new one is fetched. You can use the following script from DTML just like the original script:

```
<img src="&dtml-cached_dilbert_url;">
```

You can use Perl and DTML together to control your logic and your presentation.

### Perl-Based Script Security

Like DTML and Python-based scripts, Perl-based scripts constrain you in the Zope security system from doing anything that you are not allowed to do. Script security is similar in both languages, but some Perl-specific constraints exist.

First, the security system does not enable you to eval an expression in Perl. For example, consider this script:

```
my $context = shift;
my $input = shift;

eval $input
```

This code takes an argument and evaluates it in Perl. This means you could call this script from, say, an HTML form, and evaluate the contents of one of the form elements. This is not allowed because the form element could contain malicious code.

Perl-based scripts also cannot assign new variables to any object other than local variables that you declare with my.

# DTML Versus Python Versus Perl

Zope gives you many ways to script. For small scripting tasks, the choice of Python, Perl, or DTML probably doesn't make a big difference. For larger, logic-oriented tasks, you should use Python or Perl. You should choose the language you are most comfortable with. Of course, your boss might want to have some say in the matter too.

Just for the sake of comparison, the following is a simple script suggested by Gisle Aas, the author of Perl-based scripts, in three different languages.

In DTML:

```
<dtml-in objectValues>
  <dtml-var getId>: <dtml-var sequence-item>
</dtml-in>
done
```

In Python:

```
for item in context.objectValues():
    print "%s: %s" % (item.getId(), item)
print "done"
return printed
```

In Perl:

```
my $context = shift;
my @res;

for ($context->objectValues()) {
    push(@res, join(": ", $_->getId(), $_));
}
join("\n", @res, "done");
```

Despite the fact that Zope is implemented in Python, it follows the Perl philosophy that there's more than one way to script.

# Remote Scripting and Network Services

Web servers are used to serve content to software clients—usually people using Web browser software. The software client can also be another computer that is using your Web server to access some kind of service.

Because Zope exposes objects and scripts on the Web, it can be used to provide a powerful, well-organized, secure Web API to other remote network application clients.

You can remotely script Zope in two different ways. The first way is using a simple remote procedure call protocol called XML-RPC. XML-RPC is used to execute a procedure on a remote machine and get a result on the local machine. XML-RPC is designed to be language neutral, and in the section, "Using XML-RPC," you see examples in Python, Perl, and Java.

The second common way to remotely script Zope is with any HTTP client that can be automated with a script. Many language libraries come with simple scriptable HTTP clients and many programs let you script HTTP from the command line.

## Using XML-RPC

XML-RPC is a simple remote procedure call mechanism that works over HTTP and uses XML to encode information. XML-RPC clients have been implemented for many languages, including Python, Perl, Java, JavaScript, and TCL.

In-depth information on XML-RPC can be found at the XML-RPC Web site (http://www.xmlrpc.org/).

All Zope scripts that can be called from URLs can also be called through XML-RPC. Basically, XML-RPC provides a system to marshal arguments to scripts that can be called from the Web. Zope provides its own marshaling controls that you can use from HTTP. XML-RPC and Zope's own marshaling essentially accomplish the same thing. The advantage of XML-RPC marshaling is that it is a reasonably supported standard that also supports marshaling of return values as well as argument values.

Let's look at a fanciful example that shows you how to remotely script a mass firing of janitors using XML-RPC.

The following is the code in Python:

```
import xmlrpclib

server = xmlrpclib.Server('http://www.zopezoo.org/')
for employeeID in server.JanitorialDepartment.personnel():
    server.fireEmployee(employee)
```

In Perl:

```
use Frontier::Client;

$server = Frontier::Client->new(url => "http://www.zopezoo.org/");

$employees = $server->call("JanitorialDepartment.personnel");
foreach $employee ( @$employees ) {

  $server->call("fireEmployee",$server->string($employee));

}
```

In Java:

```
try {
    XmlRpcClient server = new XmlRpcClient("http://www.zopezoo.org/");
    Vector employees = (Vector)
server.execute("JanitorialDepartment.personnel");

    int num = employees.size();
    for (int i = 0; i < num; i++) {
        Vector args = new Vector(employees.subList(i, i+1));
        server.execute("fireEmployee", args);
    }

} catch (XmlRpcException ex) {
    ex.printStackTrace();
} catch (IOException ioex) {
    ex.printStackTrace();
}
```

Actually, the preceding examples probably will not run correctly because you most likely want to protect the fireEmployee script. This brings up the issue of security with XML-RPC. XML-RPC does not have any security provisions of its own; however, because it runs over HTTP, it can leverage existing HTTP security controls. In fact, Zope treats an XML-RPC request exactly like a normal HTTP request with respect to security controls. This means that you must provide authentication in your XML-RPC request for Zope to grant you access to protected scripts. The Python client, at the time of this writing, does not support control of HTTP Authorization headers. However, it is a fairly trivial addition. For example, an article on XML.com, *Internet Scripting: Zope and XML-RPC*, includes a patch to Python's XML-RPC support showing how to add HTTP authorization headers to your XML-RPC client (`http://www.xml.com/pub/ 2000/01/xmlrpc/index.html`).

## Remote Scripting with HTTP

Any HTTP client can be used for remotely scripting Zope.

On UNIX systems, you have a number of tools at your disposal for remotely scripting Zope. One simple example is to use wget to call Zope script URLs and use cron to schedule the script calls. For example, suppose you have a Zope script that feeds the lions and you like to call it every morning. You can use wget to call the script like so:

```
$ wget —spider http://www.zopezope.org/Lions/feed
```

The spider option tells wget not to save the response as a file. Suppose that your script is protected and requires authorization. You can pass your username and password with wget to access protected scripts:

```
$ wget —spider —http_user=ZooKeeper —http_pass=SecretPhrase
➥http://www.zopezope.org/Lions/feed
```

Now let's use cron to call this command every morning at 8 a.m. Edit your crontab file with the crontab command:

```
$ crontab -e
```

Then add a line to call wget every day at 8 a.m.:

```
0 8 * * * wget -v —spider —http_user=ZooKeeper —http_pass=SecretPhrase
➥http://www.zopezoo.org/Lions/feed
```

The only difference between using cron and calling wget manually is that you should use the v switch when using cron because you don't care about output of the wget command.

For our final example, let's get really perverse. Because networking is built into so many different systems, it's easy to find an unlikely candidate to script Zope. If you had an Internet-enabled toaster, you would probably be able to script Zope with it. Let's take Microsoft Word as our example Zope client. All that's necessary is to get Word to agree to tickle a URL.

The easiest way to script Zope with Word is to tell Word to open a document and then type a Zope script URL as the filename, as shown in Figure 8.9.

Word then loads the URL and returns the results of calling the Zope script. Despite the fact that Word doesn't let you POST arguments this way, you can pass GET arguments by entering them as part of the URL.

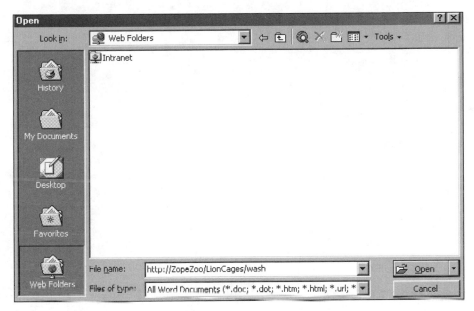

**Figure 8.9**  Calling a URL with Microsoft Word.

You can even control this behavior using Word's built-in Visual Basic scripting. For example, the following is a fragment of Visual Basic that tells Word to open a new document using a Zope script URL:

```
Documents.Open
➥FileName:="http://www.zopezoo.org/LionCages/wash?use_soap=1&water_temp=hot"
```

You can use Visual Basic to call Zope script URLs in many different ways.

Zope's URL to script call translation is the key to remote scripting. Because you can control Zope so easily with simple URLs, you can easily script Zope with almost any network-aware system.

Zope provides scripting with Python and Perl. With scripts, you can control Zope objects and glue together your application's logic, data, and presentation. You can also perform serious programming tasks, such as image processing and XML parsing.

In Chapter 9, you learn about ZCatalog, Zope's built-in search engine.

# 9

# Searching and Categorizing Content

THE CATALOG IS ZOPE'S BUILT-IN SEARCH ENGINE. It enables you to categorize and search your Zope objects. You can also use it to search external data, such as relational data, files, and remote Web pages. In addition to searching, you can use the Catalog to organize collections of objects.

The Catalog supports a rich query interface. You can perform full-text searching, and you can search multiple indexes at once. In addition, the Catalog keeps track of metadata about indexed objects. The two most common Catalog usage patterns are as follows:

- **Mass cataloging** Cataloging a large collection of objects all at once.
- **Automatic cataloging**—Cataloging objects as they are created and tracking changes made to them.

## Getting Started with Mass Cataloging

Let's take a look at how to use the Catalog to search documents. Cataloging a bunch of objects all at once is called *mass cataloging*. Mass cataloging involves three steps:

- Creating a ZCatalog
- Finding objects and cataloging them
- Creating a Web interface to search the catalog

Choose ZCatalog from the product Add list to create a ZCatalog object. This takes you to the ZCatalog Add form, as shown in Figure 9.1.

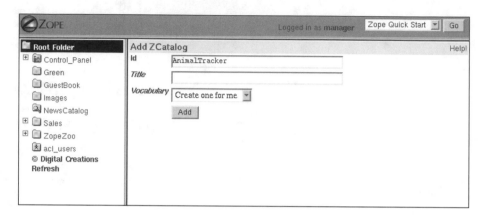

Figure 9.1   ZCatalog Add form.

The Add form asks you for an Id and a *Title*. The third form element is the *Vocabulary* select box. For now, leave this box on `Create one for me`. Give your ZCatalog the Id `AnimalTracker`, and click Add to create your new catalog. The Catalog icon looks like a folder with a small magnifying glass on it. Select the AnimalTracker icon to see the Contents view of the Catalog.

A ZCatalog looks a lot like a folder, but it has a few more tabs. Six of the tabs on the ZCatalog are the same six tabs you find on a standard folder. ZCatalog has these views: Contents, Catalog, Properties, Indexes, MetaData, Find Objects, Advanced, Undo, Security, and Ownership. When you click a ZCatalog, you are in the Contents view. You can add new objects, and the ZCatalog contains them, just as any folder does. You should note that containment does not imply that the object is searchable.

Now that you have created a ZCatalog, you can move onto the next step, finding objects and cataloging them. Suppose you have a zoo site with information about animals. To work with these examples, create two DTML documents that contain information about reptiles and amphibians:

- **Title: Chilean four-eyed frog**—The Chilean four-eyed frog has a bright pair of spots on its rump that look like enormous eyes. When seated, the frog's thighs conceal these eyespots. When predators approach, the frog lowers its head and lifts its rump, creating a much larger and more intimidating head. Frogs are amphibians.

- **Title: Carpet python**—Morelia spilotes variegata averages 2.4 meters in length. It is a medium-sized python with black-to-gray patterns of blotches, crossbands, stripes, or a combination of these markings on a light yellowish-to-dark brown background. Snakes are reptiles.

Visitors to your zoo want to be able to search for information on the zoo's animals. Eager herpetologists want to know if you have their favorite snake, so you should provide them with the ability to search for certain words and show all the documents that contain those words. Searching is one of the most useful and common Web activities.

The AnimalTracker ZCatalog you created can catalog all the documents in your Zope site and enables your users to search for specific words. To catalog your documents, go to the AnimalTracker ZCatalog and click the Find Objects tab.

In this view, you tell the ZCatalog what kind of objects you are interested in. You want to catalog all DTML documents, so select DTML Document from the Find objects of type multiple selection, and click Find and Catalog.

The ZCatalog now starts from the folder where it is located and searches for all DTML documents. It searches the folder and then descends down into all the subfolders and their subfolders. If you have a lot of objects, this might take a long time to complete, so be patient.

After a period of time, the Catalog takes you to the Catalog view automatically with a status message telling you what it just did.

Below the status information is a list of objects that are cataloged—they are all DTML documents. To confirm that these are the objects you are interested in, you can click to visit them.

You have completed the first step of searching for your objects and cataloging them into a ZCatalog. Your documents are now in the ZCatalog's database. Now you can move onto the third step, creating a Web page and a result form to query the ZCatalog.

To create search and report forms, make sure you are inside the AnimalTracker catalog, and select Z Search Interface from the Add list. Select the AnimalTracker ZCatalog as the searchable object, as shown in Figure 9.2.

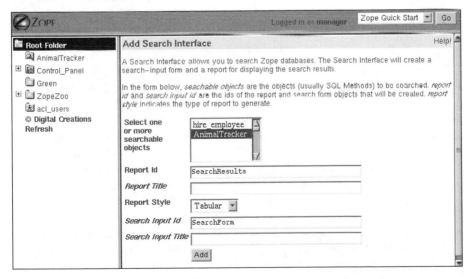

**Figure 9.2**   Creating a search form for a ZCatalog.

Name the Report Id `SearchResults` and the Search Input Id `SearchForm`, and click Add. This creates two new DTML methods in the AnimalTracker ZCatalog named SearchForm and SearchResults.

These DTML methods are *contained in* the ZCatalog, but they are not *cataloged by* the ZCatalog. The AnimalTracker has only cataloged DTML documents. The SearchForm and Report methods are just a user interface to search the animal documents in the Catalog. You can verify this by noting that the Search and Report forms are not listed in the Cataloged Objects tab.

To search the AnimalTracker ZCatalog, select the SearchForm method, and click its View tab. This form has a number of elements in it. Each index in the ZCatalog has one search element. Indexes are explained further in the following section, "Defining Indexes." For now, you want to use the PrincipiaSearchSource form element. You can leave all the other form elements blank.

By typing words into the PrincipiaSearchSource form element, you can search all the documents cataloged by the AnimalTracker ZCatalog. For example, type the word `Reptiles`. The AnimalTracker ZCatalog is searched and returns a simple table of objects that have the word Reptiles in them. The search results should include the carpet python. You can also try specifying multiple search terms, such as reptile frog. Search results for this query should include both the Chilean four-eyed frog and the carpet python. Congratulations, you have successfully created a catalog, cataloged content into it, and searched for the content through the Web.

# Configuring Catalogs

The Catalog is capable of much more powerful and complex searches than the one you just performed. Let's take a look at how the Catalog stores information. This helps you tailor your catalogs to provide the sort of searching you want.

## Defining Indexes

ZCatalogs store information about objects and their contents in fast databases called *indexes*. Indexes can store and retrieve large volumes of information very quickly. You can create different kinds of indexes that remember different kinds of information about your objects. For example, you could have one index that remembers the text content of DTML documents and another index that remembers any objects that have a specific property.

When you search a ZCatalog, you are not searching through your objects one by one. That would take far too much time, if you had a lot of objects. Before you search a ZCatalog, it looks at your objects and remembers whatever you tell it to remember about them. This process is called *indexing*. From then on, you can search for certain criteria, and the ZCatalog returns objects that match the criteria you provide.

A good way to think of an index in a ZCatalog is just like an index in a book. For example, in a book's index you can look up the word Python:

```
Python: 23, 67, 227
```

The word Python appears on three pages. Zope indexes words like this, except it maps the search term. In this case, the word Python is mapped to a list of all the objects that contain it instead of to a list of pages in a book.

These indexes are managed in the Indexes view of the ZCatalog, as shown in Figure 9.3.

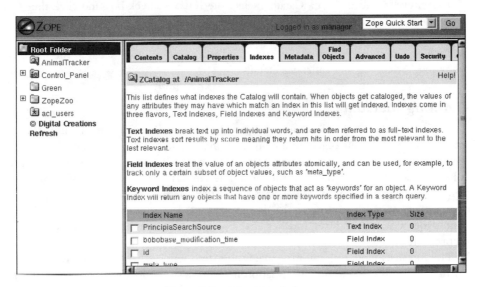

**Figure 9.3**   Managing indexes.

In Figure 9.3, you can see that ZCatalogs come with some predefined indexes. Each index has a name, such as PrincipiaSearchSource, and a type, such as Text Index.

When you catalog an object, the Catalog uses each index to examine the object. The Catalog consults attributes and methods to find an object's value for each index. For example, in the case of the DTML documents cataloged with a PrincipiaSearchSource index, the Catalog calls each document's PrincipiaSearchSource method and records the results in its PrincipiaSearchSource index. If the Catalog cannot find an attribute or method for an index, then it ignores it. In other words, it is fine if an object does not support a given index. The three kinds of indexes are as follows:

- **Text Index**—Searches text. Use this kind of index when you want a full-text search.

- **Field Index**—Searches objects for specific values. Use this kind of index when you want to search date objects, numbers, or specific strings.

- **Keyword Index**—Searches collections of specific values. This index is like a Field Index, but it enables you to search collections instead of single values.

We examine these different indexes more closely in the section, "Searching and Indexing Details," later in the chapter. New indexes can be created using the Indexes view of a ZCatalog. In the Indexes view, you can enter the name and select a type for your new index. This creates a new empty index in the ZCatalog. To populate this index with information, you need to go to the Cataloged Objects view, then to the Advanced view, and click the Update Catalog button. Recataloging your content might take a while if you have a lot of cataloged objects.

To remove an index from a Catalog, select the Indexes check box and click the Delete button. This deletes the index and all of its indexed content. As usual, this operation can be undone.

Each type of index has its own purpose and is covered in more detail in the sections following, "Searching and Indexing Details."

### Defining Metadata

The ZCatalog not only indexes information about your object, but it can also store information about your object in a tabular database called the *metadata table*. The metadata table works similarly to a relational database table. It consists of one or more columns that define the *schema* of the table. The table is filled with rows of information about cataloged objects. These rows can contain information about cataloged objects that you want to store in the table. Your metadata columns don't need to match your Catalog's indexes. Indexes enable you to search; metadata enables you to report search results.

The metadata table is useful for generating search reports. It keeps track of information about objects and that information goes on your report forms. For example, if you create a metadata table column called absolute_url, then your report forms can use this information to create links to your objects that are returned in search results.

To add a new metadata table column, type the name of the column in the metadata table view, and click Add. To remove a column from the metadata table, select the Column check box, and click the Delete button. This deletes the column and all its content for each row. As usual, this operation can be undone. Next, let's look more closely at how to search a Catalog.

## Searching Catalogs

You can search a Catalog by passing it *search terms*. These search terms describe what you are looking for in one or more indexes. The Catalog can glean this information from the Web request, or you can pass this information explicitly from DTML or Python. In response to a search request, a Catalog returns a list of records corresponding to the cataloged objects that match the search terms.

### Searching with Forms

In this chapter, you used the Z Search Interface to automatically build a Form/Action pair to query a Catalog (the Form/Action pattern is discussed in Chapter 4, "Dynamic

Content with DTML"). The Z Search Interface builds a very simple form and a very simple report. These two methods are a good place to start understanding how Catalogs are queried and how you can customize and extend your search interface.

Suppose you have a catalog that holds News Items. Each News Item has contents, an author, and a date. Your Catalog has three indexes that correspond to these attributes. The Contents index is a Text Index, and the author and date indexes are Field Indexes. The following is the search form that would enable you to query such a Catalog:

```
<dtml-var standard_html_header>

<form action="Report" method="get">
<h2><dtml-var document_title></h2>
Enter query parameters:<br><table>

<tr><th>Content</th>
    <td><input name="content" width=30 value=""></td></tr>
<tr><th>Author</th>
    <td><input name="author" width=30 value=""></td></tr>
<tr><th>Date</th>
    <td><input name="date"  width=30 value=""></td></tr>

<tr><td colspan=2 align=center>
<input type="SUBMIT" value="Submit Query">
</td></tr>
</table>
</form>

<dtml-var standard_html_footer>
```

This form consists of three input boxes named Content, Author, and Date. These input form element names match the names of the indexes in the catalog. These names must match the names of the Catalog's indexes for the Catalog to find the search terms. The following is a report form that works with the search form:

```
<dtml-var standard_html_header>

<table>
  <dtml-in NewsCatalog>
  <tr>
    <td><dtml-var author></td>
    <td><dtml-var date></td>
  </tr>
  </dtml-in>
</table>

<dtml-var standard_html_footer>
```

A few things going on in this example merit closer examination. The heart of the example is the in tag.:

```
<dtml-in NewsCatalog>
```

The in tag calls the NewsCatalog Catalog. Notice how the form parameters from the search form (Content, Author, Date) are not mentioned here at all. Zope automatically makes sure that the query parameters from the search form are given to the Catalog. All you have to do is make sure the report form calls the Catalog. Zope locates the search terms in the Web request and passes them to the Catalog.

The Catalog returns a sequence of Record Objects (just like ZSQL methods). These record objects correspond to *search hits*, which are objects that match the search criteria you typed in. For a record to match a search, it must match all criteria for each specified index. So, if you enter an author and some search terms for the contents, the Catalog only returns records that match both the author and the contents.

Record objects have an attribute for every column in the metadata table. In fact, the purpose of the metadata table is to define the schema for the Record objects that Catalog queries return.

## Searching from Python

DTML makes querying a Catalog from a form very simple. For the most part, DTML automatically makes sure your search parameters are passed properly to the Catalog.

Sometimes, however, you might not want to search a Catalog from a Web form because you might want some other part of your application to query a Catalog. For example, suppose you want to add a sidebar to the Zope zoo, which only shows News Items that relate to the animals in the section of the site that you are currently looking at. As you've seen, the Zope zoo site is built up from folders that organize all the sections according to animal. Each folder's id is a name that specifies the group or animal the folder contains. Suppose you want your sidebar to show you all the News Items that contain the id of the current section. The following is a script called relevantSectionNews that queries the news Catalog with the current folder's id:

```
## Script (Python) "relevantSectionNews"
##
""" Returns news relevant to the current folder's id """
id=context.getId()
return context.NewsCatalog({'content' : id})
```

This script queries the NewsCatalog by calling it like a method. Catalogs expect a *mapping* as the first argument when they are called. The argument maps the name of an index to the search terms you are looking for. In this case, the Content index is queried for all News Items that contain the name of the current folder. To use this in your sidebar, just edit the Zope zoo's standard_html_header to use the relevantSectionNews script:

```
<html>
<body>
<dtml-var style_sheet>
<dtml-var navigation>
<ul>
<dtml-in relevantSectionNews>
  <li><a href="&dtml-absolute_url;"><dtml-var title></a></li>
</dtml-in>
</ul>
```

This method assumes that you have defined absolute_url and title as metadata columns in the NewsCatalog. Now, when you are in a particular section, the sidebar shows a simple list of links to News Items that contain the id of the current animal section you are viewing.

# Searching and Indexing Details

Earlier in the chapter, you saw that the Catalog supports three types of indexes: Text Indexes, Field Indexes and Keyword Indexes. Now let's examine these indexes more closely to understand what they are good for and how to search them.

## Searching Text Indexes

A *Text Index* is used to index text. After indexing, you can search the index for objects that contain certain words. Text Indexes support a rich search grammar for doing more advanced searches than just looking for a word. ZCatalog's Text Index can

- Search for Boolean expressions, such as word1 AND word2. This expression searches for all objects that contain *both* word1 and word2. Valid Boolean operators include AND, OR, and AND NOT.

- Control search order with parenthetical expressions, such as (word1 AND word2) OR word3). This expression returns objects containing word1 and word2 or just objects that contain the term word3.

- If you use a special kind of vocabulary object, (explained in the section, "Current Vocabularies") you can search using simple wildcards, such as Z*, which returns all words that begin with Z.

All of these advanced features can be mixed together. For example, ((bob AND uncle) AND NOT Zoo*) returns all objects that contain the terms bob and uncle but does not include any objects that contain words that start with Zoo, such as Zoologist, Zoology, or Zoo itself.

Querying a Text Index with these advanced features works just like querying it with the original simple features. In the HTML search form for DTML documents, for example, you could enter Koala AND Lion and get all documents about Koalas and Lions. Querying a Text Index from Python with advanced features works in much the same way; suppose you want to change your relevantSectionNews script, so that it does not include any News Items that contain the word catastrophic:

```
## Script (Python) "relevantSectionNews"
##
""" Returns relevant, non-catastrophic news """
id=context.getId()
return context.NewsCatalog(
        {'content' : id + ' AND NOT catastrophic'}
        )
```

Text Indexes are very powerful. When mixed with the automatic-cataloging pattern, described later in the section, "Automatic Cataloging," Text Indexes give you the ability to automatically free-text search all your objects as you create and edit them.

## Vocabularies

Vocabularies are used by Text Indexes. A *vocabulary* is an object that manages language-specific text indexing options. For the ZCatalog to work with any kind of language, it must understand certain behaviors of that language. For example, all languages:

- Have a different concept of *words*. In English and many other languages, words are defined by white space boundaries, but in other languages, such as Chinese and Japanese, words are defined by their contextual usage.

- Have different concepts of *stop words*. A stop word is a common word that should be ignored by indexes. The French word *nous* is extremely common in French text and should probably be removed as a stop word, but in English text it might make perfect sense to catalog this word because it is very infrequent.

- Have different concepts of *synonymous*. The synonym pair automobile/car does not make sense in any language but English.

- Have different concepts of *stemming*. In English, it is common for text indexers to strip suffixes, such as *ing* from words, so that bake and baking match the same word. This is called stemming. These suffix strippings only make sense in English, and other languages need to provide their own stemming (or none at all).

### Current Vocabularies

A number of vocabularies are currently available for ZCatalog:

- **Plain vocabularies**—Plain vocabularies are very simple and do minimal English language-specific tasks.

- **Globbing vocabularies**—Globbing vocabularies are more complex vocabularies that enable wildcard searches to be performed on English text. The down side of them is that they consume a lot more memory and database space than plain vocabularies.

The idea behind vocabularies is to customize the way text is indexed in any language. Because of this, other languages might be supported in the future by people who create a vocabulary specific to their language. Creating your own vocabulary is an advanced topic and is beyond the scope of this book.

### Using Vocabularies

When you create a new ZCatalog, the ZCatalog Add form has a select box for you to choose a vocabulary. If you do not select a vocabulary, the ZCatalog automatically creates a Plain vocabulary for you, and adds it to the ZCatalog's contents (this can be seen on the Contents view of the AnimalTracker you created for the examples earlier in this chapter).

To use a Globbing vocabulary or any other kind of vocabulary, you must create it first before you create the Catalog you want to use it in. A ZCatalog can use any vocabulary inside its contents or any vocabulary higher than it in the Zope folder hierarchy.

## Searching Field Indexes

*Field Indexes* differ slightly from Text Indexes. A Text Index treats the value it finds in your object like text—for example the contents of a News Item. This means that it breaks the text up into words and then indexes all the individual words.

A Field Index does not break up the value it finds. Instead, it indexes the entire value it finds. This is very useful for tracking objects that have traits with fixed values.

In the News Item example, you created two Field Indexes, *date* and *author*. With the existing search form, these fields are not very useful. To use them more effectively, you have to customize your search form a little. Before doing that, however, let's consider some cases for these indexes.

The *date* index enables you to search for News Items by the time they were created. The existing search form is not very useful, however, because you have to type *exactly* the time you are looking for, right down to the second, in the text box to get any hits. This is obviously not very useful. It is better to search for a *range* of dates, such as all the News Items added in the last 24 hours, or even broader—all the News Items from last month.

The *author* index enables you to search for News Items by certain authors. Unless you know exactly the name of the author you are looking for, however, you do not get any results. It is better to select from a list of all the *unique* authors indexed by the author index.

Field Indexes are designed to do both range searching and searching for a unique value in the index. To take advantage of these features, you only need to change your search form a little bit. Let's try the first example, range searching, with dates.

Like Text Indexes, Field Indexes can be passed special options to enable these features. These special features need to be passed in as form elements that get turned into Catalog queries. Here is the search form used earlier in the section "Searching with Forms," but with some new form elements added to enable searching for News Items modified since Yesterday, Last Week, Last Month, Last Year or Ever:

```
<dtml-var standard_html_header>

<form action="Report" method="get">
<h2><dtml-var document_title></h2>
Search for News Items:<br><table>

<tr><th>Content</th>
    <td><input name="content" width=30 value=""></td></tr>
<tr><th>Author</th>
    <td><input name="author" width=30 value=""></td></tr>
<tr>
```

*continues*

*continued*

```
      <td><p>modified since:</p></td>
      <td>
        <input type="hidden" name="date_usage" value="range:min">
        <select name="date:date">
          <option value="<dtml-var expr="ZopeTime(0)" >">Ever</option>
          <option value="<dtml-var expr="ZopeTime() - 1" >">Yesterday</option>
          <option value="<dtml-var expr="ZopeTime() - 7" >">Last Week</option>
          <option value="<dtml-var expr="ZopeTime() - 30" >">Last Month</option>
          <option value="<dtml-var expr="ZopeTime() - 365" >">Last Year</option>
        </select>
      </td>
  </tr>

  <tr><td colspan=2 align=center>
  <input type="SUBMIT" value="Submit Query">
  </td></tr>
  </table>
  </form>
  <dtml-var standard_html_footer>
```

The preceding example should make your search form look like Figure 9.4.

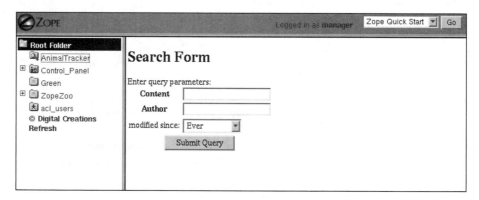

**Figure 9.4**   Range searching by date.

This HTML form changes the date format from the old search form. Instead of just a text box, it offers you a selection box where you can choose a date. But remember, this is a range search. Can you spot the code in the preceding example that tells the date Field Index to search by range? Here it is:

```
<input type="hidden" name="date_usage" value="range:min">
```

This is a special kind of HTML form element called a *hidden* element. It does not show up anywhere on the search form that you look at, but it is still passed into Zope when you submit the form. This special element, called `date_usage` tells the date Field Index that the value in the date form element is a *minimum range boundary*. This means that the Field Index does not just return objects that have that date, but it returns objects that have that date or any later date.

You can tell any kind of Field Index what kind of range specifiers to use by adding an additional search argument that suffixes the index name with _usage. In addition to specifying a minimum range boundary, you specify a *maximum range boundary* by changing the hidden form element to:

```
<input type="hidden" name="date_usage" value="range:max">
```

This script causes the search form to return all News Items modified *before* the specified date instead of after.

The _usage syntax can also be used when calling a Catalog directly from a script, such as the script, relevantRecentSectionNews:

```
## Script (Python) "relevantRecentSectionNews"
##
""" Return relevant, and recent, news for this section """
id=context.getId()
return context.NewsCatalog(
         {'content'    : id,
          'date'       : ZopeTime() - 7,
          'date_usage' : 'range:min',
         }
        )
```

This script works just like your old relevantSectionNews script, except that it only shows News Items created in the last week.

You can also supply both a minimum and maximum range boundary. There's one catch to this, however. Normally, if you specify no range boundary or just one boundary, ZCatalog uses the value you pass in as the search term. However, when you provide *two* range boundaries, the ZCatalog needs two values, not one. The following is the preceding relevantRecentSectionNews script with some slight modification to provide a list of date objects instead of just one:

```
## Script (Python) "relevantRecentSectionNews"
##
"""
Return relevant news modified in the last month, but not the
last week
"""
id=context.getId()
return context.NewsCatalog(
         {'content'    : id,
          'date'       : [ZopeTime() - 30, ZopeTime() - 7],
          'date_usage' : 'range:min:max',
         }
        )
```

This script returns all of the relevant News Items modified in the last month, but not in the last week. When using two range specifiers, it is important to make sure you get the order of the values to correctly match the order of the range specifiers. If you were to accidentally switch the min and max around, but didn't switch around the two dates, then you would not get any search results. This is because you are making a query that doesn't make sense (that is, providing a minimum value that is larger than the maximum value).

The second case you considered was being able to search from a list of all unique authors. A special method on the ZCatalog does exactly this. It is called *uniqueValuesFor*. The uniqueValuesFor method returns a list of unique values for a certain index. Let's change your search form yet again, and replace the original author input box with something a little more useful:

```
<dtml-var standard_html_header>

<form action="Report" method="get">
<h2><dtml-var document_title></h2>
Search for News Items:<br><table>

<tr><th>Content:</th>
    <td><input name="content" width=30 value=""></td></tr>

<tr valign="top">
  <td><p>Author:</p></td>

  <td>
    <select name="author:list" size=6 MULTIPLE>
    <dtml-in expr="AnimalTracker.uniqueValuesFor('author')">
      <option value="<dtml-var sequence-item>">
➥<dtml-var sequence-item></options>
    </dtml-in>
    </select>
  </td>
 </tr>

<tr>
  <td><p>modified since:</p></td>
  <td>
    <input type="hidden" name="date_usage" value="range:min">
    <select name="date:date">
      <option value="<dtml-var "ZopeTime(0)" >">Ever</option>
      <option value="<dtml-var "ZopeTime() - 1" >">Yesterday</option>
      <option value="<dtml-var "ZopeTime() - 7" >">Last Week</option>
      <option value="<dtml-var "ZopeTime() - 30" >">Last Month</option>
      <option value="<dtml-var "ZopeTime() - 365" >">Last Year</option>
    </select>
  </td>
</tr>

<tr><td colspan=2 align=center>
<input type="SUBMIT" name="SUBMIT" value="Submit Query">
</td></tr>
</table>
</form>
<dtml-var standard_html_footer>
```

The new, important bit of code added to the search form is as follows:

```
<select name="author:list" size=6 MULTIPLE>
<dtml-in expr="AnimalTracker.uniqueValuesFor('author')">
  <option value="<dtml-var sequence-item>"><dtml-var sequence-item></options>
</dtml-in>
</select>
```

The HTML was also changed a bit to make the onscreen presentation make sense.

In this example, you are changing the form element author from just a simple text box to an HTML multiple select box. This box contains a unique list of all the authors that are indexed in the author Field Index. Now, your search form should look like Figure 9.5.

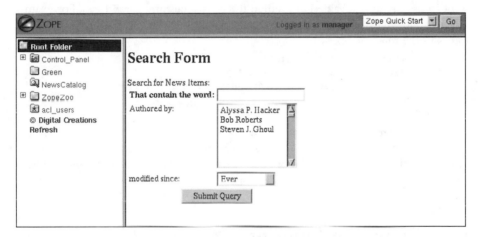

**Figure 9.5** Range searching and unique authors.

That's it. You can continue to extend this search form using HTML form elements to be as complex as you want. In the following section, we show you how to use the next kind of index, Keyword Indexes.

## Searching Keyword Indexes

A *Keyword Index* indexes a sequence of keywords for objects and can be queried for any objects that have one or more of those keywords.

Suppose that you have a number of Image objects that have a topics property. The topics property is a lines property that lists the relevant topics for a given Image, for example, the terms "Portraits," "19th Century," and "Women" are relevant topics for a picture of Queen Victoria.

The topics provide a way of categorizing Images. Each Image can belong in one or more categories, depending on its topics property. For example, the portrait of Queen Victoria belongs to three categories and, thus, it can be found by searching for any of the three terms.

You can use a Keyword Index to search the topics property. Define a Keyword Index with the name topics on your ZCatalog, and then catalog your Images. Now you should be able to find all the Images that are portraits by creating a search form and searching for "Portraits" in the topics field. You can also find all pictures that represent 19th Century subjects by searching for "19th Century."

It's important to realize that the same Image can be in more than one category. Because of this, you have much more flexibility in searching and categorizing your objects than you get with a Field Index. If you use a Field Index, your portrait of Queen Victoria can only be categorized one way. If you use a Keyword Index, however, it can be categorized a couple of different ways.

You often use a small list of terms with Keyword Indexes. In this case, you might want to use the uniqueValuesFor method to create a custom search form. For example, the following is a snippet of DTML that creates a multiple select box for all the values in the topics index:

```
<select name="topics:list" multiple>
<dtml-in expr="uniqueValuesFor('topics')">
  <option value="&dtml-sequence-item;"><dtml-var sequence-item></option>
</dtml-in>
</select>
```

Using this search form, you can provide users with a range of valid search terms. You can select as many topics as you want and Zope finds all the Images that match one or more of your selected topics. Not only can each object have several indexed terms, but you can provide several search terms and find all objects that have one or more of those values.

## Concatenating Queries

ZCatalog queries can be concatenated, or added together, to combine two queries into one with the plus (+) operator. For example, the following is a Python script that adds two queries together:

```
## Script (Python) "oldNewsandBobNews"
##
"""
All old news and news written by bob.
"""
id=context.getId()
bobs =  context.NewsCatalog('author' : 'bob')
yearold = context.NewsCatalog('data' : ZopeTime() - 365)

return bobs + yearold
```

This script demonstrates how to query for all the documents authored by bob and all News Items that are a year old. The script adds these two result sets together and returns them. The preceding query is quite different from the following query:

```
## Script (Python) "oldBobNews"
##
"""
Only old news written by bob.
"""
id=context.getId()
return context.NewsCatalog({'author' : 'bob', 'data' : ZopeTime() - 365})
```

Why are they different? Because the first example returns the results of the one query (author) and the results of the other (data). In other words, in the first example, you get all the old News Items as well as all the items authored by **bob**, regardless of how old they are.

The second example returns all the News Items that were authored by **bob** that are a year old, and puts all of that into one query. This means that you only get News Items authored by **bob** that are more than a year old. This is a much more restrictive search.

# Stored Queries

Although the main use of the Catalog is to provide interactive searching, you can also use *stored queries* to categorize and organize your site. For example, in the previous section, "Searching Keyword Indexes," you saw how you can use the Catalog and properties to search for categories of Images, such as portraits. In addition to providing interactive searching for categories of Images, you can create Web pages with canned queries. So, for example, the following is some DTML that you can use for a page that displays all your portraits:

```
<dtml-var standard_html_header>

<h1>Portraits</h1>

<dtml-in expr="ImageCatalog({'topics':'Portraits'})">
<p>
<dtml-var sequence-item>
<dtml-var title_or_id>
</p>
</dtml-in>

<dtml-var standard_html_footer>
```

The dynamic nature of this page is not visible to the viewer. However, just add another portrait, update the catalog, and this page will automatically include the new Image.

This technique can be very powerful. Not only can you organize and display public resources, but you can easily institute work flow systems by tagging objects with properties to indicate their state and cataloging them. After that, it's easy for you to create pages for different people that show what objects need their attention. This technique is even more powerful when using the automatic cataloging pattern.

# Automatic Cataloging

*Automatic cataloging* is an advanced Catalog usage pattern that keeps updating objects in the Catalog. As objects are created, changed, or destroyed, automatic Cataloging requires that they are automatically tracked by a ZCatalog. This usually involves the objects notifying the Catalog when they are created, changed, or deleted.

Automatic cataloging has a number of advantages compared to mass cataloging. Mass cataloging is simple, but it has drawbacks. The total amount of content you can index in one transaction is equivalent to the amount of free virtual memory available to the Zope process plus the amount of temporary storage the system has. In other words, the more content you want to index all at once, the better your computer hardware has to be. Mass cataloging works well for indexing up to a few thousand objects, but beyond that, automatic cataloging works much better.

Another major advantage of automatic cataloging is that it can handle objects that change. As objects evolve and change, the index information is always current, even for rapidly changing information sources, such as message boards.

In this section, we show you an example that creates "news" items that people can add to your site. These items get automatically cataloged. This example consists of two steps:

- Creating a new type of object to catalog.
- Creating a Catalog to catalog the newly created objects.

As of Zope 2.3, the "out-of-the-box" Zope objects do not support automatic cataloging. This is for backward compatibility reasons. For now, you have to define your own kind of objects that can be cataloged automatically. One of the ways this can be done is by defining a ZClass.

A ZClass is a Zope object that defines new types of Zope objects. In a way, a ZClass is like a blueprint that describes how new Zope objects are built. Consider a News Item, as discussed in previous examples in the chapter. News Items not only have content, but they also have specific properties that make them News Items. These Items often come in collections that have their own properties. You want to build a News site that collects News Items, reviews them, and posts them online to a Web site where readers can read them.

In this kind of system, you might want to create a new type of object called a News Item. This way, when you want to add a new News Item to your site, you just select it from the product Add list. If you design this object to be automatically cataloged, then you can search your news content very powerfully. For this example, we just skim a little over ZClasses, however, they are described in much more detail in Chapter 12, "Extending Zope."

New types of objects are defined in the Products section of the Control Panel. This is reached by clicking the Control Panel and then clicking Product Management. Products contain new kinds of ZClasses. In this screen, click Add to add a New product. You are taken to the Add form for new products.

Name the new product **News**, and click Generate. This takes you back to the
Products Management view where you see your new Product.

Select the News product by clicking it. This new product looks a lot like a folder. It
contains one object called Help, and it has an Add menu as well as the usual folder
tabs across the top. To add a new ZClass, pull down the Add menu and select ZClass.
This takes you to the ZClass Add form, as shown in Figure 9.6.

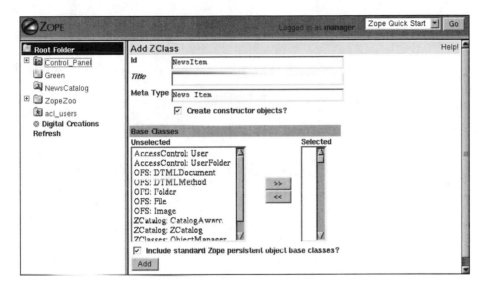

**Figure 9.6**  ZClass Add form.

This is a complicated form, which is explained in much more detail in Chapter 12.
For now, you only need to do three things to create your ZClass:

- **Specify the Id "NewsItem"**—This is the name of the new ZClass.
- **Specify the Meta_Type "News Item"**—This is used to create the Add menu
  entry for your new type of object.
- **Select ZCatalog:CatalogAware**—Select this from the left Base Classes box,
  and click the button with the arrow pointing to the right Base Classes box. This
  should cause ZCatalog:CatalogAware to show up in the right window.

When you're done, don't change any of the other settings in the form. To create your
new ZClass, click Add. This takes you back to your News product. Notice that a new
object called NewsItem exists as well as several other objects. The NewsItem object is
your new ZClass. The other objects are *helpers*, which are examined more closely in
Chapter 12.

Select the NewsItem ZClass object. Your view should now look like Figure 9.7.

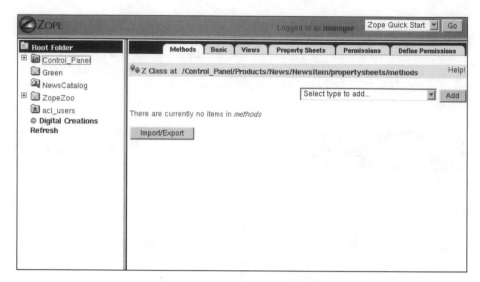

**Figure 9.7**   A ZClass Methods view.

This is the Methods view of a ZClass. Here, you can add Zope objects that act as methods on your new type of object. For example, you can create DTML methods or scripts, and these objects become methods on any new News Items that are created. Before creating any methods, however, let's review the needs of this new NewsItem object:

- **News Content**—The News Item contains news content; this is its primary purpose. This content could be any kind of plain text or marked-up content, such as HTML or XML.

- **Author Credit**—The News Item should provide some kind of credit to the author or organization that created it.

- **Date**—News Items are timely, so the date that the item was created is important.

- **Keywords**—News Items fit into various lists of categories. By convention, these lists of categories are often called *keywords*.

You might want your new News Item object to have other properties, however, this is just a suggestion. To add new properties to your News Item, click the Property Sheets tab. This takes you to the Property Sheets view.

Properties are added to new types of objects in groups called *property sheets*. Because your object has no property sheets defined, this view is empty. To add a New Property Sheet, click the Add Common Instance property sheet, and give the sheet the name News. Now click Add. This adds a new property sheet called News to your object. Clicking the new Property Sheet takes you to the Properties view of the News Property Sheet, as shown in Figure 9.8.

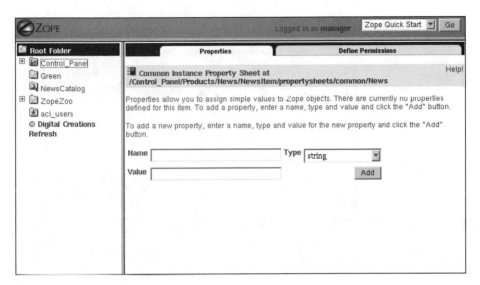

**Figure 9.8**   The Properties screen for a property sheet.

This view is almost identical to the Properties view found on folders and other objects. Here, you can create the properties of your News Item object. Create the following three new properties in this form:

- **content**—This property's type should be text. Each newly created News Item contains its own unique content property.
- **author**—This property's type should be string. This contains the name of the news author.
- **date**—This property's type should be date. This contains the time and date the News Item was last updated. A date property requires a value, so for now, you can enter the string 01/01/2000.

That's it! Now you have created a property sheet that describes your News Items and what kind of information they contain. Properties can be thought of as the data that an object contains. Now that we have the data all set, you need to create an *interface* to your new kind of objects. This is done by creating new Views for your object.

Click the Views tab. This takes you to the Views view, as shown in Figure 9.9. Here, you can see that Zope has created three default views for you. These views are described in much more detail in Chapter 12, but for now, it suffices to say that these views define the tabs that your objects will eventually have.

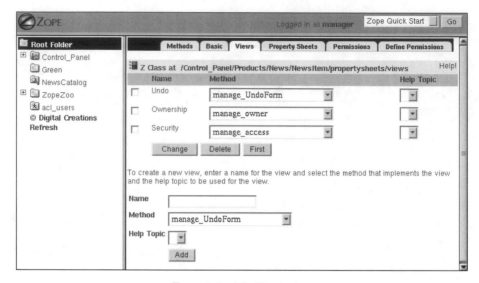

**Figure 9.9**   The Views view.

To create a new view, use the form at the bottom of the Views view. Create a new view with the name News and select propertysheets/News/manage from the select box and click Add. This creates a new view on this screen under the original three views, as shown in Figure 9.10.

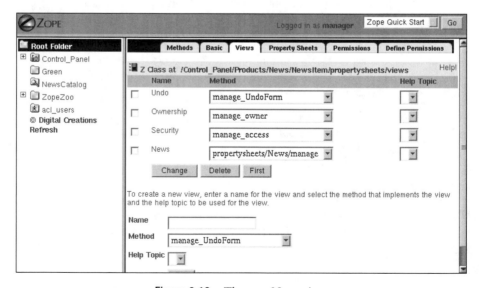

**Figure 9.10**   The new News view.

Because the News view is going to give us the ability to edit the News Item, we want to make it the first view that you see when you select a News Item object. To change the order of the views, select the newly created News view, and click the First button. This should move the new view from the bottom to the top of the list.

The final step in creating a ZClass is defining the methods for the class. Methods are defined in the Methods view. Click the Methods tab, and you are taken to the Methods view. Select DTML Method from the Add list, and add a new DTML method with the id index_html. This is the default view of your News Item. Add the following DTML to the new method:

```
<dtml-var standard_html_header>

<h1>News Flash</h1>

<p><dtml-var date></p>

<p><dtml-var author></p>

<P><dtml-var content></p>

<dtml-var standard_html_footer>
```

That's it! You've created your own kind of object called a News Item. When you go to the Root folder, you now see a new entry in your Add list.

However, do not add any new News Items yet because the second step in this exercise is to create a Catalog that catalogs your new News Items. Go to the Root folder and create a new catalog with the id Catalog.

Like the previous two examples using a ZCatalog, you need to create indexes and a metadata table that make sense for your objects. First, delete the default indexes in the new ZCatalog, and create the following indexes to replace them:

- **content**—This should be a Text Index. This indexes the content of your News Items.
- **title**—This should be a Text Index. This indexes the title of your News Items.
- **author**—This should be a Field Index. This indexes the author of the News Item.
- **date**—This should be a Field Index. This indexes the date of the News Item.

After creating these indexes, delete the default metadata columns, and add the following columns to replace them:

- author
- date
- title
- absolute_url

After creating the indexes and metadata table columns, create a search interface for the Catalog using the Z Search Interface tool, described previously in this chapter.

Now you are ready to go. Start by adding some new News Items to your Zope. Go anywhere in Zope and select News Item from the Add list. This takes you to the Add Form for News items.

Give your new News Item the id `KoalaGivesBirth`, and click Add. This creates a new News Item. Select the new News Item.

Notice how it has four tabs that match the four views that were in the ZClass. The first view is News; this view corresponds to the News Property Sheet you created in the News Item ZClass.

Enter your news in the Contents box:

```
Today, Bob the Koala bear gave birth to little baby Jimbo.
```

Enter your name in the Author box and today's date in the Date box. In Chapter 12, you see how to automate the task of entering the date.

Click Change. Your News Item should now contain some news. Because the News Item object is *CatalogAware*, it is automatically cataloged when it is changed or added. Verify this by looking at the Cataloged Objects tab of the ZCatalog you created for this example.

The News Item you added is the only object that is cataloged. As you add more News Items to your site, they automatically get cataloged here. Add a few more items, and then experiment with searching the ZCatalog. For example, if you search for `Koala`, you should get back the `KoalaGivesBirth` News Item.

At this point, you might want to use some of the more advanced search forms that you created earlier in the chapter. You can see, for example, that as you add new News Items with new authors, the authors select list on the search form changes to include the new information.

The cataloging features of ZCatalog enable you to search your objects for certain attributes very quickly. This can be very useful for sites with a lot of content that many people need to search in an efficient manner.

Searching the ZCatalog works a lot like searching a relational database, except that the searching is more object-oriented. Not all data models are object oriented, however, so in some cases you might want to use the ZCatalog, but in other cases, you might want to use a relational database. Chapter 10, "Relational Database Connectivity," goes into more detail about how Zope works with relational databases and how you can use relational data as objects in Zope.

# 10

# Relational Database Connectivity

ZOPE USES AN OBJECT DATABASE to store Zope objects. Relational databases, such as Oracle, Sybase, and PostgreSQL, store information in a different way. Relational databases store their information in tables, as shown in Figure 10.1.

| Row | First Name | Last Name | Age |
|-----|-----------|-----------|-----|
| #1 | Bob | McBob | 42 |
| #2 | John | Johnson | 24 |
| #3 | Steve | Smith | 38 |

**Figure 10.1**   Relational database table.

Information in the table is stored in rows. The table's column layout is called the *schema*. A standard language called the *Structured Query Language* (SQL) is used to query and change tables in relational databases.

Zope does not store its information this way. Zope's object database allows for many different types of objects that have many different types of relationships to each other. Relational data does not easily map onto objects because relational data assumes a much simpler table-oriented data model. Zope provides several mechanisms for taking relational data and using it in Zope's object-centric world; including Database Adapters and SQL methods, which are discussed in detail in the section, "Using Database Connections."

Zope's relational database support is most commonly used for putting existing relational databases on the Web. For example, suppose your Human Resources department has an employee database. Your database comes with tools to enable administrators to run reports and change data. However, it is hard for employees to see their own records and perform simple maintenance, such as updating their address when they move. By interfacing your relational database with Zope, your employees can use any Web browser to view and update their records from the office or home.

By using your relational data with Zope, you get all of Zope's benefits, including security, dynamic presentation, networking, and more. You can use Zope to dynamically tailor your data access, data presentation, and data management.

To use a relational database in Zope, you must create two different Zope objects: a Database Connection and a Z SQL method. Database Connections tell Zope how to connect to a relational database. Z SQL methods describe an action to take on a database. Z SQL methods use Database Connections to connect to relational databases. We look more closely at these two types of objects in the sections, "Using Database Connections" and "Using Z SQL Methods."

## Using Database Connections

Database Connections are used to establish and manage connections to external relational databases. Database Connections must be established before database methods can be defined. Moreover, every Z SQL method must be associated with a database connection. Database adapters (or DAs for short) are available for a number of databases:

- **Oracle**—Oracle is a powerful and popular commercial relational database. This DA is written and commercially supported by Zope Corporation. Oracle can be purchased or evaluated from the Oracle Web site (http://www.oracle.com/).

- **Sybase**—Sybase is another popular commercial relational database. The Sybase DA is written and commercially supported by Zope Corporation. Sybase can be purchased or evaluated from the Sybase Web site (http://www.sybase.com/).

- **ODBC**—ODBC is a cross-platform, industry standard database protocol supported by many commercial and open source databases. The ODBC DA is written and commercially supported by Zope Corporation.

- **PostgreSQL**—PostgreSQL is a leading open source relational database. Several database adapters for PostgreSQL exist, including ZpoPy, which is maintained by Zope community member Thierry Michel (http://sourceforge.net/projects/zpopyda/). You can find more information about PostgreSQL at the PostgreSQL Web site (http://www.postgresql.org/).

- **MySQL**—MySQL is a fast open source relational database. You can find more information about MySQL at the MySQL Web site (http://www.mysql.com/). The MySQL DA is maintained by Zope community member Monty Taylor.

- **Interbase**—Interbase is an open source relational database from Borland/Inprise. You can find more information about Interbase at the Borland Web site (`http://www.borland.com/interbase/`). You might also be interested in FireBird, which is a community maintained offshoot of Interbase (`http://sourceforge.net/projects/firebird`). The Zope Interbase adapter is maintained by Zope community member Bob Tierney.

- **Gadfly**—Gadfly is a relational database written in Python by Aaron Waters. Gadfly is included with Zope for demonstration purposes and small data sets. Gadfly is fast, but is not intended for large amounts of information because it reads the entire database into memory. You can find out more about Gadfly at the Chordate Web site (`http://www.chordate.com/gadfly.html`).

Other than Gadfly, all relational databases run as processes external to Zope. In fact, your relational database does not even need to run on the same machine as Zope, so long as Zope can connect to the machine that the database is running on. Installing and setting up relational databases is beyond the scope of this book. All the relational databases mentioned have their own installation and configuration documentation that you should consult for specific details.

Because Gadfly runs inside Zope, you do not need to specify any connection information for Zope to find the database. Because all other kinds of databases run externally to Zope, they require that you specify how to connect to the database. This specification, called a *connection string*, is different for each kind of database. For example, Figure 10.2 shows the PostgreSQL database connection Add form.

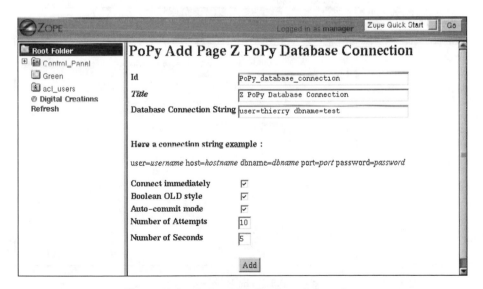

**Figure 10.2**   PostgreSQL Database Connection.

The connection string format for PostgreSQL is shown in Figure 10.2.

To use your relational database of choice from Zope, you must download and install the database adapter for your specific relational database. Database adapters can be downloaded from the Products section at Zope.org (`http://www.zope.org/Products/`). The exception to this is Gadfly, which is included with Zope. All the examples in this chapter use Gadfly. However, the procedures described apply to all databases.

After installing the database adapter product for your database, you can create a new database connection by selecting it from the Add list. All database connections are fairly similar. Select Z Gadfly Database Connection from the Add list. This takes you to the Add form for a Gadfly database connection.

Select the Demo data source, specify Gadfly_database_connection for the id, and click the Add button. This creates a new Gadfly Database Connection. Select the new connection by clicking it.

You are looking at the Status view of the Gadfly Database Connection. This view tells you whether you are connected to the database, and there is a button for connecting or disconnecting. In general, Zope manages the connection to your database for you, so there is little reason to manually control the connection. For Gadfly, connecting and disconnecting are meaningless. However, for external databases, you might want to connect or disconnect manually to do database maintenance.

The next view is the Properties view. This view shows you the data source and other properties of the Database Connection. This is useful if you want to move your Database Connection from one data source to another. Figure 10.3 shows the Properties view.

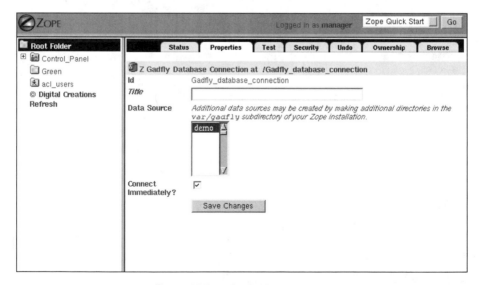

**Figure 10.3**   The Properties view.

You can test your connection to a database by going to the Test view. This view enables you to type SQL code directly and run it on your database. This view is just for testing your database and issuing one-time SQL commands (such as creating tables). This is *not* the place where you enter most of your SQL code. SQL commands reside in Z SQL methods, which are discussed later in this chapter in the section, "Using Z SQL Methods."

Let's create a table in your database to use in this chapter's examples. The Test view of the Database Connection enables you to send SQL statements directly to your database. You can create tables by typing SQL code directly into the Test view; there is no need to use a SQL method to create tables. Create a table called `employees` with the following SQL code.

```
CREATE TABLE employees
(
emp_id integer,
first varchar,
last varchar,
salary float
)
```

Click the Submit Query button to run the SQL command. Zope should return a confirmation screen that tells you what SQL code was run and the results, if any.

The SQL used here might differ, depending on your database. For the exact details on creating tables with your database, check the user documentation from your specific database vendor.

This SQL creates a new table in your Gadfly database called `employees`. This table has four columns: emp_id, first, last, and salary. The first column is the employee id, which is a unique number that identifies the employee. The next two columns have the type *varchar*, which is similar to a string. The salary column has the type *float*, which holds a floating point number. Every database supports different kinds of types, so consult your documentation to find out what types your database supports.

To ensure that the employee id is a unique number, you can create an index on your table. Type the following SQL code in the Test view:

```
CREATE UNIQUE INDEX emp_id ON employees
(
emp_id
)
```

Now you have a table and an index. To examine your table, go to the Browse view. This view enables you to view your database's tables and their schemas. Here, you can see the employee's table, and if you click the plus symbol, the table expands to show the four columns: emp_id, first, last, and salary, as shown in Figure 10.4.

This information is very useful when creating complex SQL applications with a lot of large tables because it enables you to discover the schemas of your tables. Not all databases support browsing of tables.

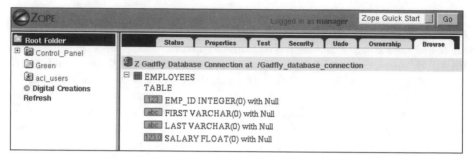

**Figure 10.4**   Browsing the Database Connection.

Now that you created a Database Connection and have defined a table, you can create Z SQL methods to operate on your database.

## Using Z SQL Methods

Z SQL methods are Zope objects that execute SQL code through a Database Connection. All Z SQL methods must be associated with a Database Connection. Z SQL methods can both query databases and change data. Z SQL methods can also contain more than one SQL command.

For example, create a new Z SQL method called hire_employee that inserts a new employee in the employees table. When a new employee is hired, this method is called, and a new record is inserted in the employees table that contains the information about the new employee. Select Z SQL Method from the Add list. This takes you to the Add form for Z SQL methods, as shown in Figure 10.5.

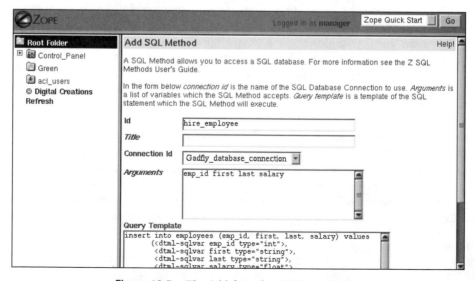

**Figure 10.5**   The Add form for Z SQL methods.

As usual, you must specify an id and title for the Z SQL method. In addition, you need to select a Database Connection to use with this Z SQL method. Give this new method the id `hire_employee`, and select the Gadfly_database_connection that you created in the previous section.

Next, you can specify *arguments* to the Z SQL method. Just like scripts, Z SQL methods can take arguments. Arguments are used to construct SQL statements. In this case, your method needs four arguments: the employee id number, the first name, the last name, and the employee's salary. Type `emp_id first last salary` into the Arguments field. You can put each argument on its own line, or you can put more than one argument on the same line separated by spaces. You can also provide default values for arguments just like with Python scripts. For example, `empid=100` gives the empid argument a default value of 100.

The last form field is the Query template. This field contains the SQL code that is executed when the Z SQL method is called. In this field, enter the following code:

```
insert into employees (emp_id, first, last, salary) values
(<dtml-sqlvar emp_id type="int">,
 <dtml-sqlvar first type="string">,
 <dtml-sqlvar last type="string">,
 <dtml-sqlvar salary type="float">
 )
```

Notice that this SQL code also contains DTML. The DTML code in this template is used to insert the values of the arguments into the SQL code that gets executed on your database. So, if the emp_id argument had the value 42, the first argument had the value Bob, the last argument had the value Uncle, and the salary argument had the value 50000.00, then the query template would create the following SQL code:

```
insert into employees (emp_id, first, last, salary) values
(42,
 'Bob',
 'Uncle',
 50000.00
 )
```

The query template and SQL-specific DTML tags are explained further in the following section, "Calling Z SQL Methods."

You have your choice of three buttons to add your new Z SQL method. The Add button creates the method and takes you back to the folder containing the new method. The Add and Edit button creates the method and makes it the currently selected object in the Workspace. The Add and Test button creates the method and takes you to the method's Test view so that you can test the new method. To add your new Z SQL method, click the Add button.

Now you have a Z SQL method that inserts new employees in the employees table. You need another Z SQL method to query the table for employees. Create a new Z SQL method with the id list_all_employees. It should not have arguments and should contain the following SQL code:

```
select * from employees
```

This simple SQL code selects all the rows from the employees table. Now you have two Z SQL methods—one to insert new employees and one to view all the employees in the database. Let's test your two new methods by inserting some new employees in the employees table and then listing them. To do this, click the hire_employee method, and click the Test tab. This takes you to the Test view of the method, as shown in Figure 10.6.

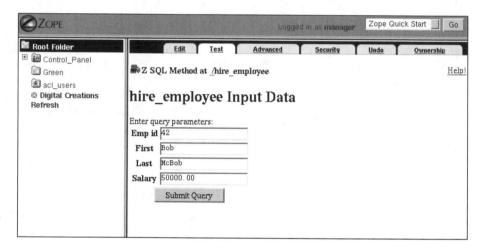

**Figure 10.6**   The hire_employee Test view.

Here, you see a form with four input boxes, one for each argument to the hire_employee Z SQL method. Zope automatically generates this form for you based on the arguments of your Z SQL method. Because the hire_employee method has four arguments, Zope creates this form with four input boxes. You can test the method by entering an employee number, a first name, a last name, and a salary for your new employee. Enter the employee id 42, Bob for the first name, McBob for the last name, and a salary of 50000.00. Then click the Test button. This shows you the results of your test.

The screen says This statement returned no results. This is because the hire_employee method only inserts new information in the table, it does not select any information outside of the table, so no records were returned. The screen also shows you how the query template gets rendered into SQL. As expected, the sqlvar DTML tags rendered the four arguments into valid SQL code that your database executed. You can add as many employees as you want by repeatedly testing this method.

To verify that the information you added is being inserted into the table, select the list_all_employees Z SQL method, and click its Test tab.

This view says This query requires no input, indicating the list_all_employees does not have any arguments, and thus, requires no input to execute. Click the Submit Query button to test the method.

The list_all_employees method returns the contents of your employees table. You can see all the new employees that you added. Zope automatically generates this tabular report screen for you. Next, we show you how to create your own user interface on your Z SQL methods to integrate them into your Web site.

## Calling Z SQL Methods

Querying a relational database returns a sequence of results. The items in the sequence are called *result rows*. SQL query results are always a sequence. Even if the SQL query returns only one row, that row is the only item contained in a list of results. Hence, Z SQL methods *always* return a sequence of results, which contain zero or more results records.

The items in the sequence of results returned by a Z SQL method are called *result objects*. Result objects can be thought of as rows from the database table turned into Zope objects. These objects have attributes that match the schema of the database results.

An important difference between result objects and other Zope objects is that result objects do not get created and permanently added to Zope. Result objects are not persistent. They exist for only a short period of time, just long enough for you to use them in a result page or to use their data for some other purpose. As soon as you are done with a request that uses result objects, they go away, and the next time you call a Z SQL method, you get a new set of fresh result objects.

Result objects can be used from DTML to display the results of calling a Z SQL method. For example, add a new DTML method to your site called listEmployees with the following DTML content:

```
<dtml-var standard_html_header>

<ul>
<dtml-in list_all_employees>
  <li><dtml-var emp_id>: <dtml-var last>, <dtml-var first>
    makes <dtml-var salary fmt=dollars-and-cents> a year.
  </li>
</dtml-in>
</ul>

<dtml-var standard_html_footer>
```

This method calls the list_all_employees Z SQL method from DTML. The in tag is used to iterate over each result object returned by the list_all_employees Z SQL method. Z SQL methods always return a list of objects, so you almost certainly use them from the DTML in tag, unless you are not interested in the results, or if the SQL code never returns any results, such as in the hire_employee example.

The body of the in tag is a template that defines what gets rendered for each result object in the sequence returned by list_all_employees. In the case of a table with three employees in it, listEmployees might return HTML that looks like this:

```
<html>
  <body>

  <ul>
    <li>42: Roberts, Bob
      makes $50,000 a year.
    </li>
    <li>101: leCat, Cheeta
      makes $100,000 a year.
    </li>
    <li>99: Junglewoman, Jane
      makes $100,001 a year.
    </li>
  </ul>

  </body>
</html>
```

The in tag rendered an HTML list item for each result object returned by list_all_employees.

Next, let's look at how to create user interfaces to collect data and pass it to Z SQL methods.

## Providing Arguments to Z SQL Methods

So far, you have the ability to display employees with the listEmployees DTML method, which calls the list_all_employees Z SQL method. Now, let's look at how to build a user interface for the hire_employee Z SQL method. Recall that hire_employee accepts four arguments: emp_id, first, last, and salary. The Test tab on the hire_employee method enables you to call this method, but this is not very useful for integrating into a Web application. You need to create your own input form for your Z SQL method or call it manually from your application.

The Z Search Interface can create an input form for you automatically. In Chapter 9, "Searching and Categorizing Content," you used the Z Search Interface to build a form/action pair of methods that automatically generated an HTML search form and report screen that queried the Catalog and returned results. The Z Search Interface also works with Z SQL methods to build a similar set of search/result screens.

Select Z Search Interface from the Add list, and specify hire_employee as the Searchable object. Enter the value `hireEmployee` for the Report Id, and `hireEmployeeForm` for the Search Id, and click Add.

Click the newly created hireEmployeeForm, and click the View tab. Enter an employee_id, a first name, a last name, and a salary for a new employee, and click Submit. Zope returns a screen that says `There was no data matching this query`. Because the report form generated by the Z Search Interface is meant to display the result of a Z SQL method, and the hire_employee Z SQL method does not return any results, it just inserts a new row in the table. Edit the hireEmployee DTML method a little to make it more informative. Select the hireEmployee method. It should contain the following long stretch of DTML:

```
<dtml-var standard_html_header>

<dtml-in hire_employee size=50 start=query_start>

    <dtml-if sequence-start>

        <dtml-if previous-sequence>

          <a href="<dtml-var URL><dtml-var sequence-query
                  >query_start=<dtml-var
                  previous-sequence-start-number>">
          (Previous <dtml-var previous-sequence-size> results)
          </a>

        </dtml-if previous-sequence>

        <table border>
          <tr>
          </tr>

    </dtml-if sequence-start>

          <tr>
          </tr>

    <dtml-if sequence-end>

        </table>
        <dtml-if next-sequence>

            <a href="<dtml-var URL><dtml-var sequence-query
               >query_start=<dtml-var
               next-sequence-start-number>">
            (Next <dtml-var next-sequence-size> results)
            </a>

        </dtml-if next-sequence>

    </dtml-if sequence-end>

<dtml-else>

  There was no data matching this <dtml-var title_or_id> query.

</dtml-in>

<dtml-var standard_html_footer>
```

This is a pretty big piece of DTML! All of this DTML is meant to dynamically build a batch-oriented tabular result form. Because we don't need this, let's change the hireEmployee method to be much simpler:

```
<dtml-var standard_html_header>

<dtml-call hire_employee>

<h1>Employee <dtml-var first> <dtml-var last> was Hired!</h1>

<p><a href="listEmployees">List Employees</a></p>

<p><a href="hireEmployeeForm">Back to hiring</a></p>

<dtml-var standard_html_footer>
```

Now view the hireEmployeeForm, and hire another new employee. Notice how the hire_employee method is called from the DTML `call` tag. This is because we know there is no output from the hire_employee method. Because there are no results to iterate over, the method does not need to be called with the `in` tag. It can be called simply with the `call` tag.

Now you have a complete user interface for hiring new employees. Using Zope's security system, you can now restrict access to this method to only a certain group of users who you want to have permission to hire new employees. Keep in mind, the search and report screens generated by the Z Search Interface are just guidelines that you can easily customize to suit your needs.

Next, let's take a closer look at precisely controlling SQL queries. You've already seen how Z SQL methods enable you to create basic SQL query templates. Now let's learn how to make the most of your query templates.

# Dynamic SQL Queries

A Z SQL method query template can contain DTML that is evaluated when the method is called. This DTML can be used to modify the SQL code that is executed by the relational database. Several SQL-specific DTML tags exist to assist you in the construction of complex SQL queries. In the following sections, you learn about the `sqlvar`, `sqltest`, and `sqlgroup` tags.

## Inserting Arguments with the *sqlvar* Tag

It's pretty important to make sure you insert the right kind of data into a column in a database. Your database will complain if you try to use the string "12" where the integer 12 is expected. SQL requires that different types be quoted differently. To make matters worse, different databases have different quoting rules.

In addition to avoiding errors, SQL quoting is important for security. Suppose you had a query that makes a select:

```
select * from employees
  where emp_id=<dtml-var emp_id>
```

This query is unsafe because someone could slip SQL code into your query by entering something, such as 12; drop table employees, as an emp_id. To avoid this problem you need to make sure that your variables are properly quoted. The sqlvar tag does this for you. The following is a safe version of the preceding query that uses sqlvar:

```
select * from employees
  where emp_id=<dtml-sqlvar emp_id type=int>
```

The sqlvar tag operates similarly to the regular DTML var tag in that it inserts values. However, it has some tag attributes targeted at SQL-type quoting and dealing with null values. The sqlvar tag accepts a number of arguments:

- **name**—The name argument is identical to the name argument for the var tag. This is the name of a Zope variable or Z SQL method argument. The value of the variable or argument is inserted into the SQL Query Template. A name argument is required, but the "name=" prefix can be omitted.

- **type**—The type argument determines the way the sqlvar tag should format the value of the variable or argument being inserted in the query template. Valid values for type are string, int, float, or nb. nb stands for non-blank and means a string with at least one character in it. The sqlvar tag type argument is required.

- **optional**—The optional argument tells the sqlvar tag that the variable or argument can be absent or a null value. If the variable or argument does not exist or is a null value, the sqlvar tag does not try to render it. The sqlvar tag optional argument is optional.

The type argument is the key feature of the sqlvar tag. It is responsible for correctly quoting the inserted variable. See Appendix A, "DTML Reference," for complete coverage of the sqlvar tag.

You should always use the sqlvar tag instead of the var tag when inserting variables into a SQL code because it correctly quotes variables and keeps your SQL safe.

## Equality Comparisons with the *sqltest* Tag

Many SQL queries involve equality comparison operations. These are queries that ask for all values from the table that are in some kind of equality relationship with the input. For example, you might want to query the employees table for all employees with a salary greater than a certain value.

To see how this is done, create a new Z SQL method named employees_paid_more_than. Give it one argument, salary, and the following SQL template:

```
select * from employees
  where <dtml-sqltest salary op=gt type=float>
```

Now, click Add and Test. The `op` tag attribute is set to `gt`, which stands for greater than. This Z SQL method only returns records of employees that have a higher salary than what you enter in this input form. The `sqltest` builds the SQL syntax necessary to safely compare the input to the table column. Type "10000" into the salary input, and click the Test button. As you can see, the `sqltest` tag renders this SQL code:

```
select * from employees
  where salary > 10000
```

The `sqltest` tag renders these comparisons to SQL, taking into account the type of variable and the particularities of the database. The `sqltest` tag accepts the following tag parameters:

- **name**—The name of the variable to insert.

- **type**—The data type of the value to be inserted. This attribute is required and can be one of these types: string, int, float, or nb. The nb data type stands for not blank and indicates a string that must have a length that is greater than 0.

- **column**—The name of the SQL column, if different from the name attribute.

- **multiple**—A flag indicating whether multiple values can be provided. This enables you to test if a column is in a set of variables. For example, when name is a list of strings, such as "Bob", "Billy", '<dtml-sqltest name type="string" multiple>', it renders to this SQL: `name in ("Bob", "Billy")`.

- **optional**—A flag indicating if the test is optional. If the test is optional and no value is provided for a variable, or the value provided is an invalid empty string, then no text is inserted.

- **op**—A parameter used to choose the comparison operator that is rendered. The comparisons are eq (equal to), gt (greater than), lt (less than), ge (greater than or equal to), le (less than or equal to), and ne (not equal to).

See Appendix A for more information on the `sqltest` tag. If your database supports additional comparison operators, such as `like`, you can use them with `sqlvar`. For example, if `name` is the string "Mc%", the SQL code

```
<dtml-sqltest name type="string" op="like">
```

would render to

```
name like 'Mc%'
```

The `sqltest` tag helps you build correct SQL queries. In general, your queries are more flexible and work better with different types of input and different databases, if you use `sqltest` rather than hand coding comparisons.

## Creating Complex Queries with the *sqlgroup* Tag

The `sqlgroup` tag enables you to create SQL queries that support a variable number of arguments. Based on the arguments specified, SQL queries can be made more specific by providing more arguments or less specific by providing fewer or no arguments.

The following is an example of an unqualified SQL query:

```
select * from employees
```

The following is an example of a SQL query qualified by salary:

```
select * from employees
where(
  salary > 100000.00
)
```

The following is an example of a SQL query qualified by salary and first name:

```
select * from employees
where(
  salary > 100000.00
  and
  first in ('Jane', 'Cheetah', 'Guido')
)
```

The following is an example of a SQL query qualified by a first and a last name:

```
select * from employees
where(
  first = 'Old'
  and
  last = 'McDonald'
)
```

All three of these queries can be accomplished with one Z SQL method that creates more specific SQL queries as more arguments are specified. The following SQL template can build all three of the preceding queries:

```
select * from employees
<dtml-sqlgroup where>
  <dtml-sqltest salary op=gt type=float optional>
<dtml-and>
  <dtml-sqltest first op=eq type=string multiple optional>
<dtml-and>
  <dtml-sqltest last  op=eq type=string multiple optional>
</dtml-sqlgroup>
```

The `sqlgroup` tag renders the string *where*, if the contents of the tag body contain any text, and it builds the qualifying statements into the query. This `sqlgroup` tag does not render the where clause if no arguments are present.

The `sqlgroup` tag consists of three blocks separated by and tags. These tags insert the string *and*, if the enclosing blocks render a value. This way, the correct number of *ands* are included in the query. As more arguments are specified, more qualifying statements are added to the query. In this example, qualifying statements restricted the search with and tags, however, or tags can be used to expand the search.

This example also illustrates multiple attributes on `sqltest` tags. If the value for first or last is a list, then the right SQL is rendered to specify a group of values instead of a single value.

You can also nest `sqlgroup` tags. For example:

```
select * from employees
<dtml-sqlgroup where>
  <dtml-sqlgroup>
     <dtml-sqltest first op=like type=string>
  <dtml-and>
     <dtml-sqltest last op=like type=string>
  </dtml-sqlgroup>
<dtml-or>
  <dtml-sqltest salary op=gt type=float>
</dtml-sqlgroup>
```

Given sample arguments, this template renders to SQL like so:

```
select * from employees
where
( (name like 'A%'
   and
   last like 'Smith'
   )
   or
   salary > 20000.0
   )
```

You can construct very complex SQL statements with the `sqlgroup` tag. For simple SQL code, you don't need to use the `sqlgroup` tag. However, if you find yourself creating a number of different but related Z SQL methods, you should see if you can't accomplish the same thing with one method that uses the `sqlgroup` tag.

# Advanced Techniques

So far you've seen how to connect to a relational database, send it queries and commands, and create a user interface. These are the basics of relational database conductivity in Zope.

In the following sections, you learn how to integrate your relational queries more closely with Zope and enhance performance. We start by looking at how to pass arguments to Z SQL methods both explicitly and by acquisition. Then, you find out how you can call Z SQL methods directly from URLs using traversal to result objects. Next, you learn how to make results objects more powerful by binding them to classes. Finally, we look at caching to improve performance and how Zope handles database transactions.

## Calling Z SQL Methods with Explicit Arguments

If you call a Z SQL method without an argument from DTML, the arguments are automatically collected from the environment. This is the technique that we have used so far in this chapter. It works well when you want to query a database from a search form, but sometimes you want to manually or programmatically query a database.

Z SQL methods can be called with explicit arguments from DTML or Python. For example, to query the employee_by_id Z SQL method manually, the following DTML can be used:

```
<dtml-var standard_html_header>

  <dtml-in expr="employee_by_id(emp_id=42)">
    <h1><dtml-var last>, <dtml-var first></h1>

    <p><dtml-var first>'s employee id is <dtml-var emp_id>.  <dtml-var
    first> makes <dtml-var salary fmt=dollars-and-cents> per year.</p>
  </dtml-in>

<dtml-var standard_html_footer>
```

Remember, the employee_by_id method returns only one record, so the body of the in tag in this method only executes once. In this example, you are calling the Z SQL method like any other method and are passing it a keyword argument for emp_id. The following example shows how the same can be done easily from Python:

```
## Script (Python) "join_name"
##parameters=id
##
for result in context.employee_by_id(emp_id=id):
    return result.last + ', ' + result.first
```

This script accepts an id argument and passes it to employee_by_id as the emp_id argument. It then iterates over the single result and joins the last name and the first name with a comma.

You can provide more control over your relational data by calling Z SQL methods with explicit arguments. It's also worth noting that from DTML and Python, Z SQL methods can be called with explicit arguments—just like you call other Zope methods.

## Acquiring Arguments from Other Objects

Z SQL can acquire information from other objects and use it to modify the SQL query. Consider Figure 10.7, which shows a collection of folders in an organization's Web site.

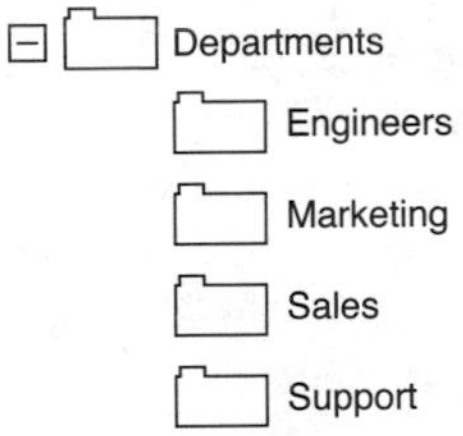

**Figure 10.7**   Folder structure of an organizational Web site.

Suppose each department folder has a department_id string property that identifies the accounting ledger id for that department. This property could be used by a shared Z SQL method to query information for just that department. To illustrate, create various nested folders with different department_id string properties. Then create a Z SQL method with the id requisition_something in the Root folder, which takes three arguments: description, quantity, and unit_cost, and takes the following query template:

```
INSERT INTO requisitions
  (
    department_id, description, quantity, unit_cost
  )
VALUES
  (
    <dtml-sqlvar department_id type=string>,
    <dtml-sqlvar description type=string>,
    <dtml-sqlvar quantity type=int>,
    <dtml-sqlvar unit_cost type=float>
  )
```

Now create a Z Search Interface with a Search Id of requisitionSomethingForm and the Report id of requisitionSomething. Select the requisition_something Z SQL method as the Searchable Object, and click Add.

Edit the requisitionSomethingForm, and remove the first input box for the department_id field. We don't want the value of department_id to come from the form, we want it to come from a property that is acquired.

Now you should be able to go to a URL, such as:

```
http://example.org/Departments/Support/requisitionSomethingForm
```

and requisition some punching bags for the Support department. Alternatively, you could go to

```
http://example.org/Departments/Sales/requisitionSomethingForm
```

and requisition some tacky rubber keychains with your logo on them for the Sales department. Using Zope's security system as described in Chapter 6, "Users and Security," you can now restrict access to these forms so that personnel can requisition items just for their department and not any other.

The interesting thing about this example is that department_id was not one of the arguments provided to the query. Instead of getting the value of this variable from an argument, it *acquires* the value from the folder where the Z SQL method is accessed. In the case of the previous URLs, the requisition_something Z SQL method acquires the value from the Sales and Support folders. This enables you to tailor SQL queries for different purposes. All the departments can share a query, but it is customized for each department.

By using acquisition and explicit argument passing, you can tailor your SQL queries to your Web application.

## Traversing to Result Objects

So far you've provided arguments to Z SQL methods from Web forms, explicit argument and acquisition. You can also provide arguments to Z SQL methods by calling them from the Web with special URLs. This is called *traversing* to results objects. Using this technique you can walk directly up to result objects using URLs.

To traverse to result objects with URLs, you must be able to ensure that the SQL method returns only one result object given one argument. For example, create a new Z SQL method named employee_by_id that accepts one argument, emp_id, and has the following SQL template:

```
select * from employees where
  <dtml-sqltest emp_id op=eq type=int>
```

This method selects one employee out of the employees table based on their employee id. Because each employee has a unique id, only one record is returned. Relational databases can provide these kinds of uniqueness guarantees.

At this point, you can pass the Z SQL method the emp_id argument with a value of 42 by accessing this query with this URL `http://localhost:8080/employee_by_id?emp_id=42`. This URL simply passes an argument with the HTTP query string. However, Zope provides a special URL syntax for this type of URL. Rather than using a query string, you can add the argument name and the value as additional path elements. For example, `http://localhost:8080/employee_by_id/emp_id/42`. This URL returns a result object.

Unfortunately, the result object you get with this URL is not very interesting to look at. It has no way to display itself in HTML. You still need to display the result object. To do this, you can call a DTML method on the result object. This can be done using the normal URL acquisition rules described in Chapter 8, "Advanced Zope Scripting." For example, consider the following URL:

```
http://localhost:8080/employee_by_id/emp_id/42/viewEmployee
```

Here we see the employee_by_id Z SQL method being passed the emp_id argument by the URL. The viewEmployee method is then called on the result object. Let's create a viewEmployee DTML method and try it out. Create a new DTML method named viewEmployee and give it the following content:

```
<dtml-var standard_html_header>

  <h1><dtml-var last>, <dtml-var first></h1>

  <p><dtml-var first>'s employee id is <dtml-var emp_id>.  <dtml-var
  first> makes <dtml-var salary fmt=dollars-and-cents> per year.</p>

<dtml-var standard_html_footer>
```

Now when you go to the URL `http://localhost:8080/employee_by_id/emp_id/42/viewEmployee` the viewEmployee DTML method binds the result object that is returned by employee_by_id. The viewEmployee method can be used as a generic template used by many different Z SQL methods that all return employee records.

Because the employee_by_id method only accepts one argument, it isn't even necessary to specify emp_id in the URL to qualify the numeric argument. If your Z SQL method has one argument, then you can configure the Z SQL method to accept only one extra path element argument instead of a pair of arguments. This example can be simplified even more by selecting the employee_by_id Z SQL method, and clicking the Advanced tab. Here, you can see a check box called Allow "Simple" Direct Traversal. Check this box, and click Change. Now you can browse employee records with simpler URLs, such as `http://localhost:8080/employee_by_id/42/viewEmployee`. Notice how no emp_id qualifier is declared in the URL.

Traversal gives you an easy way to provide arguments and bind methods to Z SQL methods and their results. Next, we show you how to bind whole classes to result objects to make them even more powerful.

## Binding Classes to Result Objects

A result object has an attribute for each column in the results row. However, result objects do not have any methods, just attributes.

A method can be bound to a result object in two ways. As you saw in the previous section, you can bind DTML and other methods to Z SQL method result objects using traversal to the results object coupled with the normal URL-based acquisition bind mechanism, described in Chapter 8. You can also bind methods to result objects by defining a Python class that gets *mixed in* with the normal, simple result object class. These classes are defined in the same location as external methods in the file system in Zope's Extensions directory. Python classes are collections of methods and attributes. By associating a class with a result object, you can make the result object have a rich API and user interface.

Classes that are used to bind methods and other class attributes to result classes are called *Pluggable Brains*, or just *Brains*. Consider the example Python class:

```
class Employee:

    def fullName(self):
        """ The full name in the form 'John Doe' """
        return self.first + ' ' + self.last
```

When result objects with this Brains class are created, as the result of a Z SQL method query, the results objects have Employee as a base class. This means that the record objects have all the methods defined in the Employee class, giving them behavior, as well as data.

To use this class, create the Employee class in the Employee.py file in the Extensions directory. Go to the Advanced tab of the employee_by_id Z SQL method, and enter Employee in the Class Name field, enter Employee in the Class File field, and click Save Changes. Now you can edit the employeeView DTML method to contain:

```
<dtml-var standard_html_header>

  <h1><dtml-var fullName></h1>

  <p><dtml-var first>'s employee id is <dtml-var emp_id>.  <dtml-var
  first> makes <dtml-var salary fmt=dollars-and-cents> per year.</p>

<dtml-var standard_html_footer>
```

Now when you go to the URL, http://localhost:8080/employee_by_id/42/
viewEmployee the fullName method is called by the viewEmployee DTML method.
The fullName method is defined in the Employee class of the Employee module and
is bound to the result object returned by employee_by_id.

Brains provide a very powerful facility, which enables you to treat your relational
data in a more object-centric way. For example, not only can you access the fullName
method using direct traversal, but you can use it anywhere you handle result objects.
For example:

```
<dtml-in employee_by_id>
  <dtml-var fullName>
</dtml-in>
```

For all practical purposes, your Z SQL method returns a sequence of smart objects,
not just data.

This example only scratches the surface of what can be done with Brains classes.
Python programming is beyond the scope of this book, so we will only go a little
farther here. However, you could create Brains classes that access network resources,
call other Z SQL Methods, and perform all kinds of business logic.

The following is a more powerful example of Brains. Suppose that you have a managers table to go with the employees table that you've used so far. Suppose also that
you have a manager_by_id Z SQL method that returns a manager id manager given
an emp_id argument:

```
select manager_id from managers where
  <dtml-sqltest emp_id type=int op=eq>
```

You could use this Z SQL method in your Brains class like so:

```
class Employee:

    def manager(self):
        """
        Returns this employee's manager or None if the
        employee does not have a manager.
        """
        # Calls the manager_by_id Z SQL Method.
        records=self.manager_by_id(emp_id=self.emp_id)
        if records:
            manager_id=records[0].manager_id
            # Return an employee object by calling the
            # employee_by_id Z SQL Method with the manager's emp_id
            return self.employee_by_id(emp_id=manager_id)[0]
```

This `Employee` class shows how methods can use other Zope objects to weave together relational data to make it seem like a collection of objects. The `manager` method calls two Z SQL methods, one to figure out the emp_id of the employee's manager, and another to return a new result object, representing the manager. You can now treat employee objects as though they have simple references to their manager objects. For example, you could add something like this to the viewEmployee DTML method:

```
<dtml-if manager>
  <dtml-with manager>
    <p> My manager is <dtml-var first> <dtml-var last>.</p>
  </dtml-with>
</dtml-if>
```

As you can see, Brains can be both complex and powerful. When designing relational database applications, you should try to keep things simple and add complexity slowly. It's important to make sure that your Brains classes don't add a lot of unneeded overhead.

## Caching Results

You can increase the performance of your SQL queries with caching. Caching stores Z SQL method results, so if you call the same method with the same arguments frequently, you don't have to connect to the database every time. Depending on your application, caching can dramatically improve performance.

To control caching, go to the Advanced tab of an SQL method. You have three different cache controls, as shown in Figure 10.8.

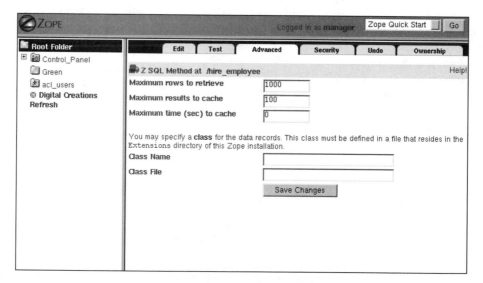

**Figure 10.8**   Caching controls for Z SQL methods.

The Maximum rows to retrieve field controls how much data to cache for each query. The Maximum results to cache field controls how many queries to cache. The Maximum time (sec) to cache controls how long cached queries are saved. In general, the larger you set these values, the greater your performance increase. However, Zope will consume more memory. As with any performance tuning, you should experiment to find the optimum settings for your application.

In general, you want to set the Maximum results to cache to be just high enough, and the Maximum time to cache to be just long enough for your application. For a site with few hits, you should cache results for longer, and for sites with lots of hits you should cache results for a shorter period of time. For machines with lots of memory, you should increase the number of cached results. To disable caching, set the cache time to zero seconds. For most queries, the default value of 1000 for the Maximum number of rows retrieved is adequate. For extremely large queries, you may have to increase this number to retrieve all your results.

## Transactions

A *transaction* is a group of operations that can be undone all at once. As you saw in Chapter 1, "Introducing Zope," all changes done to Zope are done within transactions. Transactions ensure data integrity. When using a system that is not transactional, for example, one of your Web actions changes ten objects and then fails to change the eleventh, your data is inconsistent. Transactions enable you to revert all the changes you made during a request if an error occurs.

Imagine the case where you have a Web page that bills a customer for goods received. This page first deducts the goods from the inventory, and then deducts the amount from the customers account. If the second operations fails for some reason, you want to make sure the change to the inventory doesn't take effect.

Most commercial and open source relational databases support transactions. If your relational database supports transactions, Zope makes sure that they are tied to Zope transactions. This ensures data integrity across both Zope and your relational database. If either Zope or the relational database aborts the transaction, the entire transaction is aborted.

Zope enables you to build Web applications with relational databases. Unlike many Web application servers, Zope has its own object database and does not require the use of relational databases to store information.

Zope enables you to use relational data just like you use other Zope objects. You can connect your relational data to business logic with scripts and Brains, you can query your relational data with Z SQL methods and presentation tools, such as DTML, and you can even use advanced Zope features, such as URL traversal, acquisition, undo, and security while working with relational data.

# Developing Advanced Web
# Applications with Zope

# 11

# Scalability and ZEO

WHEN A WEB SITE GETS MORE REQUESTS than it can handle, it can become slow
and unresponsive. In the worst case, too many requests to a Web site can cause the
server to completely overload, stop handling requests, and possibly even crash. This can
be a problem for any kind of server application, not just Zope. The obvious solution to
this problem is to use more than one computer, so in case one computer fails, another
computer can continue to serve up your Web site.

Using multiple computers has obvious benefits, but it also has some drawbacks. For
example, if you have five computers running Zope, then you must ensure that all five
Zope installations have the same information on them. This is not a very hard task if
you're the only user, and you have only a few static objects, but for large organizations
with thousands of rapidly changing objects, keeping five separate Zope installations
synchronized manually would be a nightmare. To solve this problem, Zope Corporation
created *Zope Enterprise Objects* (ZEO) (`http://www.zope.org/Products/ZEO`). This
chapter gives you a brief overview on installing ZEO, but many other options are not
covered. For more in-depth information, see the documentation that comes with the
ZEO package, and also take a look at the ZEO discussion area (`http://www.zope.org/
Wikis/ZODB/FrontPage`).

# What is ZEO?

*ZEO* is a system that enables you to run your site on more than one computer. This is often called *clustering* and *load balancing*. By running Zope on multiple computers, you can spread the requests evenly around and add more computers as the number of requests grows. Further, if one computer fails or crashes, other computers can still service requests while you fix the broken one.

ZEO runs Zope on multiple computers and takes care of making sure all the Zope installations share the exact same database at all times. ZEO uses a client/server architecture. Zope installations on multiple computers are known as *ZEO clients*. All the clients connect to one central *ZEO storage server*, as shown in Figure 11.1.

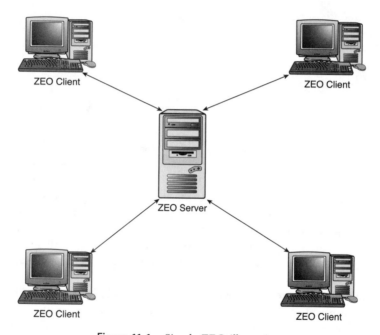

**Figure 11.1**   Simple ZEO illustration.

The terminology can be a bit confusing because normally you think of Zope as a server, not a client. When using ZEO, your Zope processes act as both servers (for Web requests) and clients (for data from the ZEO server).

ZEO clients and servers communicate using standard Internet protocols, so they can be in the same room or in different countries. In fact, ZEO can distribute a Zope site all over the world. In this chapter, we explore some interesting ways you can distribute your ZEO clients.

# When You Should Use ZEO

ZEO serves many hits in a fail-safe way. If your site does not get millions of hits, then you probably don't need ZEO. There is no hard-and-fast rule about when you should and should not use ZEO, but for the most part, you should not need to run ZEO unless:

- Your site is getting too many hits for your computer to handle them quickly. Zope is a high-performance system, and one Zope can handle many thousands of hits per day (depending on your hardware, of course). If you need to serve more hits than that, then you should use ZEO.

- Your site is very critical and requires constant 24/7 uptime. In this case, ZEO enables you to have multiple fail-over servers.

- You want to distribute your site globally to many different mirror ZEO clients.

- You want to debug one ZEO client while others are still serving requests. This is a very advanced technique for Python developers, and it is not covered in this book.

All of these cases are fairly advanced, high-end uses of Zope. Installing, configuring, and maintaining systems, such as these, requires advanced system administration knowledge and resources. Most Zope users do not need ZEO, or might not have the expertise necessary to maintain a distributed server system, such as ZEO. ZEO is fun, and can be very useful, but before jumping head-first and installing ZEO in your system, you should weigh the extra administrative burden ZEO creates against the simplicity of running just a simple, standalone Zope.

# Installing and Running ZEO

The most common ZEO setup is one ZEO server and multiple ZEO clients. Before installing and configuring ZEO, however, consider the following issues:

- All the ZEO clients and servers must run the same version of Zope. Make sure all your computers use the latest version. This is necessary. Otherwise, Zope might behave abnormally or not work at all.

- All your ZEO clients must have the same third-party products installed, and they must be the same version. This is necessary. Otherwise, your third-party objects might behave abnormally or not work at all.

- If your Zope system requires access to external resources, such as mail servers or relational databases, ensure that all your ZEO clients have access to those resources.

- Slow or intermittent network connections between clients and server degrades the performance of your ZEO clients. Your ZEO clients should have a good connection to their server.

ZEO is not distributed with Zope, you must download it from the Products section of Zope.org (`http://www.zope.org/Products/ZEO`).

Installing ZEO requires a little bit of manual preparation. To install ZEO, download the ZEO-1.0.tgz from the Zope.org Web site, and place it in your Zope installation directory. Now, unpack the tarball. In UNIX, this can be done with the following command:

```
$ tar -zxf ZEO-1.0.tgz
```

In Windows, you can unpack the archive with WinZip. Before installing ZEO, make sure you back up your Zope system first.

Now you should have a ZEO-1.0 directory. Next, you have to copy some files into your Zope top-level lib/python directory. This can be done in UNIX with:

```
$ cp -R ZEO-1.0/ZEO lib/python
```

If you're running Windows, you can use the following DOS command to copy ZEO:

```
C:\...Zope\>xcopy ZEO-1.0\* lib\python /S
```

Now, you have to create a special file in your Zope root directory called custom_zodb.py. In that file, put the following Python code:

```
import ZEO.ClientStorage
Storage=ZEO.ClientStorage.ClientStorage(('localhost',7700))
```

This configures your Zope to run as a ZEO client. If you pass `ClientStorage` a tuple, as this code does, the tuple must have two elements: a string that contains the address to the server, and the port on which the server is listening. In this example, we're going to show you how to run both the clients and the servers on the same machine so that the machine name is set to `localhost`.

Now you have ZEO properly configured to run on one computer. Try it out by starting the server. Go to your Zope top-level directory in a terminal window or DOS box and type

```
python lib/python/ZEO/start.py -p 7700
```

This starts the ZEO server listening on port `7700` on your computer. Now, in another window, start up Zope like you normally would with the z2.py script:

```
$ python z2.py -D


— — —
2000-10-04T20:43:11 INFO(0) client Trying to connect to server
— — —
2000-10-04T20:43:11 INFO(0) ClientStorage Connected to storage
— — —
2000-10-04T20:43:12 PROBLEM(100) ZServer Computing default pinky
— — —
2000-10-04T20:43:12 INFO(0) ZServer Medusa (V1.19) started
➥at Wed Oct  4 15:43:12 2000
        Hostname: pinky.zopezoo.org
        Port:8080
```

Notice how in the preceding example, Zope tells you `client Trying to connect to server` and then `ClientStorage Connected to storage`. This means your ZEO client has successfully connected to your ZEO server. Now, you can visit `http://localhost:8080/manage` (or whatever URL your ZEO client is listening on and log into Zope as usual.

As you can see, everything looks the same. If you go to the Control Panel and click Database Management, you see that Zope is connected to a ZEO storage, and that its state is connected.

Running ZEO on one computer is a great way to familiarize yourself with ZEO and how it works. Running ZEO on one computer does not, however, improve the speed of your site. In fact, it might slow it down just a little. To really get the speed benefits that ZEO provides, you need to run ZEO on several computers, which is explained in the following section.

## How to Run ZEO on Many Computers

Setting up ZEO to run on multiple computers is similar to running ZEO on one computer. Generally, the two steps are as follows: the first step is to start the ZEO server, and the second step is to start one or more ZEO clients.

For example, let's say you have four computers. One computer named zooserver is your ZEO server, and the other three computers named zeoclient1, zeoclient2, and zeoclient3 are your ZEO clients.

The first step is to run the server on zooserver. To tell your ZEO server to listen on the tcp socket at port 9999 on the zooserver interface, run the server with the start.py script like this:

```
$ python lib/python/ZEO/start.py -p 9999 -h zooserver.zopezoo.org
```

This starts the ZEO server. Now, you can start up your clients by going to each client and configuring each of them with the following custom_zodb.py:

```
import ZEO.ClientStorage
Storage=ZEO.ClientStorage.ClientStorage(('zooserver.zopezoo.org',7700))
```

Now, you can start each client's z2.py script as shown in the previous section, "Installing and Running ZEO." Notice how the host and port for each client is the same. This is so that they all connect to the same server. By following this procedure for each of your three clients, you will have three different Zopes all serving the same Zope site. You can verify this by visiting port 8080 on all three of your ZEO client machines.

You probably want to run ZEO on more than one computer so that you can take advantage of the speed increase this gives you. Running more computers means that you can serve more hits per second than with just one computer. Distributing the load of your Web site's visitors, however, does require a bit more elaboration in your system. The following section describes why, and how, you distribute the load of your visitors among many computers.

# How to Distribute Load

In the previous example, you have a ZEO server named zooServer and three ZEO clients named zeoclient1, zeoclient2, and zeoclient3. The three ZEO clients are connected to the ZEO server and each client is verified to work properly.

Now you have three computers that serve content to your users. The next problem is how to actually spread the incoming Web requests evenly among the three ZEO clients. Your users only know about www.zopezoo.org, not zeoclient1, zeoclient2 or zeoclient3. It would be a hassle to tell only some users to use zeoclient1, and others to use zeoclient3, and it wouldn't be very good use of your computing resources. You want to automate, or at least make very easy, the process of evenly distributing requests to your various ZEO clients.

A number of solutions exist for this problem—some easy, some advanced, and some expensive. The following section goes over the more common ways of spreading Web requests around various computers using different kinds of technology, some of which are based on freely available or commercial software, and some others that are based on special hardware.

## User Chooses a Mirror

The easiest way to distribute requests across many Web servers is to pick from a list of *mirrored sites*, each of which is a ZEO client. Using this method requires no extra software or hardware, it just requires the maintenance of a list of mirror servers. By presenting your users with a menu of mirrors, they can choose what server to use.

Note, that this method of distributing requests is passive (you have no active control over which clients are used) and it is voluntary (your users need to make a voluntary choice to use another ZEO client). If your users do not use a mirror, then the requests go to your ZEO client that serves www.zopezoo.org.

If you do not have any administrative control over your mirrors, then this can be a pretty easy solution. If your mirrors go offline, your users can always choose to come back to the master site, which you *do* have administrative control over, and choose a different mirror.

On a global level, this method improves performance. Your users can choose to use a server that is geographically closer to them, which probably results in faster access. For example, if your main server is in Portland, Oregon on the west coast of the U.S., and you have users in London, England, they could choose your London mirror, and their request would not have to go halfway across the world and back.

To use this method, create a property in your Root folder with the type lines named mirror_servers. On each line of this property, put the URL to your various ZEO clients, as shown in Figure 11.2.

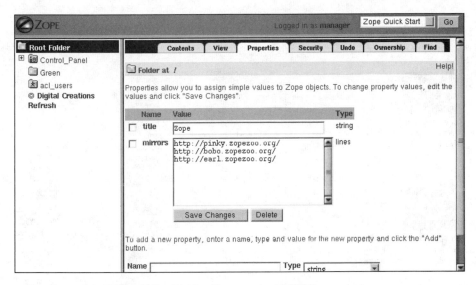

Figure 11.2   Figure of property with URLs to mirrors.

Now, add some simple DTML to your site to display a list of your mirrors:

```
<h2>Please choose from the following mirrors:
<ul>
  <dtml-in mirror_servers>
  <li><a href="&dtml-sequence-item;"><dtml-var
  sequence-item></a></li>
  </dtml-in>
</ul>
```

This DTML displays a list of all mirrors your users can choose from. When using this model, it is good to name your computers in ways that assist your users in their choice of mirror. For example, if you spread the load geographically, then choose names of countries for your computer names.

Alternatively, if you do not want users voluntarily choosing a mirror, you can have the index_html method of your www.zopezoo.org site issue HTTP redirects. For example, use the following code in your www.zopezoo.org site's index_html method:

```
<dtml-call expr="RESPONSE.redirect(_.whrandom.choice(mirror_servers))">
```

This code redirects any visitors from www.zopezoo.org to a random mirror server.

## Using Round-Robin DNS to Distribute Load

The *Domain Name System* (DNS) is the Internet mechanism that translates computer names (such as www.zope.org) into numeric addresses. This mechanism can map one name to many addresses.

The simplest method for load balancing is to use round-robin DNS, as illustrated in Figure 11.3.

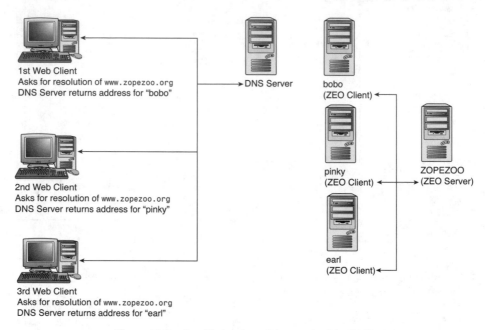

**1st Web Client**
Asks for resolution of www.zopezoo.org
DNS Server returns address for "bobo"

**2nd Web Client**
Asks for resolution of www.zopezoo.org
DNS Server returns address for "pinky"

**3rd Web Client**
Asks for resolution of www.zopezoo.org
DNS Server returns address for "earl"

DNS Server

bobo
(ZEO Client)

pinky
(ZEO Client)

earl
(ZEO Client)

ZOPEZOO
(ZEO Server)

**Figure 11.3**   Load balancing with round-robin DNS.

When www.zopezoo.org gets resolved, BIND answers with the address of either zeo-client1, zeoclient2, or zeoclient3—but it does so in a rotated order every time. For example, one user might resolve www.zopezoo.org and get the address for zeoclient1, and another user might resolve www.zopezoo.org and get the address for zeoclient2. This way your users are spread over the various ZEO clients.

This is not a perfect load balancing scheme because DNS resolve information gets cached by the other nameservers on the Net. After a client has resolved www.zopezoo.org to a particular ZEO client, all subsequent requests also go to the same ZEO client. The final result is generally acceptable because the total sum of the requests are spread over your various ZEO clients.

One downside to this solution is that it can take hours or days for name servers to refresh their cached copy of the address for www.zopezoo.org. If you are not responsible for the maintenance of your ZEO clients and one fails, then $1/N$th of your users (where $N$ is the number of ZEO clients) will not be able to reach your site until their name server cache refreshes.

Configuring your DNS server to do round-robin name resolution is a pretty advanced technique that is not covered in this book. A good reference on how to do this can be found in the Apache documentation at (http://www.engelschall.com/pw/apache/rewriteguide/#ToC29).

Distributing the load with round-robin DNS is useful and cheap, but not 100 percent effective. DNS servers can have strange caching policies, and you are relying on a particular quirk in the way DNS works to distribute the load. The following section describes a more complex, but much more powerful way, of distributing load called Layer 4 switching.

## Using Layer 4 Switching to Distribute Load

*Layer 4 switching* enables one computer to transparently hand requests to a farm of computers. This is a pretty advanced technique that is beyond the scope of this book. However, it is worth pointing out several products that do Layer 4 switching for you.

According to your preferences, Layer 4 switching involves a switch that chooses from a group of ZEO clients whenever a request comes in, as shown in Figure 11.4.

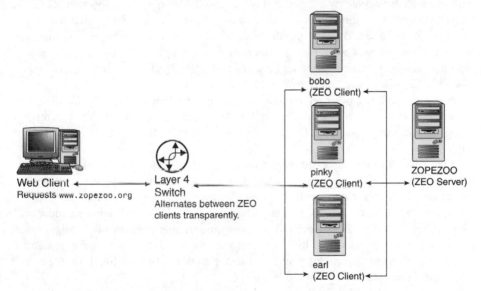

**Figure 11.4**   Illustration of Layer 4 switching.

Both hardware and software Layer 4 switches are shown. A number of software solutions exist, but one in general that stands out is the *Linux Virtual Server* (LVS). This is an extension to the free Linux operating system that enables you to turn a Linux computer into a Layer 4 switch. More information on LVS can be found on its Web site (http://www.linuxvirtualserver.org).

A number of hardware solutions also claim higher performance than software-based solutions, such as LVS. Cisco Systems has a hardware router called *LocalDirector* that works as a Layer 4 switch, and Alteon also makes a popular Layer 4 switch.

## Dealing with a Single Point of Failure

Without ZEO, your entire Zope system is a single point of failure. ZEO enables you to spread that point of failure around to many different computers. If one of your ZEO clients fails, other clients can answer requests on the failed clients behalf.

Note that as of this writing, the single point of failure can't be entirely eliminated because there is still one central storage server. The methods described in this section, however, do minimize the risks of failure by spreading most of Zope across many computers.

What this means is that, although this does remove a lot of risk from your Web servers as a single point of failure, it does not eliminate all risk because now the ZEO server is a single point of failure. This issue can be dealt with in several ways.

One popular method is to accept the single point of failure risk and mitigate that risk as much as possible by using very high-end, reliable equipment for your ZEO server, frequently backing up your data, and using inexpensive, off-the-shelf hardware for your ZEO clients. By investing the bulk of your infrastructure budget on making your ZEO server rock solid, (using redundant power supplies, RAID, and other fail-safe methods) you can be pretty well assured that your ZEO server will remain up, even if a handful of your inexpensive ZEO clients fail.

Some applications, however, require absolute 100 percent up-time. A chance still exists, with the solution described previously, that your ZEO server will fail. If this happens, you want a backup ZEO server to jump in and take over for the failed server right away.

Like Layer 4 switching, a number of software and hardware products help you mitigate this kind of risk. One popular software solution for Linux is called fake (`http://vergenet.net/linux/fake/`). Fake is a Linux-based utility that can make a backup computer take over for a failed primary computer by "faking out" network addresses. When fake is used in conjunction with monitoring utilities, such as mon (http://www.kernel.org/software/mon/) or heartbeat (`http://www.linux-ha.org/`), it can guarantee almost 100 percent up-time of your ZEO server and Layer 4 switches. Using fake in this way is beyond the scope of this book.

So far, we explained the following techniques for mitigating a single point of failure:

- Various tools (mirrors, round-robin DNS, Layer 4 switching) can be used to multiplex requests across multiple computers.
- ZEO can be used to distribute your database (ZEO server) to multiple ZEO clients.
- Fake and other tools can be used to provide redundant servers and Layer 4 switches.

The final piece of the puzzle is the ZEO server itself and where it stores its information. If your primary ZEO server fails, how can your backup ZEO server ensure it has the most recent information that was contained in the primary server? As usual, there are several ways to solve this problem, and they are covered in the following section.

## ZEO Server Details

Before explaining the details of how the ZEO server works, it is worth understanding some details about how Zope *storages* work in general.

Zope does not save any of its object or information directly to disk. Instead, Zope uses a storage component that takes care of all the details of where objects should be saved.

This is a very flexible model because Zope no longer needs to be concerned about opening files, reading and writing from databases, or sending data across a network (in the case of ZEO). Each particular storage takes care of that task on Zope's behalf.

For example, a plain, standalone Zope system is illustrated in Figure 11.5.

**Figure 11.5**  Zope connected to a FileStorage.

You can see only one Zope application, which plugs into a FileStorage. This storage, as its name implies, saves all of its information to a file on the computer's file system.

When using ZEO, you simply replace the FileStorage with a ClientStorage, as illustrated in Figure 11.6.

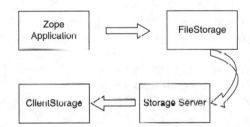

**Figure 11.6**  Zope with a ClientStorage and Storage Server.

Instead of saving objects to a file, a ClientStorage sends objects over a network connection to a Storage Server. As you can see in Figure 11.6, the Storage Server uses a FileStorage to save that information to a file on the ZEO server's file system.

Storages are interchangeable and easy to implement. Because of their interchangeable nature, ZEO Storage Servers can use ZEO ClientStorages to pass on object data to yet another ZEO Storage Server. This is illustrated in Figure 11.7.

Here you can see a number of ZEO clients funnel down through three ZEO servers, which in turn act as ZEO clients themselves. They funnel down into the final, central ZEO server, which saves its information in a FileStorage. If the Central ZEO Server were the single point of failure in the system, or if any of your other clients or intermediate servers fail, the system would still continue to work. However, if the Central Server fails, then you need an alternative.

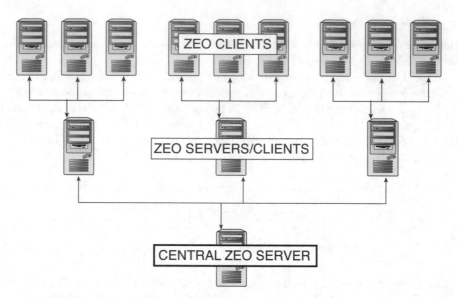

**Figure 11.7**   Multitiered ZEO system.

By using fake, you can have a back-up storage server strategy, however this method is not very well proven and hasn't been explored by the authors. In the future, ZEO will have a multiple-server feature that enables a group of storage servers to act as a quorum, so if one or more storage servers fail, the remaining servers in the quorum can continue to serve objects.

There are a number of advantages to approaches such as these, especially if you are interested in creating a massively distributed network object database. Of course, with any system there are some drawbacks as well, which are discussed in the following section.

## ZEO Caveats

For the most part, running ZEO is exactly like running Zope by itself, but there are a few issues to keep in mind.

First, it takes longer for information to be written to the Zope object database. This does not slow down your ability to use Zope, (because Zope does not block you during this write operation) but it does increase your chances of getting a ConflictError. *ConflictErrors* happen when two ZEO clients try to write to the same object at the same time. One of the ZEO clients wins the conflict and continues on normally. The other ZEO client loses the conflict and has to try again.

ConflictErrors should be as infrequent as possible because they could slow down your system. Although it's normal to have a few ConflictErrors, (due to the concurrent nature of Zope) it is abnormal to have a lot of ConflictErrors. The pathological case is when more than one ZEO client tries to write to the same object over and over again very quickly. In this case, there are lots of ConflictErrors, and therefore lots of retries. If a ZEO client tries to write to the database three times and gets three ConflictErrors in a row, then the request is aborted and the data is not written.

Because ZEO takes longer to write this information, the chances of getting a ConflictError are higher than if you are not running ZEO. Because of this, ZEO is more *write sensitive* than Zope without ZEO. You might have to keep this in mind when you are designing your network or application. As a rule of thumb, more and more frequent writes to the database increase your chances of getting a ConflictError. On the flip side, faster and more reliable network connections and computers lower your chances of getting a ConflictError. By taking these two factors into account, ConflictErrors can be mostly avoided.

Finally, as of this writing, no built-in encryption or authentication between ZEO servers and clients exists. This means that you must be very careful about who you expose your ZEO servers to. If you leave your ZEO servers open to the whole Internet, then anyone can connect to your ZEO server and write data into your database, and that can be bad news.

This is a solveable problem, however, because you can use other tools, such as firewalls, to protect your ZEO servers. If you are running a ZEO client/server connection over an unsecure network, and you want a guarantee that your information is kept private, you can use tools, such as OpenSSH (`http://www.openssh.org`) and stunnel (`http://www.stunnel.org/`) to set up secure, encrypted communication channels between your ZEO clients and servers. How these tools work and how to set them up is beyond the scope of this book. However, both packages are adequately documented on their Web sites. For more information on firewalls, with Linux in particular, we recommend the book *Linux Firewalls*, by Robert Ziegler, which is published by New Riders Publishing.

In this chapter we looked at ZEO, and how ZEO can substantially increase the capacity of your Web site. In addition to getting familiarized with running ZEO on one computer, we looked at running ZEO on many computers and various techniques for spreading the load of your visitors among those many computers.

ZEO is not a magic bullet solution, and like other systems designed to work with many computers, it adds another level of complexity to your Web site. This complexity pays off, however, when you need to serve up a lot of dynamic content to your audience.

# 12

# Extending Zope

Y OU CAN EXTEND ZOPE BY CREATING your own types of objects that are customized to your application's needs. Zope is extended using products. Products can be installed in Zope to add new kinds of objects. *Products* are extensions to Zope created by the Zope Corporation and many other third-party developers. Hundreds of different products exist—many of which serve very specific purposes. A complete library of products can be found at the download section of Zope.org (http://www.zope.org/Products/).

Products can be developed two ways: through the Web using ZClasses and in the Python programming language. Products can also be a hybrid of both Web products and Python code. This chapter discusses building new products through the Web, a topic which you've already had some brief exposure to in Chapter 9, "Searching and Categorizing Content." Developing a product entirely in Python product programming is beyond the scope of this book. You should visit Zope.org for specific product developer documentation.

This chapter shows you how to:

- Create new products in Zope
- Define ZClasses in products
- Integrate Python with ZClasses

- Distribute products to other Zope users

The first step to customizing Zope starts in the next section where you learn how to create new Zope products.

# Creating Zope Products

The Web products are stored in the Product Management folder in the Control Panel.

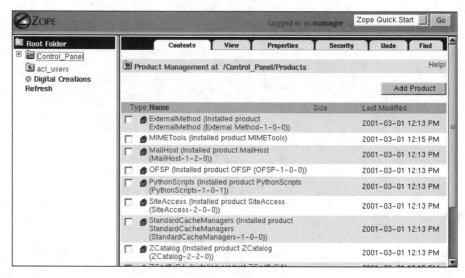

Click the Control_Panel in the Root folder, and then click Products. You should now see the screen shown in Figure 12.1.

**Figure 12.1**    Installed products.

Each blue box represents an installed product. From this screen, you can manage these products. Some products are built into Zope by default, while others have been installed by you or your administrator. These products have a closed box icon, as shown in Figure 12.1. Closed-box products cannot be managed through the Web. You can get information about these products by clicking them, but you cannot change them.

You can also create your own products that you can manage through the Web. Your products enable you to create new kinds of objects in Zope. These products managed through the Web have open-box icons. If you followed the examples in Chapter 9, then you have a News open-box product.

Why do you want to create products? Let's say for example, all the various caretakers at the zoo want an easy way to build simple online exhibits. The exhibits must all be in the same format and contain a similar information structure, and each is specific to a certain animal in the zoo.

To accomplish this, you could build an exhibit for one animal, and then copy and paste it for each exhibit, however this would be a difficult and manual process. All the information and properties would have to be changed for each new exhibit. Further, there could be thousands of exhibits.

To add to this problem, let's say you want to add information to each exhibit that tells whether or not the animal is endangered. You would have to change each exhibit, one by one, to add this if you used copy and paste. Clearly, copying and pasting does not work well for a very large zoo, and it could be very expensive.

You also need to ensure each exhibit is easy to manage. The caretakers of the individual exhibits should be the ones providing information, but none of the zoo caretakers know much about Zope or how to create Web sites, and you certainly don't want to waste their time making them learn. You just want them to type some simple information into a form about their topic of interest, click submit, and walk away.

By creating a Zope product, you can accomplish these goals quickly and easily. You can create easy-to-manage objects that your caretakers can use. You can define exhibit templates, that you can change once, that effect all the exhibits. You can do these things by creating Zope products.

# Creating a Simple Product

Using products can solve the exhibit creation and management problems. Let's begin with an example that shows how to create a simple product that enables you to collect information about exhibits and create a customized exhibit.

The chief value of Zope products is that they enable you to create objects in a central location, and they give you access to your objects through the product Add list. This gives you the ability to build global services and make them available through a standard part of the Zope management interface. In other words, a product enables you to customize Zope.

Begin by going to the products folder in the Control Panel. To create a new product, click the Add Product button on the Product Management folder. This takes you to the Product Add form. Enter the id `ZooExhibit`, and click Generate. You can see your new product in the Product Management folder. It should be a blue box with an open lid. The open lid means you can click the product and manage it through the Web.

Select the ZooExhibit product. This takes you to the Product Management screen.

The management screen for a product looks and acts just like a folder except for a few differences:

- There is a new view called Distribution to the far right. This gives you the ability to package and distribute your product. This view is discussed in the section, "Distributing Products," later in this chapter.

- If you select the Add list, you see some new types of objects that you can add, including ZClass, Factory, and Permission.

- The folder with a question mark on it is the ZooExhibit product's Help folder. This folder can be used to contain help topics that tell people how to use your product.

- There is also a new view called Define Permissions, which defines the permissions associated with this product. This is advanced and is not necessary for this example.

In the Contents view, create a DTML method named `hello` with these contents:

```
<dtml-var standard_html_header>

<h2>Hello from the Zoo Exhibit Product</h2>

<dtml-var standard_html_footer>
```

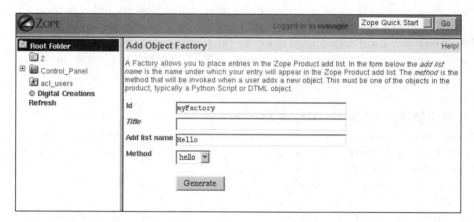

This method enables you to test your product. Next, create a factory. Select Zope Factory from the product Add list. You are taken to a Factory Add form, as shown in Figure 12.2.

**Figure 12.2**   Adding a Factory.

Factories create a bridge from the product Add list to your product. Give your factory an id of `myFactory`. In the Add list name field, enter `Hello`, and in the Method selection, choose `hello`. Click Generate. Now, click the new factory, and change the Permission to Add Document, Images, and Files, and click Save Changes. This tells Zope that you must have the Add Documents, Images, and Files permission to use the factory. Congratulations, you just customized the Zope management interface. Go to the Root folder and click the product Add list. Notice that it now includes an entry named Hello. Choose Hello from the product Add list. It calls your `hello` method.

Copying objects into the current folder is one of the most common uses of methods that are linked to factories. In other words, your methods can get access to the location from which they were called, and they can perform operations on that folder, including copying objects into it. Just because you can do all kinds of crazy things with factories and products does not mean you should. In general, people expect to be taken to an Add form when they specify the id of a new object from the product Add list. They also expect a new object to be created in their folder, with the id they specified, when they click Add. So, let's see how to fulfill these expectations.

First create a new folder named exhibitTemplate in your product. This serves as a template for exhibits. Also, in the Product folder, create a DTML method named addForm and a Python script named add. These objects create new exhibit instances. Now, go back to your factory and change it so that the Add list name is `Zoo Exhibit` and the method is `addForm`.

Now when someone chooses Zoo Exhibit from the product Add list, the addForm method runs. This method should collect information about the id and title of the exhibit. When the user clicks Add, the addForm method should call the add script, which copies the exhibitTemplate folder into the calling folder, and it should rename it to have the specified id. The next step is to edit the addForm method to have these contents:

```
<dtml-var manage_page_header>

  <h2>Add a Zoo Exhibit</h2>

  <form action="add" method="post">
  id <input type="text" name="id"><br>
  title <input type="text" name="title"><br>
  <input type="submit" value=" Add ">
  </form>

<dtml-var manage_page_footer>
```

Admittedly, this is a rather bleak Add form. It doesn't collect much data, and it doesn't tell the user what a Zoo Exhibit is or why she wants to add one. When you create your own Web applications, you'll want to do better than this example.

Notice that this method doesn't include the standard HTML headers and footers. By convention, Zope management screens do not use the same headers and footers that your site uses. Instead, management screens use `manage_page_header` and `manage_page_footer`. The management view header and footer ensure that management views have a common look and feel.

Also, notice that the action of the form is the add script. Paste the following body into the add script:

```
## Script (Python) "add"
##parameters: id ,title, REQUEST=None
##
"""
Copy the exhibit template to the calling folder
"""

# Clone the template, giving it the new ID. This will be placed
```

*continues*

*continued*

```
# in the current context (the place the factory was called from).
exhibit=context.manage_clone(container.exhibitTemplate,id)

# Change the clone's title
exhibit.manage_changeProperties(title=title)

# If we were called through the web, redirect back to the context
if REQUEST is not None:
    try: u=context.DestinationURL()
    except: u=REQUEST['URL1']
    REQUEST.RESPONSE.redirect(u+'/manage_main?update_menu=1')
```

This script clones the exhibitTemplate and copies it to the current folder with the specified id. Then it changes the title property of the new exhibit. Finally, it returns the current folder's main management screen by calling manage_main.

Congratulations, you've now extended Zope by creating a new product. You've created a way to copy objects into Zope through the product Add list. However, this solution still suffers from some of the problems discussed earlier in this chapter. Even though you can edit the exhibit template in a centralized place, it is still only a template. So, if you add a new property to the template, it will not affect any of the existing exhibits. To change existing exhibits, you have to modify each one manually.

ZClasses take you one step further by enabling you to have one central template that defines a new type of object, and when you change that template, all the objects of that type change along with it. This central template is called a ZClass. In the next section, we show you how to create ZClasses that define a new Exhibit ZClass.

## Creating ZClasses

ZClasses are tools that help you build new types of objects in Zope by defining a *class*. A class is like a blueprint for objects. When you define a class, you define what an object will be like when it is created. A class can define methods, properties, and other attributes.

Objects that you create from a certain class are called *instances* of that class. For example, there is only one Folder class, but you might have many Folder instances in your application.

Instances have the same methods and properties as their class. If you change the class, then all the instances reflect that change. Unlike the templates that you created in the last section, classes continue to exert control over instances. Keep in mind that this only works one way; if you change an instance, no changes are made to its class or any other instances.

A good real-world analogy to ZClasses are word processor templates. Most word processors come with a set of predefined templates that you can use to create a certain kind of document, such as a resumé. Hundreds of thousands of resumes in the world might be based on the Microsoft Word Resume template, but only one template exists.

Microsoft Word Resume is the template for all those resumes, and in the same way, a ZClass is the template for any number of similar Zope objects.

ZClasses are classes you can build through the Web using Zope's management interface. Classes can also be written in Python, however this is not covered in this book.

ZClasses can inherit attributes from other classes. Inheritance enables you to define a new class based on another class. For example, say you wanted to create a new kind of document object that had special properties you were interested in. Instead of building all the functionality of a document from scratch, you can just inherit that functionality from the DTML Document class and add only the new information you are interested in.

Inheritance also enables you to build generalization relationships between classes. For example, you could create a class called `Animal`, which contains information that all animals have in general. Then, you could create Reptile and Mammal classes that

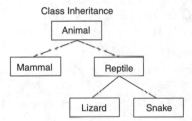

inherit from Animal. Taking it even further, you could create two additional classes, Lizard and Snake, that inherit from Reptile, as shown in Figure 12.3.

**Figure 12.3** An example of class inheritance.

ZClasses can inherit from most of the objects you've used in this book. In addition, ZClasses can inherit from other ZClasses defined in the same product. We will use this technique and others in this chapter.

Before going on with the next example, you should rename the existing ZooExhibit product in your Zope products folder to something else, such as ZooTemplate so that it does not conflict with this example. Now, create a new product in the Product folder named `ZooExhibit`.

Select ZClass from the Add list of the ZooExhibit Contents view, and go to the ZClass Add form. This form is complex, and it has a lot of elements. Let's go through them one by one:

- **Id**—This is the name of the class to create. For this example, choose the name ZooExhibit.
- **Metatype**—This is the name of the type of object. This should be something short, but descriptive, about what the object does. For this example, choose the metatype `Zoo Exhibit`.
- **Base classes**—Base classes define a sequence of classes from which you want

your class to inherit attributes. Your new class can be thought of as extending or being derived from the functionality of your base classes. You can choose one or more classes from the list on the left, and click the -> button to put them in your base class list. The <- button removes any base classes you select on the right. For this example, don't select any base classes. Later in this chapter, we explain some of the more interesting base classes, such as ObjectManager.

- **Create constructor objects?**—You usually want to leave this option checked unless you want to take care of creating form/action constructor pairs and a Factory object yourself. If you want Zope to do this task for you, leave this checked. Checking this box means that this Add form creates five objects: a Class, a Constructor Form, a Constructor Action, a Permission, and a Factory. For this example, leave this box checked.

- **Include standard Zope persistent object base classes?**—This option should be checked unless you do not want your object to be saved in the database. This is an advanced option and should only be used for Plugable Brains. For this example, leave this box checked.

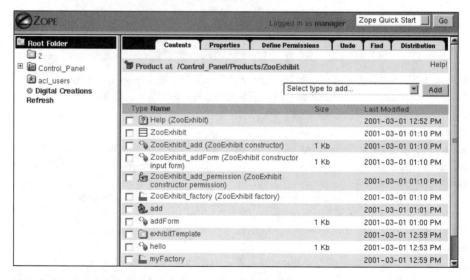

Now click Add. This takes you back to the ZooExhibit product where you see five new objects, as shown in Figure 12.4.

**Figure 12.4** Product with a ZClass.

The five objects Zope created are all automatically configured to work properly—you do not need to change them for now. The following is a brief description of each object that was created:

- **ZooExhibit**—This is the ZClass itself. Its icon is a white box with two horizontal lines in it. This is the traditional symbol for a class.

- **ZooExhibit_addForm**—This DTML method is the constructor form for the ZClass. It is a simple form that accepts an id and title. You can customize this form to accept any kind of input your new object requires. The is very similar to the Add form we created in the first example.

- **ZooExhibit_add**—This DTML method gets called by the constructor form ZooExhibit_addForm. This method actually creates your new object and sets its id and title. You can customize this form to do more advanced changes to your object based on input parameters from the ZooExhibit_addForm. This has the same functionality as the Python script we created in the previous example.

- **ZooExhibit_add_permission**—The curious looking stick-person carrying the blue box is a permission. This defines a permission that you can associate with adding new ZooExhibit objects. This enables you to protect the ability to add new zoo exhibits. If you click this permission, you can see the name of this new permission is Add ZooExhibits.

- **ZooExhibit_factory**—The little factory with a smokestack icon is a Factory object. If you click this object, you can change the text that shows up in the Add list for this object in the Add list name box. The Method is the method that gets called when a user selects the Add list name from the Add list. This is usually the constructor form for your object, in this case, ZooExhibit_ addForm. You can associate the permission the user must have to add this object, in this case, ZooExhibit_add_permission. You can also specify a regular Zope permission instead.

That's it, you've created your first ZClass. Click the new ZClass and click its Basic tab. The Basic view on your ZClass enables you to change some of the information you specified on the ZClass Add form. You cannot change the base classes of a ZClass. As you learned earlier in the chapter, these settings include

- **metatype**—The name of your ZClass as it appears in the product Add list.

- **class id**—A unique identifier for your class. You should only change this if you want to use your class definition for existing instances of another ZClass. In this case, you should copy the class id of the old class into your new class.

- **icon**—The path to your class' icon image. There is little reason to change this. If you want to change your class' icon, upload a new file with the Browse button.

At this point, you can start creating new instances of the ZooExhibit ZClass. However, first you probably want to create a common place where all exhibits are defined, so go to your Root folder and select Folder from the Add list. Create a new folder with the id Exhibits. Now, click the Exhibits folder you just created, and pull down the Add list. As you can see, ZooExhibit is now in the Add list.

Select ZooExhibit from the Add list, and create a new exhibit with the id
FangedRabbits. After creating the new exhibit, select it by clicking it.

As you can see, your object already has three views: Undo, Ownership, and
Security. You don't have to define these parts of your object, Zope does that for you.
In the next section, we add some more views for you to edit your object.

## Creating Views of Your ZClass

All Zope objects are divided into logical screens called *views*. Views are used commonly when you work with Zope objects in the management interface—the tabbed
screens on all Zope objects are views. Some views, such as Undo, are standard and
come with Zope.

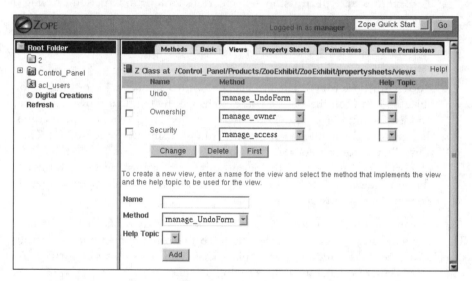

Views are defined on the Views view of a ZClass. Go to your ZooExhibit ZClass,
and click the Views tab. The Views view looks like Figure 12.5.

**Figure 12.5**   The Views view.

In this view, you can see the three views that come automatically with your new object:
Undo, Ownership, and Security. They are automatically configured for you as a convenience because almost all objects have these interfaces; however, you can change them
or remove them from this view if you really want to, but generally you will not need to.

The table of views is broken into three columns: Name, Method, and Help Topic.
The Name is the name of the view and is the label that gets drawn on the view's tab
in the management interface. The Method is the method of the class or property sheet
that gets called to render the view. The help topic is where you associate a Help Topic

object with this view. Help topics are explained in more detail in the section, "Providing Context-Sensitive Help for Your ZClass."

Views also work with the security system to make sure users only see views on an object that they have permission to see. Security is explained in detail in the section, "ZClass Security Controls," but it is good to know at this point that views not only divide object management interfaces into logical chunks, but they also control who can see which view.

The Method column on the Methods view has select boxes that enable you to choose what method generates what view. The method associated with a view can be either an object in the Methods view or a property sheet in the Property Sheets view.

## Creating Properties on Your ZClass

*Properties* are collections of variables that your object uses to store information. A Zoo-Exhibit object, for example, would need properties to contain information about the exhibit, such as what animal is in the exhibit, a description, and who the caretakers are.

Properties for ZClasses work a little differently from properties on Zope objects. In ZClasses, properties come in named groups called property sheets. A property sheet is a way of organizing a related set of properties together. Go to your ZooExhibit ZClass, and click the Property Sheets tab. To create a new sheet, click Add Common Instance Property Sheet. This takes you to the Property Sheet Add form. Call your new Property Sheet ExhibitProperties, and click Add.

Now you can see that your new sheet, ExhibitProperties, has been created in the

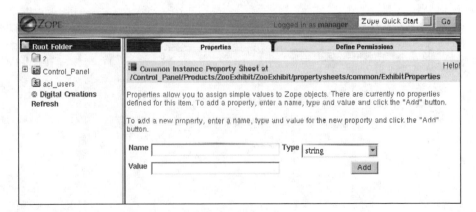

Property Sheets view of your ZClass. Click the new sheet to manage it, as shown in Figure 12.6.

**Figure 12.6**  A property sheet.

As you can see, this sheet looks very much like the Properties view on Zope objects.

You can create new properties on this sheet. Properties on property sheets are exactly like properties on Zope objects—they have a name, a type, and a value.

Create the following three new properties on this sheet:

- **animal**—This property type should be string. It holds the name of the animal this exhibit features.

- **description**—This property type should be text. It holds the description of the exhibit.

- **caretakers**—This property type should be lines. It holds a list of names for the exhibit caretakers.

Property sheets have two uses. As you've seen with this example, they are a tool for organizing related sets of properties about your objects, and second to that, they are used to generate HTML forms and actions to edit those set of properties. The HTML edit forms are generated automatically for you, so you only need to associate a view with a property sheet to see the sheet's edit form. For example, return to the ZooExhibit ZClass, click the Views tab, create a new view with the name Edit, and associate it with the method `propertysheets/ExhibitProperties/manage_edit`.

Because you can use property sheets to create editing screens, you might want to create more than one property sheet for your class. By using more than one sheet, you can control which properties are displayed together for editing purposes. You can also separate private from public properties on different sheets by associating them with different permissions.

Now, go back to your Exhibits folder and either look at an existing ZooExhibit

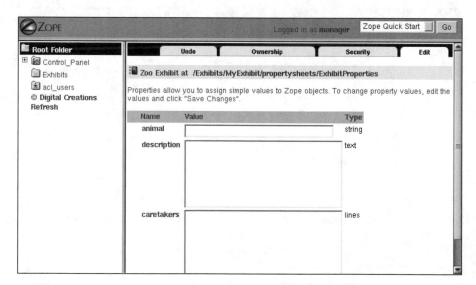

instance or create a new one. As you can see, a new view called Edit has been added to your object, as shown in Figure 12.7.

**Figure 12.7**    A ZooExhibit Edit view.

This edit form has been generated for you automatically. You only needed to create the property sheet and associate it with a View. If you add another property to the Exhibit-Properties property sheet, all your instances automatically get a new updated edit form, because when you change a ZClass, all the instances of that class inherit the change.

It is important to understand that changes made to the class are reflected by all the instances. However, changes to an instance are *not* reflected in the class or in any other instance. For example, on the Edit view for your ZooExhibit instance, (not the class) enter `Fanged Rabbit` for the animal property, enter `Fanged, carnivorous rabbits plagued early medieval knights. They are known for their sharp, pointy teeth.` as the description, and enter two caretakers, `Tim` and `Somebody Else`. Now click Save Changes.

As you can see, your changes have obviously effected this instance, but what happened to the class? Go back to the ZooExhibit ZClass, and look at the ExhibitProperties Property Sheet. Nothing has changed! Changes to instances have no effect on the class.

You can also provide default values for properties on a property sheet. You could, for example, enter the text `Describe your exhibit in this box` in the description property of the ZooExhibit ZClass. Now, go back to your Exhibits folder and create a new ZooExhibit object, and click its Edit view. Here, you see that the value provided in the property sheet is the default value for the instance. Remember, if you change this instance, the default value of the property in the property sheet is *not* changed. Default values enable you to set up useful information in the ZClass for properties that can later be changed on an instance-by-instance basis.

You might want to go back to your ZClass, click the Views tab, and click the First button, so the Edit view is the first view shown. Now, when you click your instances, they show the Edit view first.

## Creating Methods on Your ZClass

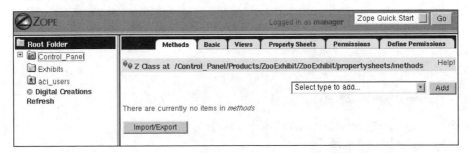

The Methods view of your ZClass enables you to define the methods for the instances of your ZClass. Go to your ZooExhibit ZClass, and click the Methods tab. The Methods view is shown in Figure 12.8.

**Figure 12.8**    The Methods view.

You can create any kind of Zope object on the Methods view, but generally, only callable objects (DTML methods and scripts, for example) are added.

Methods are used for several purposes:

- **Presentation**—When you associate a view with a method, the method is called when a user selects that view on an instance. For example, if you had a DTML method called showAnimalImages and a view called Images, you could associate the showAnimalImages method with the Images view. Whenever anyone clicked the Images view on an instance of your ZClass, the showAnimalImages method would get called.

- **Logic**—Methods are not necessarily associated with views. Methods that define how you can work with your object are often created. For example, consider the isHungry method of the ZooExhibit ZClass, which is defined later in this section. It does not define a view for a ZooExhibit, it just provides very specific information about the ZooExhibit. Methods in a ZClass can call each other just like any other Zope methods, so logic methods could be used from a presentation method even though they do not define a view.

- **Shared objects**—As was pointed out earlier, you can create any kind of object on the Methods view of a ZClass. All instances of your ZClass share the objects on the Methods view. For example, if you create a Z Gadfly Connection in the Methods view of your ZClass, then all instances of that class will share the same Gadfly connection. Shared objects can be useful to your class' logic or presentation methods.

A good example of a presentation method is a DTML method that displays a Zoo Exhibit to your Web site viewers. This is often called the *public interface* to an object, and it is usually associated with the View view found on most Zope objects.

Create a new DTML method on the Methods tab of your ZooExhibit ZClass called index_html. Like all objects named index_html, this will be the default representation for the object in which it is defined, namely, instances of your ZClass. Put the following DTML in the index_html method you just created:

```
<dtml-var standard_html_header>

  <h1><dtml-var animal></h1>

  <p><dtml-var description></p>

  <p>The <dtml-var animal> caretakers are:<br>
    <dtml-in caretakers>
```

```
    <dtml-var sequence-item><br>
  </dtml-in>
</p>
```

```
<dtml-var standard_html_footer>
```

Now you can visit one of your ZooExhibit instances directly through the Web, for example, `http://www.zopezoo.org/Exhibits/FangedRabbits/` shows you the public interface for the Fanged Rabbit exhibit.

You can use Python-based or Perl-based scripts, and even Z SQL methods, to implement logic. Your logic objects can call each other, and they can be called from your presentation methods. To create the isHungry method, first create two new properties in the ExhibitProperties property sheet named last_meal_time, which is of the type date and isDangerous, which is of the type boolean. This adds two new fields to your Edit view where you can enter the last time the animal was fed and select whether or not the animal is dangerous.

The following is an example of an implementation of the isHungry method in Python:

```
## Script (Python) "isHungry"
##
"""
Returns true if the animal hasn't eaten in over 8 hours
"""
from DateTime import DateTime
if (DateTime().timeTime()
    - self.last_meal_time.timeTime() >  60 * 60 * 8):
    return 1
else:
    return 0
```

You could call this method from your index_html display method using this snippet of DTML:

```
<dtml-if isHungry>
  <p><dtml-var animal> is hungry</p>
</dtml-if>
```

You can even call a number of logic methods from your display methods. For example, you could improve the hunger display like so:

```
<dtml-if isHungry>

  <p><dtml-var animal> is hungry.

  <dtml-if isDangerous>

    <a href="notify_hunger">Tell</a> an authorized
    caretaker.

  <dtml-else>

    <a href="feed">Feed</a> the <dtml-var animal>.
```

```
</dtml-if>

</p>

</dtml-if>
```

Your display method now calls logic methods to decide what actions are appropriate, and it creates links to those actions. For more information on Properties, see Chapter 3, "Using Basic Zope Objects."

## ObjectManager ZClasses

If you choose ZClasses:ObjectManager as a base class for your ZClass, then instances of your class are able to contain other Zope objects, just like folders. Container classes are identical to other ZClasses with the exception that they have an additional view, Subobjects.

From the Subobjects view, you can control what kinds of objects your instances contain. For example, if you created a FAQ container class, you might restrict it to holding Question and Answer objects. Select one or more metatypes from the select list, and click the Change button. The Objects should appear in folder lists check box controls whether or not instances of your container class are shown in the Navigator pane as expandable objects.

Container ZClasses can be very powerful. A very common pattern for Web applications is to have two classes that work together. One class implements the basic behavior and hold data. The other class contains instances of the basic class and provides methods to organize and list the contained instances. You can model many problems this way. For example, a ticket manager can contain problem tickets, a document repository can contain documents, an object router can contain routing rules, and so on. Typically, the container class provides methods to add, delete, query, or locate contained objects.

## ZClass Security Controls

Security can play an important role when you are building new types of objects. For example, the following three roles are needed in your zoo:

- **Manager**—This role exists by default in Zope. This is you and anyone else you want to be able to completely manage your Zope system.

- **Caretaker**—After you create a ZooExhibit instance, you want users with the Caretaker role to be able to edit exhibits. Only users with this role should be able to see the Edit view of a ZooExhibit instance.

- **Anonymous**—This role exists by default in Zope. People with the Anonymous role should be able to view the exhibit, but not manage it or change it in any way.

As you learned in Chapter 6, "Users and Security," creating new roles is easy, but how can you control who is allowed to create and edit new ZooExhibit instances? To control this, you must define some security policies on the ZooExhibit ZClass, which controls access to the ZClass and its methods and property sheets.

## Controlling Access to Methods and Property Sheets

By default, Zope tries to be sensible about ZClasses and security. You might, however, want to control access to instances of your ZClass in special ways.

For example, zoo caretakers are really only interested in seeing the Edit view, (and perhaps the Undo view, which we'll show later) but definitely not the Security or Ownership views. You do not want zoo caretakers changing the security settings on your Exhibits—you do not even want them to *see* those aspects of an Exhibit—you just want to give them the ability to edit an exhibit and nothing else.

To do this, you need to create a new Zope Permission object in the ZooExhibit Product (not in the ZClass, permissions are defined in Products only). To do this, go to

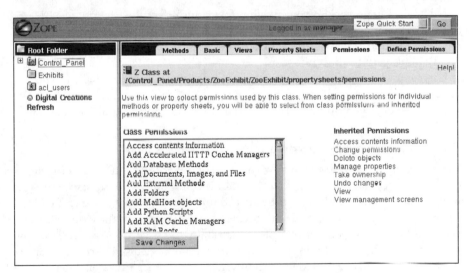

the ZooExhibit Product, and select Zope Permission from the Add list. Give the new permission the id `edit_exhibit_permission` and the name `Edit Zoo Exhibits`, and click Generate.

Now, select your ZooExhibit ZClass, and click the Permissions tab. This takes you to the Permissions view, as shown in Figure 12.9.

**Figure 12.9**   The Permissions view.

This view shows you what permissions your ZClass uses and lets you choose additional permissions to use. On the right is a list of all the default Zope permissions your ZClass inherits automatically. On the left is a multiple select box where you can add new permissions to your class. Select the Edit Zoo Exhibits permission in this box, and click Save Changes. This tells your ZClass that it is interested in this permission as well as the permissions on the right.

Now, click the Property Sheets tab, and select the ExhibitProperties property sheet. Click the Define Permissions tab.

You want to tell this property sheet that only users who have the Edit Zoo Exhibits permission, which you just created, are allowed to manage the properties on the ExhibitProperties sheet. On this view, pull down the select box, and choose Edit Zoo Exhibits. This maps the Edit Zoo Exhibits to the Manage Properties permission on the sheet. This list of permissions, from which you can select, comes from the ZClass Permissions view you were just on, and because you selected the Edit Zoo Exhibits permission on that screen, it shows up on this list for you to select. Notice that all options default to disabled, which means that the property sheet cannot be edited by anyone.

Now, you can go back to your Exhibits folder and select the Security view. Here you can see your new permission is on the left in the list of available permission. Now you need to create a new role called Caretaker and map that new Role to the Edit Zoo Exhibits permission.

Users must have the Caretaker role to see or use the Edit view on any of your ZooExhibit instances.

Access to objects on your ZClass' Methods view are controlled in the same way.

## Controlling Access to Instances of Your ZClass

The preceding section explained how you can control access to instances of your ZClass' methods and properties. Access control is controlling who can create new instances of your ZClass. As you saw earlier in this chapter, instances are created by factories. Factories are associated with permissions. In the case of the Zoo Exhibit, the Add Zoo Exhibits permission controls the capability to create Zoo Exhibit instances.

Normally, only Managers have the Add Zoo Exhibits permission, so only Managers are able to create new Zoo Exhibits. However, like all Zope permissions, you can change which roles have this permissions in different locations of your site. It is important to realize that this permission is controlled separately from the Edit Zoo Exhibits permission. This makes it possible to allow some people, such as caretakers, to change without creating Zoo Exhibits.

## Providing Context-Sensitive Help for Your ZClass

On the View screen of your ZClass, you see that each view can be associated with a help topic. This enables you to provide a link to different help topics, depending on which view the user is looking at. For example, let's create a help topic for the Edit view of the ZooExhibit ZClass.

First, you need to create an actual help topic object. This is done by going to the ZooExhibit Product, which contains the ZooExhibit ZClass, and clicking the Help folder. The icon should look like a folder with a blue question mark on it.

Inside this special folder, pull down the Add list and select Help Topic. Give this topic the id `ExhibitEditHelp` and the title `Help for Editing Exhibits`, and click Add.

Now the Help folder contains a new help topic object called ExhibitEditHelp. You can click this object and edit it; it works just like a DTML document. In this document, you should place the help information you want to show to your users:

```
<dtml-var standard_html_header>

  <h1>Help!</h1>

  <p>To edit an exhibit, click on either the <b>animal</b>,
  <b>description</b>, or <b>caretakers</b> boxes to edit
  them.</p>

<dtml-var standard_html_footer>
```

Now that you have created the help topic, you need to associate with the Edit view of your ZClass. To do this, select the ZooExhibit ZClass, and click the Views tab. At the right, in the same row the Edit view is defined, pull down the help select box, select ExhibitEditHelp, and click Change. Now, go to one of your ZooExhibit instances. The Edit view now has a Help! link that you can click to look at your help topic for this view.

In the next section, you see how ZClasses can be combined with standard Python classes to extend their functionality into raw Python.

# Using Python Base Classes

ZClasses give you a Web-manageable interface to design new kinds of objects in Zope. In the beginning of this chapter, we showed you how you can select from a list of base classes to subclass your ZClass. Most of these base classes are actually written in Python, and in this section, you see how to take your own Python classes and include them in that list so that your ZClasses can extend their methods.

Writing Python base classes is easy, but it involves a few installation details. To create a Python base class, you need access to the file system. Create a directory inside your lib/python/Products directory named AnimalBase. In this directory, create a file named Animal.py with these contents:

```
class Animal:
    """
    A base class for Animals
    """

    _hungry=0
```

*continues*

*continued*

```
        def eat(self, food, servings=1):
            """
            Eat food
            """
            self._hungry=0

        def sleep(self):
            """
            Sleep
            """
            self._hungry=1

        def hungry(self):
            """
            Is the Animal hungry?
            """
            return self._hungry
```

This class defines a couple of related methods and one default attribute. Notice that like external methods, the methods of this class can access private attributes.

Next, you need to register your base class with Zope. Create an \_\_init\_\_.py file in the AnimalBase directory with these contents:

```
from Animal import Animal

def initialize(context):
    """
    Register base class
    """
    context.registerBaseClass(Animal)
```

You need to restart Zope for it to recognize your base class. After Zope restarts, you can verify that your base class has been registered in a couple of different ways. First, go to the Products Folder in the Control Panel and look for an AnimalBase package. You should see a closed-box product. If you see a broken box, it means that there is something wrong with your AnimalBase product.

Click the Traceback view to see a Python traceback, which shows you what problem Zope ran into trying to register your base class. After you resolve any problems that your base class might have, you need to restart Zope again. Continue this process until Zope successfully loads your product. Now you can create a new ZClass, and you should see AnimalBase:Animal as a choice in the base classes selection field.

To test your new base class, create a ZClass that inherits from AnimalBase:Animal. Embellish your animal however you want. Create a DTML method named care with these contents:

```
<dtml-var standard_html_header>

<dtml-if give_food>
  <dtml-call expr="eat('cookie')">
```

```
</dtml-if>

<dtml-if give_sleep>
  <dtml-call sleep>
</dtml-if>

<dtml-if hungry>
  <p>I am hungry</p>
<dtml-else>
  <p>I am not hungry</p>
</dtml-if>

<form>
<input type="submit" value="Feed" name="give_food">
<input type="submit" value="Sleep" name="give_sleep">
</form>

<dtml-var standard_html_footer>
```

Now, create an instance of your animal class and test its care method. The care method lets you feed your animal and give it sleep by calling methods defined in its Python base class. Also, notice how after you feed your animal it is not hungry, but if you give it a nap, it wakes up hungry.

As you can see, creating your own products and ZClasses is an involved process, but it is simple to understand after you grasp the basics. With ZClasses alone, you can create some pretty complex Web applications right in your Web browser.

In the next section, you create a distribution of your product so that you can share it with others or deliver it to a customer.

## Distributing Products

Now you have created your own product that enables you to create any number of exhibits in Zope. Suppose you have a buddy at another zoo who is impressed by your new online exhibit system, and he wants to get a similar system for his zoo.

Perhaps you even belong to the Zoo Keeper's Association of America, and you want to be able to give your product to anyone interested in an exhibit system similar to yours. Zope enables you to distribute your products as one, easy-to-transport package that other users can download from you and install in their Zope system.

To distribute your product, click the ZooExhibit product, and select the Distribution tab. This takes you to the Distribution view.

The form on this view enables you to control the distribution you want to create. The Version box enables you to specify the version for your product distribution. For every distribution you make, Zope increments this number for you, but you might want to specify it yourself. Just leave it at the default of 1.0, unless you want to change it.

The next two radio buttons enable you to select whether or not you want others to be able to customize or redistribute your product. If you want to give them the ability to customize or redistribute your product with no restrictions, select the Allow Redistribution button. If you want to disallow their ability to redistribute your product, select the Disallow redistribution and allow the user to configure only the selected objects button. If you disallow redistribution, you can choose on an object-by-object basis what your users can customize in your product. If you don't want them to be able to change anything, then don't select any of the items in this list. If you want them to be able to change the ZooExhibit ZClass, then select only that ZClass. If you want them to be able to change everything, (but still not be able to redistribute your product) then select all the objects in this list.

Now, you can create a distribution of your product by clicking Create a distribution archive. Zope now automatically generates a file called ZooExhibit-1.0.tar.gz. This product can be installed in any Zope, just like any other product, by unpacking it into the Root directory of your Zope installation.

Don't forget that when you distribute your product, you also need to include any files, such as external method files and Python base classes, that your class relies on. This requirement makes distribution more difficult, and for this reason, folks try to avoid relying on Python files when creating the Web products for distribution.

# IV

# Appendixes

# DTML Reference

D OCUMENT TEMPLATE MARKUP LANGUAGE (DTML) is a handy presentation and templating language that comes with Zope. This appendix is a reference to all of DTML's markup tags and how they work.

## *call*: Call a Method

The call tag enables you to call a method without inserting the results into the DTML output.

### Syntax

call tag syntax:

```
<dtml-call Variable|expr="Expression">
```

If the call tag uses a variable, the method's arguments are passed automatically by DTML—just the same as the var tag. If the method is specified in an expression, then you must pass the arguments yourself.

## Examples

Calling by variable name:

```
<dtml-call UpdateInfo>
```

This calls the UpdateInfo object automatically by passing arguments.
Calling by expression:

```
<dtml-call expr="RESPONSE.setHeader('content-type', 'text/plain')">
```

## See Also

var tag

# *comment*: Comments DTML

The comment tag enables you to document your DTML with comments. You can also use it to temporarily disable DTML tags by commenting them out.

## Syntax

comment tag syntax:

```
<dtml-comment>
</dtml-comment>
```

The comment tag is a block tag. The contents of the block are not executed, nor are they inserted into the DTML output.

## Examples

Documenting DTML:

```
<dtml-comment>
  This content is not executed and does not appear in the
  output.
</dtml-comment>
```

Commenting out DTML:

```
<dtml-comment>
  This DTML is disabled and will not be executed.
  <dtml-call someMethod>
</dtml-comment>
```

# Functions: DTML Functions

DTML utility functions provide some Python built-in functions and some DTML-specific functions.

## Functions

- **abs(number)**—Returns the absolute value of a number. The argument might be a plain or long integer or a floating point number. If the argument is a complex number, its magnitude is returned.

- **chr(integer)**—Returns a string of one character whose ASCII code is the integer. For example, chr(97) returns the string a. This is the inverse of ord(). The argument must be in the range 0 to 255, inclusively; a ValueError is raised if the integer is outside of that range.

- **DateTime()**—Returns a Zope DateTime object given constructor arguments. See the section "class DateTime" in Appendix B, "API Reference," for more information on constructor arguments.

- **divmod(number, number)**—Takes two numbers as arguments and returns a pair of numbers consisting of their quotient and remainder when using long division. With mixed operand types, the rules for binary arithmetic operators apply. For plain and long integers, the result is the same as (a / b, a % b). For floating point numbers, the result is (q, a % b), where q is usually math.floor(a / b); however, it might be 1 less than that. In any case, q * b + a % b is very close to a. If a % b is non-zero, it has the same sign as b and 0 <= abs(a % b) < abs(b).

- **float(number)**—Converts a string or a number to floating point. If the argument is a string, it must contain a possibly signed decimal or floating point number that is embedded in white space; this behaves identical to string.atof(number). Otherwise, the argument might be a plain or long integer or a floating point number, in which case, a floating point number with the same value (within Python's floating point precision) is returned.

- **getattr(object, string)**—Returns the value of the named attribute of the object. The name must be a string. If the string is the name of one of the object's attributes, the result is the value of that attribute. For example, getattr(x, "foobar") is equivalent to x.foobar. If the named attribute does not exist, the default is returned if provided, otherwise an AttributeError is raised.

- **getitem(variable, render=0)**—Returns the value of a DTML variable. If render is true, the variable is rendered. See the render function.

- **hasattr(object, string)**—The arguments are an object and a string. The result is 1 if the string is the name of one of the object's attributes, if not, it is 0. (This is implemented by calling getattr(object, name) and seeing whether or not it raises an exception.)

- **hash(object)**—Returns the hash value of the object (if it has one). Hash values are integers. They are used to quickly compare dictionary keys during a dictionary lookup. Numeric values that are equal have the same hash value (even if they are of different types, for example, 1 and 1.0).

- **`has_key(variable)`**—Returns true if the DTML namespace contains the named variable.

- **`hex(integer)`**—Converts an integer number (of any size) to a hexadecimal string. The result is a valid Python expression. Note: This always yields an unsigned literal. For example, on a 32-bit machine, `hex(-1)` yields `0xffffffff`. When evaluated on a machine with the same word size, this literal is evaluated as –1; with a different word size, it might turn up as a large positive number or raise an `OverflowError` exception.

- **`int(number)`**—Converts a string or number to a plain integer. If the argument is a string, it must contain a possibly signed decimal number that can be represented as a Python integer and that is embedded in white space; this behaves identical to `'string.atoi(number[, radix]')`. The `radix` parameter gives the base for the conversion and might be any integer in the range 2 to 36. If `radix` is specified and the number is not a string, a `TypeError` is raised. Otherwise, the argument might be a plain or long integer or a floating point number. Conversion of floating point numbers to integers is defined by the C semantics; normally, the conversion truncates toward zero.

- **`len(sequence)`**—Returns the length (the number of items) of an object. The argument might be a sequence (string, tuple, or list) or a mapping (dictionary).

- **`max(s)`**—Returns the largest item of a non-empty sequence with a single `s` argument (for example, a string, tuple, or list). When there is more than one argument, it returns the largest of the arguments.

- **`min(s)`**—Returns the smallest item of a non-empty sequence with a single `s` argument (for example, a string, tuple, or list). When there is more than one argument, it returns the smallest of the arguments.

- **`namespace([name=value]...)`**—Returns a new DTML namespace object. Keyword argument `name=value` pairs are pushed into the new namespace.

- **`oct(integer)`**—Converts an integer number (of any size) to an octal string. The result is a valid Python expression. Note: This always yields an unsigned literal. For example, on a 32-bit machine, `oct(-1)` yields `037777777777`. When evaluated on a machine with the same word size, this literal is evaluated as –1; with a different word size, it may turn up as a large positive number or raise an `OverflowError` exception.

- **`ord(character)`**—Returns the ASCII value of a string of one character. For example, `ord("a")` returns the integer 97. This is the inverse of `chr()`.

- **`pow(x, y [,z])`**—Returns x to the power y. If z is present, it returns x to the power y modulo z (computed more efficiently than `'pow(x, y) % z'`). The arguments must have numeric types. With mixed operand types, the rules for binary arithmetic operators apply. The effective operand type is also the type of the result; if the result is not expressible in this type, the function raises an exception; for example, `pow(2, -1)` or `pow(2, 35000)` is not allowed.

- **range([start,] stop [,step])**—This is a versatile function to create lists containing arithmetic progressions. The arguments must be plain integers. If the step argument is omitted, it defaults to 1. If the start argument is omitted, it defaults to 0. The full form returns a list of plain integers '[start, start + step, start + 2 * step, ...]'. If step is positive, the last element is the largest 'start + i step' less than stop; if step is negative, the last element is the largest 'start + i step' greater than stop. step must not be zero (or else a ValueError is raised).

- **round(x [,n])**—Returns the floating point value x rounded to n digits after the decimal point. If n is omitted, it defaults to zero. The result is a floating point number. Values are rounded to the closest multiple of 10 to the power minus n; if two multiples are equally close, rounding is done away from 0 (for example, round (0.5) is 1.0 and round (-0.5) is -1.0).

- **render(object)**—Renders object. For DTML objects, this evaluates the DTML code with the current namespace. For other objects, this is equivalent to str(object).

- **reorder(s [,with] [,without])**—Reorders the items in s according to the order given in with and without the items mentioned in without. Items from s not mentioned in with are removed. s, with, and without are all either sequences of strings or sequences of key-value tuples, with ordering done on the keys. This function is useful for constructing ordered select lists.

- **SecurityCalledByExecutable()**—Returns a true if the current object (for example, DTML document or method) is being called by an executable (such as another DTML document or method, a script, or an SQL method).

- **SecurityCheckPermission(permission, object)**—Checks whether the security context allows the given permission on the given object. For example, 'Security CheckPermission("Add Documents, Images, and Files", this())' would return true if the current user was authorized to create documents, images, and files in the current location.

- **SecurityGetUser()**—Returns the current user object. This is normally the same as the REQUEST.AUTHENTICATED_USER object. However, the AUTHENTICATED_USER object is insecure because it can be replaced.

- **SecurityValidate([object] [,parent] [,name] [,value])**—Returns true if the value is accessible to the current user. object is the object the value was accessed in, parent is the container of the value, and name is the name used to access the value (for example, if it were obtained through 'getattr'). You might omit some of the arguments. However, it is best to provide all available arguments.

- **SecurityValidateValue(object)**—Returns true if the object is accessible to the current user. This function is the same as calling SecurityValidate(None, None, None, object).

- **str(object)**—Returns a string containing a nicely printable representation of an object. For strings, this returns the string itself.

- **test(condition, result [,condition, result]... [,default])**—Takes one or more **condition, result** pairs and returns the result of the first true condition. Only one result is returned, even if more than one condition is true. If no condition is true and a default is given, the default is returned. If no condition is true and there is no default, None is returned.

### Attributes

- **None**—The None object is equivalent to the Python built-in object None. This is generally used to represent a null or false value.

### See Also

string module
random module
math module
Built-in Python functions (http://www.python.org/doc/current/lib/built-in-funcs.html)

# *if*: Tests Conditions

The if tag enables you to test conditions and take different actions, depending on the conditions. The if tag mirrors Python's if/elif/else condition testing statements.

### Syntax

if tag syntax:

```
<dtml-if ConditionVariable|expr="ConditionExpression">
[<dtml-elif ConditionVariable|expr="ConditionExpression">]
  ...
[<dtml-else>]
</dtml-if>
```

The if tag is a block tag. The if tag and optional elif tags take a condition variable name or a condition expression, but not both. If the condition name or expression evaluates are true, then the if block is executed. True means not zero, an empty string or an empty list. If the condition variable is not found, then the condition is considered false.

If the initial condition is false, each elif condition is tested in turn. If any elif condition is true, its block is executed. Finally, the optional else block is executed if none of the if and elif conditions were true. Only one block is executed.

### Examples

Testing for a variable:

```
<dtml-if snake>
  The snake variable is true
</dtml-if>
```

Testing for expression conditions:

```
<dtml-if expr="num > 5">
  num is greater than five
<dtml-elif expr="num < 5">
  num is less than five
<dtml-else>
  num must be five
</dtml-if>
```

## See Also

Python Tutorial: if Statements (`http://www.python.org/doc/current/tut/`
`node6.html#SECTION006100000000000000000`)

# *in*: **Loops Over Sequences**

The in tag gives you powerful controls for looping over sequences and performing
batch processing.

## Syntax

in tag syntax:

```
<dtml-in SequenceVariable|expr="SequenceExpression">
[<dtml-else>]
</dtml-in>
```

The in block is repeated once for each item in the sequence variable or sequence
expression. The current item is pushed on to the DTML namespace during each
executing of the in block.

If no items in the sequence are variable or expression, the optional else block
is executed.

## Attributes

- **mapping**—Iterates over mapping objects rather than instances. This enables values
  of the mapping objects to be accessed as DTML variables.
- **reverse**—Reverses the sequence.
- **sort=string**—Sorts the sequence by the given attribute name.
- **start=int**—The number of the first item to be shown, where items are
  numbered from 1.
- **end=int**—The number of the last item to be shown, where items are
  numbered from 1.

- **size=int**—The size of the batch.
- **skip_unauthorized**—Does not raise an exception if an unauthorized item is encountered.
- **orphan=int**—The desired minimum batch size.
- **overlap=int**—The number of items to overlap between batches. The default value is 3.
- **previous**—Iterates once if there is a previous batch. Sets batch variables for previous sequence.
- **next**—Iterates once if there is a next batch. Sets batch variables for the next sequence.

## Tag Variables

### Current Item Variables

These variables describe the current item:

- *sequence-item*—The current item.
- *sequence-key*—The current key. When looping over tuples of the form (key,value), the in tag interprets them as (sequence-key, sequence-item).
- *sequence-index*—The index starting with 0 of the current item.
- *sequence-number*—The index starting with 1 of the current item.
- *sequence-roman*—The index in lowercase Roman numerals of the current item.
- *sequence-Roman*—The index in uppercase Roman numerals of the current item.
- *sequence-letter*—The index in lowercase letters of the current item.
- *sequence-Letter*—The index in uppercase letters of the current item.
- *sequence-start*—True if the current item is the first item.
- *sequence-end*—True if the current item is the last item.
- *sequence-even*—True if the index of the current item is even.
- *sequence-odd*—True if the index of the current item is odd.
- *sequence-length*—The length of the sequence.
- *sequence-var-variable*—A variable in the current item. For example, sequence-var-title is the title variable of the current item. Normally, you can access these variables directly because the current item is pushed on the DTML namespace. However, these variables can be useful when displaying previous and next batch information.
- *sequence-index-variable*—The index of a variable of the current item.

## Summary Variables

These variables summarize information about numeric item variables. To use these variables, you must loop over objects (such as database query results) that have numeric variables.

- *total-variable*—The total of all occurrences of an item variable.
- *count-variable*—The number of occurrences of an item variable.
- *min-variable*—The minimum value of an item variable.
- *max-variable*—The maximum value of an item variable.
- *mean-variable*—The mean value of an item variable.
- *variance-variable*—The variance of an item variable with count-1 degrees of freedom.
- *variance-n-variable*—The variance of an item variable with *n* degrees of freedom.
- *standard-deviation-variable*—The standard-deviation of an item variable with count-1 degrees of freedom.
- *standard-deviation-n-variable*—The standard-deviation of an item variable with *n* degrees of freedom.

## Grouping Variables

These variables enable you to track changes in current item variables:

- *first-variable*—True if the current item is the first with a particular value for a variable.
- *last-variable*—True if the current item is the last with a particular value for a variable.

## Batch Variables

- *sequence-query*—The query string with the *start* variable removed. You can use this variable to construct links to next and previous batches.
- *sequence-step-size*—The batch size.
- *previous-sequence*—True if the current batch is not the first one. Note, this variable is only true for the first loop iteration.
- *previous-sequence-start-index*—The starting index of the previous batch.
- *previous-sequence-start-number*—The starting number of the previous batch. Note, this is the same as `previous-sequence-start-index` + 1.
- *previous-sequence-end-index*—The ending index of the previous batch.
- *previous-sequence-end-number*—The ending number of the previous batch. Note, this is the same as `previous-sequence-end-index` + 1.

- *previous-sequence-size*—The size of the previous batch.
- *previous-batches*—A sequence of mapping objects with information about all previous batches. Each mapping object has these keys: `batch-start-index`, `batch-end-index`, and `batch-size`.
- *next-sequence*—True if the current batch is not the last batch. Note, this variable is only true for the last loop iteration.
- *next-sequence-start-index*—The starting index of the next sequence.
- *next-sequence-start-number*—The starting number of the next sequence. Note, this is the same as `next-sequence-start-index` + 1.
- *next-sequence-end-index*—The ending index of the next sequence.
- *next-sequence-end-number*—The ending number of the next sequence. Note, this is the same as `next-sequence-end-index` + 1.
- *next-sequence-size*—The size of the next index.
- *next-batches*—A sequence of mapping objects with information about all following batches. Each mapping object has these keys: `batch-start-index`, `batch-end-index`, and `batch-size`.

## Examples

Looping over subobjects:

```
<dtml-in objectValues>
  title: <dtml-var title><br>
</dtml-in>
```

Looping over a list of (key, value) tuples:

```
<dtml-in objectItems>
  id: <dtml-var sequence-key>, title: <dtml-var title><br>
</dtml-in>
```

Creating alternate colored table cells:

```
<table>
<dtml-in objectValues>
<tr <dtml-if sequence-odd>bgcolor="#EEEEEE"
    <dtml-else>bgcolor="#FFFFFF"
    </dtml-if>
  <td><dtml-var title></td>
</tr>
</dtml-in>
</table>
```

Basic batch processing:

```
<p>
<dtml-in largeSequence size=10 start=start previous>
  <a href="<dtml-var absolute_url><dtml-var sequence-query>
➥start=<dtml-var previous-sequence-start-number>">Previous</a>
```

```
</dtml-in>

<dtml-in largeSequence size=10 start=start next>
  <a href="<dtml-var absolute_url><dtml-var sequence-query>
➥start=<dtml-var next-sequence-start-number>">Next</a>
</dtml-in>
</p>

<p>
<dtml-in largeSequence size=10 start=start>
  <dtml-var sequence-item>
</dtml-in>
</p>
```

This example creates *Previous* and *Next* links to navigate between batches. Note, by using
sequence-query, you do not lose any *GET* variables as you navigate between batches.

# *let*: Defines DTML Variables

The let tag defines variables in the DTML namespace.

## Syntax

let tag syntax:

```
<dtml-let [Name=Variable][Name="Expression"]...>
</dtml-let>
```

The let tag is a block tag. Variables are defined by tag arguments. Defined variables are
pushed onto the DTML namespace while the let block is executed. Variables are
defined by attributes. The let tag can have one or more attributes with arbitrary
names. If the attributes are defined with double quotes, they are considered expressions. Otherwise, they are looked up by name. Attributes are processed in order, so
later attributes can reference and overwrite earlier ones.

## Examples

Basic use:

```
<dtml-let name="'Bob'" ids=objectIds>
  name: <dtml-var name>
  ids: <dtml-var ids>
</dtml-let>
```

Using the let tag with the in tag:

```
<dtml-in expr="(1,2,3,4)">
  <dtml-let num=sequence-item
            index=sequence-index
            result="num*index">
    <dtml-var num> * <dtml-var index> = <dtml-var result>
  </dtml-let>
</dtml-in>
```

This yields:

```
1 * 0 = 0
2 * 1 = 2
3 * 2 = 6
4 * 3 = 12
```

### See Also

with tag

# *math*: DTML Math Functions

The math module provides trigonometric and other math functions. It is a standard Python module.

## Functions

- **acos(x)**—Returns the arc cosine of $x$.
- **asin(x)**—Returns the arc sine of $x$.
- **atan(x)**—Returns the arc tangent of $x$.
- **atan2(x, y)**—Returns atan(y / x).
- **ceil(x)**—Returns the ceiling of $x$ as a real.
- **cos(x)**—Returns the cosine of $x$.
- **cosh(x)**—Returns the hyperbolic cosine of $x$.
- **exp(x)**—Returns e**x.
- **fabs(x)**—Returns the absolute value of the real $x$.
- **floor(x)**—Returns the floor of $x$ as a real.
- **fmod(x, y)**—Returns fmod(x, y) as defined by the platform C library. Note, that the Python expression x % y might not return the same result.
- **fexp(x)**—Returns mantissa and exponent of $x$ as the pair (m, e). $m$ is a float and e is an integer such that 'x == m * 2*e'. If x is zero, it returns (0.0, 0), otherwise 0.5 <= abs(m) < 1.
- **hypot(x, y)**—Returns the Euclidean distance, sqrt(x*x + y*y).
- **ldexp(x, y)**—Returns x * (2**i).
- **log(x)**—Returns the natural logarithm of $x$.
- **log10(x)**—Returns the base-10 logarithm of $x$.
- **modf(x)**—Returns the fractional and integer parts of $x$. Both results carry the sine of $x$. The integer part is returned as a real.
- **pow(x, y)**—Returns x to the power of $y$.

- **sin(x)**—Returns the sine of *x*.
- **sinh(x)**—Returns the hyperbolic sine of *x*.
- **sqrt(x)**—Returns the square root of *x*.
- **tan(x)**—Returns the tangent of *x*.
- **tanh(x)**—Returns the hyperbolic tangent of *x*.

## Attributes

- **e**—The mathematical constant *e*.
- **pi**—The mathematical constant *pi*.

## See Also

Python `math` module (`http://www.python.org/doc/current/lib/module-math.html`)

# *mime*: Formats Data with MIME

The `mime` tag enables you to create MIME encoded data. It is chiefly used to format email inside the `sendmail` tag.

## Syntax

mime tag syntax:

```
<dtml-mime>
[<dtml-boundry>]
...
</dtml-mime>
```

The `mime` tag is a block tag. The block can be divided by one or more `boundry` tags to create a multi-part MIME message. `mime` tags can be nested. The `mime` tag is most often used inside the `sendmail` tag.

## Attributes

Both the `mime` and `boundry` tags have the same attributes:

- **encode=string**—MIME Content-Transfer-Encoding header, defaults to `base64`. Valid encoding options include `base64`, `quoted-printable`, `uuencode`, `x-uuencode`, `uue`, `x-uue`, and `7bit`. If the encode attribute is set to `7bit`, no encoding is done on the block and the data is assumed to be in a valid MIME format.
- **type=string**—MIME Content-Type header.
- **type_expr=string**—MIME Content-Type header as a variable expression. You cannot use both `type` and `type_expr`.

- **name=string**—MIME Content-Type header name.
- **name_expr=string**—MIME Content-Type header name as a variable expression. You cannot use both name and name_expr.
- **disposition=string**—MIME Content-Disposition header.
- **disposition_expr=string**—MIME Content-Disposition header as a variable expression. You cannot use both disposition and disposition_expr.
- **filename=string**—MIME Content-Disposition header filename.
- **filename_expr=string**—MIME Content-Disposition header filename as a variable expression. You cannot use both filename and filename_expr.
- **skip_expr=string**—A variable expression that if true, skips the block. You can use this attribute to selectively include MIME blocks.

## Examples

Sending a file attachment:

```
<dtml-sendmail>
To: <dtml-recipient>
Subject: Resume
<dtml-mime type="text/plain" encode="7bit">

Hi, please take a look at my resume.

<dtml-boundary type="application/octet-stream" disposition="attachment"
encode="base64" filename_expr="resume_file.getId()">
➥<dtml-var expr="resume_file.read()"></dtml-mime>
</dtml-sendmail>
```

## See Also

Python Library: mimetools (http://www.python.org/doc/current/lib/module-mimetools.html)

# *raise*: **Raises an Exception**

The raise tag raises an exception, mirroring the Python raise statement.

## Syntax

raise tag syntax:

```
<dtml-raise ExceptionName|ExceptionExpression>
</dtml-raise>
```

The raise tag is a block tag. It raises an exception. Exceptions can be an exception class or a string. The contents of the tag are passed as the error value.

## Examples

Raising a KeyError:

```
<dtml-raise KeyError></dtml-raise>
```

Raising an HTTP 404 error:

```
<dtml-raise NotFound>Web Page Not Found</dtml-raise>
```

## See Also

try tag

Python Tutorial: Errors and Exceptions
(http://www.python.org/doc/current/tut/node10.html)

Python Built-in Exceptions (http://www.python.org/doc/current/lib/
module-exceptions.html)

# *random*: DTML Pseudo-Random Number Functions

The random module provides pseudo-random number functions. With it, you can generate random numbers and select random elements from sequences. This module is a standard Python module.

## Functions

- **choice(seq)**—Chooses a random element from the non-empty sequence seq and returns it.
- **randint(a, b)**—Returns a random integer N such that a<=N<=b.
- **random()**—Returns the next random floating point number in the range [0.0…1.0).
- **seed(x, y, z)**—Initializes the random number generator from the integers x, y, and z. When the module is first imported, the random number is initialized using values derived from the current time.
- **uniform(a, b)**—Returns a random real number N such that a<=N<b.

## See Also

Python random module (http://www.python.org/doc/current/lib/
module-whrandom.html)

## *return*: Returns Data

The `return` tag stops executing DTML and returns data. It mirrors the Python `return` statement.

### Syntax

`return` tag syntax:

```
<dtml-return ReturnVariable|expr="ReturnExpression">
```

This stops execution of DTML and returns a variable or expression. The DTML output is not returned. Usually, a return expression is more useful than a return variable. Scripts largely make this tag obsolete.

### Examples

Returning a variable:

```
<dtml-return result>
```

Returning a Python dictionary:

```
<dtml-return expr="{'hi':200, 'lo':5}">
```

## *sendmail*: Sends Email with SMTP

The `sendmail` tag sends an email message using SMTP.

### Syntax

`sendmail` tag syntax:

```
<dtml sendmail>
</dtml-sendmail>
```

The `sendmail` tag is a block tag. It either requires a `mailhost` or an `smtphost` argument, but not both. The tag block is sent as an email message. The beginning of the block describes the email headers. The headers are separated from the body by a blank line. Alternately the `To`, `From`, and `Subject` headers can be set with tag arguments.

### Attributes

- **`mailhost`**—The name of a Zope MailHost object used to send email. You cannot specify both a mailhost and a smtphost.
- **`smtphost`**—The name of an SMTP server used to send email. You cannot specify both a mailhost and an smtphost.
- **`port`**—If the smtphost attribute is used, then the port attribute is used to specify a port number to connect to. If not specified, then port 25 is used.

- **mailto**—The recipient address or a list of recipient addresses separated by commas. This can also be specified with the To header.

- **mailfrom**—The sender address. This can also be specified with the From header.

- **subject**—The email subject. This can also be specified with the Subject header.

## Examples

Sending an email message using a mailhost:

```
<dtml-sendmail mailhost="mailhost">
To: <dtml-var recipient>
From: <dtml-var sender>
Subject: <dtml-var subject>

Dear <dtml-var recipient>,

You order number <dtml-var order_number> is ready.
Please pick it up at your soonest convenience.
</dtml-sendmail>
```

## See Also

RFC 821 (SMTP Protocol) (http://www.ietf.org/rfc/rfc0821.txt)

mime tag

# *sqlgroup*: Formats Complex SQL Expressions

The sqlgroup tag formats complex boolean SQL expressions. You can use it along with the sqltest tag to build dynamic SQL queries that tailor themselves to the environment. This tag is used in SQL methods.

## Syntax

sqlgroup tag syntax:

```
<dtml-sqlgroup>
[<dtml-or>]
[<dtml-and>]
...
</dtml-sqlgroup>
```

The sqlgroup tag is a block tag. It is divided into blocks with one or more optional or and and tags. sqlgroup tags can be nested to produce complex logic.

## Attributes

- **required=boolean**—Indicates whether the group is required. If it is not required and contains nothing, it is excluded from the DTML output.

- **`where=boolean`**—If true, includes the string "where". This is useful for the outer-most `sqlgroup` tag in an SQL `select` query.

## Examples

Sample use:

```
select * from employees
<dtml-sqlgroup where>
  <dtml-sqltest salary op=gt type=float optional>
<dtml-and>
  <dtml-sqltest first op=eq type=string multiple optional>
<dtml-and>
  <dtml-sqltest last  op=eq type=string multiple optional>
</dtml-sqlgroup>
```

If `first` is `Bob` and `last` is `Smith, McDonald`, it renders:

```
select * from employees
where
(first='Bob'
 and
 last in ('Smith', 'McDonald')
 )
```

If `salary` is 50000 and `last` is `Smith`, it renders:

```
select * from employees
where
(salary > 50000.0
 and
 last='Smith'
 )
```

Nested `sqlgroup` tags:

```
select * from employees
<dtml-sqlgroup where>
  <dtml-sqlgroup>
    <dtml-sqltest first op=like type=string>
  <dtml-and>
    <dtml-sqltest last op=like type=string>
  <dtml-sqlgroup>
<dtml-or>
  <dtml-sqltest salary op=gt type=float>
</dtml-sqlgroup>
```

Given sample arguments, this template renders to SQL like so:

```
select * form employees
where
(
  (
  name like 'A*'
  and
  last like 'Smith'
```

```
   )
 or
 salary > 20000.0
 )
```

## See Also

sqltest tag

# *sqltest*: Formats SQL Condition Tests

The sqltest tag inserts a condition test into SQL code. It tests a column against a variable. This tag is used in SQL methods.

## Syntax

sqltest tag syntax:

```
<dtml-sqltest Variable|expr="VariableExpression">
```

The sqltest tag is a singleton. It inserts a SQL condition test statement. It is used to build SQL queries. The sqltest tag correctly escapes the inserted variable. The named variable or variable expression is tested against a SQL column using the specified comparison operation.

## Attributes

- **type=string**—The type of the variable. Valid types include string, int, float, and nb. nb means non-blank string. The type attribute is required and is used to properly escape an inserted variable.

- **column=string**—The name of the SQL column to test against. This attribute defaults to the variable name.

- **multiple=boolean**—If true, then the variable might be a sequence of values to test the column against.

- **optional=boolean**—If true, then the test is optional, and it will not be rendered if the variable is empty or non-existent.

- **op=string**—The comparison operation. Valid comparisons include the following:

    - **eq**—equal to
    - **gt**—greater than
    - **lt**—less than
    - **ne**—not equal to
    - **ge**—greater than or equal to
    - **le**—less than or equal to

The comparison defaults to equal to. If the comparison is not recognized, it is used anyway. Thus, you can use comparisons, such as like.

## Examples

Basic use:

```
select * from employees
  where <dtml-sqltest name type="string">
```

If the name variable is Bob, then this renders:

```
select * from employees
  where name = 'Bob'
```

Multiple values:

```
select * from employees
  where <dtml-sqltest empid type=int multiple>
```

If the empid variable is (12,14,17), then this renders:

```
select * from employees
  where empid in (12, 14, 17)
```

## See Also

sqlgroup tag
sqlvar tag

# *sqlvar*: Inserts SQL Variables

The sqlvar tag safely inserts variables into SQL code. This tag is used in SQL methods.

## Syntax

sqlvar tag syntax:

```
<dtml-sqlvar Variable|expr="VariableExpression">
```

The sqlvar tag is a singleton. Like the var tag, the sqlvar tag looks up a variable and inserts it. Unlike the var tag, the formatting options are tailored for SQL code.

## Attributes

- **type=string**—The type of the variable. Valid types include string, int, float, and nb. nb means non-blank string. The type attribute is required and is used to properly escape an inserted variable.

- **optional=boolean**—If true, and the variable is null or non-existent, then nothing is inserted.

## Examples

Basic use:

```
select * from employees
  where name=<dtml-sqlvar name type="string">
```

This SQL quotes the name string variable.

## See Also

sqltest tag

# *string*: DTML String Functions

The string module provides string manipulation, conversion, and searching functions. It is a standard Python module.

## Functions

- **atof(s)**—Converts a string to a floating point number. The string must have the standard syntax for a floating point literal in Python, optionally preceded by a sign ("+" or "-"). Note, that this behaves identical to the built-in function float() when passed a string.

- **atoi(s [,base])**—Converts string s to an integer in the given base. The string must consist of one or more digits, optionally preceded by a sign ("+" or "-"). The base defaults to 10. If it is 0, a default base is chosen, depending on the leading characters of the string (after stripping the sign): "0x" or "0X" means 16, "0" means 8, anything else means 10. If base is 16, a leading "0x" or "0X" is always accepted, although not required.

- **atol(s, [,base])**—Converts string s to a long integer in the given base. The string must consist of one or more digits, optionally preceded by a sign ("+" or "-"). The base argument has the same meaning as it does for atoi(). A trailing "l" or "L" is not allowed, except if the base is 0.

- **capitalize(word)**—Capitalizes the first character of the argument.

- **capwords(s)**—Splits the argument into words using split(), capitalizes each word using capitalize(), and joins the capitalized words using join(). Note, that this replaces runs of white space characters with a single space and removes leading and trailing white space.

- **find(s, sub [,start [,end]])**—Returns the lowest index in s where the substring sub is found such that sub is wholly contained in s[start:end]. It returns a –1 on failure. Defaults for start, end, and interpretation of negative values are the same as for slices.

- **rfind(s, sub [,start [,end]])**—Similar to find(), however it finds the highest index.

- **index(s, sub [,start [,end]])**—Similar to find(), however it raises a ValueError when the substring is not found.

- **rindex(s, sub [,start [,end]])**—Similar to rfind(), however it raises a ValueError when the substring is not found.

- **count(s, sub [,start [,end]])**—Returns the number of (non-overlapping) occurrences of substring sub in string s[start:end]. Defaults for start, end, and interpretation of negative values are the same as for slices.

- **lower(s)**—Returns a copy of s, but with uppercase letters converted to lowercase.

- **makestrans(from, to)**—Returns a translation table suitable for passing to translate() that maps each character in from into the character at the same position in to. from and to must have the same length.

- **split(s, [,sep [,maxsplit]])**—Returns a list of the words of the string s. If the optional second argument sep is absent or None, the words are separated by arbitrary strings of white space characters (such as space, tab, newline, return, formfeed). If the second argument sep is present and not None, it specifies a string to be used as the word separator. The returned list will then have one more item than the number of non-overlapping occurrences of the separator in the string. The optional third argument maxsplit defaults to 0. If it is nonzero, at most a maxsplit number of splits occur, and the remainder of the string is returned as the final element of the list (thus, the list will have at most maxsplit+1 elements).

- **join(words [,sep])**—Concatenates a list or tuple of words with intervening occurrences of sep. The default value for sep is a single space character. It is always true that string.join(string.split(s, sep), sep) equals s.

- **lstrip(string)**—Returns a copy of s without leading white space characters.

- **rstrip(string)**—Returns a copy of s without trailing white space characters.

- **strip(string)**—Returns a copy of s without leading or trailing white space.

- **swapcase(s)**—Returns a copy of s with lowercase letters converted to uppercase and vice versa.

- **translate(s, table [,deletechars])**—Deletes all characters from s that are in deletechars (if present), and then translates the characters using table, which must be a 256-character string giving the translation for each character value and indexed by its ordinal.

- **upper(s)**—Returns a copy of string with lowercase letters converted to uppercase.

- **ljust(string, width)**—Left-justifies a string in a field of given width. Returns a string that is at least *width* characters wide created by padding the string with spaces until the given width. The string is never truncated.

- `rjust(string, width)`—Right-justifies a string in a field of given width. Returns a string that is at least *width* characters wide created by padding the string with spaces until the given width. The string is never truncated.

- `center(string, width)`—Centers a string in a field of given width. Returns a string that is at least *width* characters wide created by padding the string with spaces until the given width. The string is never truncated.

- `zfill(s, width)`—Pads a numeric string on the left with zero digits until the given width is reached. Strings starting with a sign are handled correctly.

- `replace(s, old, new [,maxsplit])`—Returns a copy of string s with all occurrences of substring old replaced by new. If the optional argument maxsplit is given, the first maxsplit occurrences are replaced.

## Attributes

- `digits`—The string 0123456789.
- `hexdigits`—The string 0123456789abcdefABCDEF.
- `letters`—The concatenation of the strings lowercase and uppercase described next.
- `lowercase`—A string containing all the characters that are considered lowercase letters. On most systems, this is the string abcdefghijklmnopqrstuvwxyz.
- `octdigits`—The string 01234567.
- `uppercase`—A string containing all the characters that are considered uppercase letters. On most systems, this is the string ABCDEFGHIJKLMNOPQRSTUVWXYZ.
- `whitespace`—A string containing all characters that are considered white space. On most systems, this includes the characters space, tab, linefeed, return, formfeed, and vertical tab.

## See Also

Python `string` module (`http://www.python.org/doc/current/lib/module-string.html`)

# *tree*: Inserts a Tree Widget

The `tree` tag displays a dynamic tree widget by querying Zope objects.

## Syntax

tree tag syntax:

```
<dtml-tree [VariableName|expr="VariableExpression"]>
</dtml-tree>
```

The `tree` tag is a block tag. It renders a dynamic tree widget in HTML. The root of the tree is given by variable name or expression if present. Otherwise, it defaults to the current object. The `tree` block is rendered for each tree node with the current node pushed onto the DTML namespace.

The tree state is set in HTTP cookies. Thus, for trees to work, cookies must be enabled. Also, you can only have one tree per page.

## Attributes

- **branches=string**—Finds tree branches by calling the named method. The default method is `tpValues`, which most Zope objects support.

- **branches_expr=string**—Finds tree branches by evaluating the expression.

- **id=string**—The name of a method or id to determine tree state. It defaults to `tpId`, which most Zope objects support. This attribute is for advanced use only.

- **url=string**—The name of a method or attribute to determine tree item URLs. It defaults to `tpURL`, which most Zope objects support. This attribute is for advanced use only.

- **leaves=string**—The name of a DTML document or method used to render nodes that do not have any children. Note: This document should begin with `<dtml-var standard_html_header>` and end with `<dtml-var standard_html_footer>` to ensure proper display in the tree.

- **header=string**—The name of a DTML document or method displayed *before* expanded nodes. If the header is not found, it is skipped.

- **footer=string**—The name of a DTML document or method displayed *after* expanded nodes. If the footer is not found, it is skipped.

- **nowrap=boolean**—If true, then rather than wrap, nodes can be truncated to fit available space.

- **sort=string**—Sorts the branches by the named attribute.

- **reverse**—Reverses the order of the branches.

- **assume_children=boolean**—Assumes that nodes have children. This is useful if fetching and querying child nodes is a costly process. This results in plus boxes being drawn next to all nodes.

- **single=boolean**—Allows only one branch to be expanded at a time. When you expand a new branch, any other expanded branches close.

- **skip_unauthorized**—Skips nodes that the user is unauthorized to see, rather than raising an error.

- **urlparam=string**—A query string that is included in the expanding and contracting widget links. This attribute is for advanced use only.

## Tag Variables

- **`tree-item-expanded`**—True if the current node is expanded.
- **`tree-item-url`**—The URL of the current node.
- **`tree-root-url`**—The URL of the root node.
- **`tree-level`**—The depth of the current node. Top-level nodes have a depth of zero.
- **`tree-colspan`**—The number of levels deep the tree is being rendered. This variable along with the `tree-level` variable can be used to calculate table rows and colspan settings when inserting table rows into the tree table.
- **`tree-state`**—The tree state expressed as a list of ids and sublists of ids. This variable is for advanced use only.

## Tag Control Variables

You can control the tree tag by setting these variables.

- *expand_all*—If this variable is true, then the entire tree is expanded.
- *collapse_all*—If this variable is true, then the entire tree is collapsed.

## Examples

The following displays a tree rooted in the current object:

```
<dtml-tree>
  <dtml-var title_or_id>
</dtml-tree>
```

The following displays a tree rooted in another object using a custom branches method:

```
<dtml-tree expr="folder.object" branches="objectValues">
  Node id : <dtml-var getId>
</dtml-tree>
```

# *try*: **Handles Exceptions**

The `try` tag enables exception handling in DTML, mirroring the Python `try`/`except` and `try`/`finally` constructs.

## Syntax

The `try` tag has two different syntaxes, `try`/`except`/`else` and `try`/`finally`.

`try`/`except`/`else` syntax:

```
<dtml-try>
<dtml-except [ExceptionName] [ExceptionName]...>
...
[<dtml-else>]
</dtml-try>
```

The `try` tag encloses a block in which exceptions can be caught and handled. There can be one or more `except` tags that handle zero or more exceptions. If an `except` tag does not specify an exception, then it handles all exceptions.

When an exception is raised, control jumps to the first `except` tag that handles the exception. If there is no `except` tag to handle the exception, then the exception is raised normally.

If no exception is raised, and there is an `else` tag, then the `else` tag is executed after the body of the `try` tag.

The `except` and `else` tags are optional.

`try/finally` syntax:

```
<dtml-try>
<dtml-finally>
</dtml-try>
```

The `finally` tag cannot be used in the same `try` block as the `except` and `else` tags. If there is a `finally` tag, its block is executed whether or not an exception is raised in the `try` block.

## Attributes

- **except**—Zero or more exception names. If no exceptions are listed, then the `except` tag handles all exceptions.

## Tag Variables

Inside the `except` block these variables are defined:

- *error_type*—The exception type.

- *error_value*—The exception value.

- *error_tb*—The traceback.

## Examples

Catching a math error:

```
<dtml-try>
<dtml-var expr="1/0">
<dtml-except ZeroDivisionError>
You tried to divide by zero.
</dtml-try>
```

Returning information about the handled exception:

```
<dtml-try>
<dtml-call dangerousMethod>
<dtml-except>
An error occurred.
Error type: <dtml-var error_type>
```

```
Error value: <dtml-var error_value>
</dtml-try>
```

Using `finally` to make sure to perform clean up regardless of whether or not an error is raised:

```
<dtml-call acquireLock>
<dtml-try>
<dtml-call someMethod>
<dtml-finally>
<dtml-call releaseLock>
</dtml-try>
```

## See Also

`raise` tag

Python Tutorial: Errors and Exceptions
(`http://www.python.org/doc/current/tut/node10.html`)

Python Built-in Exceptions (`http://www.python.org/doc/current/lib/module-exceptions.html`)

# *unless*: Tests a Condition

The `unless` tag provides a shortcut for testing negative conditions. For more complete condition testing, use the `if` tag.

## Syntax

`unless` tag syntax:

```
<dtml-unless ConditionVariable|expr-"ConditionExpression">
</dtml-unless>
```

The `unless` tag is a block tag. If the condition variable or expression evaluates to false, then the contained block is executed. Like the `if` tag, variables that are not present are considered false.

## Examples

Testing a variable:

```
<dtml-unless testMode>
  <dtml-call dangerousOperation>
</dtml-unless>
```

The block is executed if `testMode` does not exist, or exists but is false.

## See Also

`if` tag

## *var*: Inserts a Variable

The var tag enables you to insert variables into DTML output.

### Syntax

var tag syntax:

```
<dtml-var Variable|expr="Expression">
```

The var tag is a singleton tag. The var tag finds a variable by searching the DTML namespace, which usually consists of the current object, the current object's containers, and finally, the Web request. If the variable is found, it is inserted into the DTML output. If it is not found, Zope raises an error.

var tag entity syntax:

```
&dtml-variableName;
```

Entity syntax is a shortcut that inserts and HTML quotes the variable. It is useful when inserting variables into HTML tags.

var tag entity syntax with attributes:

```
&dtml.attribute1[.attribute2]...-variableName;
```

To a limited degree, you can specify attributes with the entity syntax. You can include zero or more attributes delimited by periods. You cannot provide arguments for attributes using the entity syntax. If you provide zero or more attributes, then the variable is not automatically HTML quoted. Thus, you can avoid HTML quoting with this syntax, `&dtml.-variableName;`.

### Attributes

- **html_quote**—Converts characters that have special meaning in HTML to HTML character entities.

- **missing=string**—Specifies a default value in case Zope cannot find the variable.

- **fmt=string**—Formats a variable. Zope provides a few built-in formats, including C-style format strings. For more information on C-style format strings, see the Python Library Reference (`http://www.python.org/doc/current/lib/type-sseq-strings.html`). If the format string is not a built-in format, then it is assumed to be a method of the object, and it is called.

  - **whole-dollars**—Formats the variable as dollars.

  - **dollars-and-cents**—Formats the variable as dollars and cents.

  - **collection-length**—The length of the variable, assuming it is a sequence.

  - **structured-text**—Formats the variable as Structured Text. For more information on Structured Text, see the Structured Text How-To (`http://www.zope.org/Members/millejoh/structuredText`) at the Zope.org Web site.

- **null=string**—A default value to use if the variable is None.

- **lower**—Converts uppercase letters to lowercase.
- **upper**—Converts lowercase letters to uppercase.
- **capitalize**—Capitalizes the first character of the inserted word.
- **spacify**—Changes underscores in the inserted value to spaces.
- **thousands_commas**—Inserts commas every three digits to the left of a decimal point in values containing numbers, for example `12000` becomes `12,000`.
- **url**—Inserts the URL of the object by calling its `absolute_url` method.
- **url_quote**—Converts characters that have special meaning in URLs to HTML character entities.
- **url_quote_plus**—URL quotes character, such as `url_quote`, but it also converts spaces to plus signs.
- **sql_quote**—Converts single quotes to pairs of single quotes. This is needed to safely include values in SQL strings.
- **newline_to_br**—Converts newlines (including carriage returns) to HTML break tags.
- **size=arg**—Truncates the variable at the given length (Note: If a space occurs in the second half of the truncated string, then the string is further truncated to the right-most space).
- **etc=arg**—Specifies a string to add to the end of a string that has been truncated (by setting the `size` attribute listed earlier). By default, this is ...

## Examples

Inserting a simple variable into a document:

```
<dtml-var standard_html_header>
```

Truncation:

```
<dtml-var colors size=10 etc=", etc.">
```

produces the following output if `colors` is the string `red yellow green`:

```
red yellow, etc.
```

C-style string formatting:

```
<dtml-var expr="23432.2323" fmt="%.2f">
```

renders to

```
23432.23
```

Inserting a variable link inside an HTML A tag with the entity syntax:

```
<a href="&dtml-link;">Link</a>
```

Inserting a link to a document doc using entity syntax with attributes:

```
<a href="&dtml.url-doc;"><dtml-var doc fmt="title_or_id"></a>
```

This creates an HTML link to an object using its URL and title. This example calls the object's `absolute_url` method for the URL (using the `url` attribute) and its `title_or_id` method for the title.

# *with*: Controls DTML Variable Look Up

The `with` tag pushes an object onto the DTML namespace. Variables are looked up in the pushed object first.

## Syntax

with tag syntax:

```
<dtml-with Variable|expr="Expression">
</dtml-with>
```

The `with` tag is a block tag. It pushes the named variable or variable expression onto the DTML namespace for the duration of the `with` block. Thus, names are looked up in the pushed object first.

## Attributes

- **only**—Limits the DTML namespace to only include the namespace defined in the `with` tag.

- **mapping**—Indicates that the variable or expression is a mapping object. This ensures that variables are looked up correctly in the mapping object.

## Examples

Looking up a variable in the REQUEST:

```
<dtml-with REQUEST only>
  <dtml-if id>
    <dtml-var id>
  <dtml-else>
    'id' was not in the request.
  </dtml-if>
</dtml-with>
```

Pushing the first child on the DTML namespace:

```
<dtml-with expr="objectValues()[0]">
  First child's id: <dtml-var id>
</dtml-with>
```

## See Also

let tag

# B

# API Reference

$\mathbf{T}$ HIS APPENDIX DESCRIBES THE INTERFACES of the most common set of basic Zope objects. This reference is useful while writing DTML, Perl, and Python scripts that create and manipulate Zope objects.

## Class *AuthenticatedUser*

This interface needs to be supported by objects that are returned by user validation and are used for access control.

### *getUserName()*

Returns the name of a user.

- **Permission**—Always available.

### *getId()*

Gets the ID of the user. The ID can be used, at least in Python, to get the user from the user's UserDatabase.

- **Permission**—Python only.

### *getDatabasePath()*

Gets a physical path to the user's UserDatabase. A traversal facility can be used to get the user database from the path returned by this method.

- **Permission**—Python only.

### *hasRole(object, roles)*

Returns a value that is true if the user has the given roles on the given object; otherwise, it returns a false value.

- **Permission**—Always available.

### *getRoles(object)*

Returns a list of the roles the user has on the given object.

- **Permission**—Always available.

## Class *DTMLDocument(ObjectManagerItem, PropertyManager)*

A DTML document is a Zope object that contains and executes DTML code. It is useful to represent Web pages.

### *manage_edit(data, title)*

Changes the DTML document, replacing its contents with `data`, and changing its `title`. The `data` argument can be a file object or a string.

- **Permission**—Change DTML documents.

### *document_src()*

Returns the unrendered source text of the DTML document.

- **Permission**—View management screens.

### *__call__(client=None, REQUEST={}, RESPONSE=None, **kw)*

Calling a DTML document causes the document to interpret the DTML code that it contains. The method returns the result of the interpretation, which can be any kind of object.

To accomplish its task, DTML documents often need to resolve various names into objects. For example, when the code `<;dtml-var spam>;` is executed, the DTML engine tries to resolve the name `spam`.

To resolve names, the document must be passed a namespace in which to look them up. This can be done several ways:

- **By passing a `client` object**—If the argument `client` is passed, then names are looked up as attributes on the argument.

- **By passing a `REQUEST` mapping**—If the argument `REQUEST` is passed, then names are looked up as items on the argument. If the object is not a mapping, a TypeError is raised when a name lookup is attempted.

- **By passing keyword arguments**—Names and their values can be passed as keyword arguments to the document.

The namespace given to a DTML document is the composite of these three methods. You can pass any number of them or none at all. Names are looked up first in the keyword arguments, then in the client, and finally in the mapping.

A DTML document implicitly passes itself as a `client` argument, in addition to the specified client, so names are looked up in the DTML document itself.

Passing in a namespace to a DTML document is often referred to as providing the document with a *context*.

DTML documents can be called three ways.

## From DTML

A DTML document can be called from another DTML method or document:

```
<dtml-var standard_html_header>
  <dtml-var aDTMLDocument>
<dtml-var standard_html_footer>
```

In this example, the document aDTMLDocument is being called from another DTML object by name. The calling method passes the value this as the client argument, and it passes the current DTML namespace as the REQUEST argument. The preceding code is identical to the following use in a DTML Python expression:

```
<dtml-var standard_html_header>
  <dtml-var "aDTMLDocument(_.None, _)">
<dtml-var standard_html_footer>
```

## From Python

Products, external methods, and scripts can call a DTML document in the same way they call a DTML document from a Python expression in DTML (as shown in the preceding example).

## By the Publisher

When the URL of a DTML document is fetched from Zope, the DTML document is called by the publisher. The REQUEST object is passed as the second argument to the document.

- **Permission**—View.

## *get_size()*

Returns the size of the unrendered source text of the DTML document in bytes.

- **Permission**—View.

### ObjectManager Constructor

*manage_addDocument(id, title)*

Adds a DTML document to the current ObjectManager.

# Class *DTMLMethod(ObjectManagerItem)*

A DTML method is a Zope object that contains and executes DTML code. It can act as a template to display other objects. It can also hold small pieces of content, which are inserted into other DTML documents or DTML methods.

The DTML method's id is available through the `document_id` variable, and the title is available through the `document_title` variable.

## *manage_edit(data, title)*

Changes the DTML method, replacing its contents with `data`, and changes its `title`.

The `data` argument can be a file object or a string.

- **Permission**—Change DTML methods.

## *document_src()*

Returns the unrendered source text of the DTML method.

- **Permission**—View management screens.

## *__call__(client=None, REQUEST={}, **kw)*

Calling a DTML method causes the method to interpret the DTML code that it contains. The method returns the result of the interpretation, which can be any kind of object.

To accomplish its task, DTML method often needs to resolve various names into objects. For example, when the code `<;dtml-var spam>;` is executed, the DTML engine tries to resolve the name `spam`.

To resolve names, the method must be passed a namespace in which to look them up. This can be done several ways:

- **By passing a `client` object**—If the argument `client` is passed, then names are looked up as attributes on the argument.

- **By passing a `REQUEST` mapping**—If the argument `REQUEST` is passed, then names are looked up as items on the argument. If the object is not a mapping, a TypeError is raised when a name lookup is attempted.
- **By passing keyword arguments**—Names and their values can be passed as keyword arguments to the method.

The namespace given to a DTML method is the composite of these three methods. You can pass any number of them or none at all. Names are looked up first in the keyword argument, next in the client, and finally in the mapping.

Unlike DTML documents, DTML methods do not look up names in their own instance dictionary.

Passing in a namespace to a DTML method is often referred to as providing the method with a *context*.

DTML methods can be called three ways:

### From DTML

A DTML method can be called from another DTML method or document:

```
<dtml-var standard_html_header>
  <dtml-var aDTMLMethod>
<dtml-var standard_html_footer>
```

In this example, the method aDTMLMethod is being called from another DTML object by name. The calling method passes the value this as the client argument, and it passes the current DTML namespace as the REQUEST argument. The preceding code is identical to the following use in a DTML Python expression:

```
<dtml-var standard_html_header>
  <dtml-var "aDTMLMethod(_.None, _)">
<dtml-var standard_html_footer>
```

### From Python

Products, external methods, and scripts can call a DTML method in the same way they call a DTML method from a Python expression in DTML (as shown in the preceding example).

### By the Publisher

When the URL of a DTML method is fetched from Zope, the DTML method is called by the publisher. The REQUEST object is passed as the second argument to the method.

- **Permission**—View.

## *get_size()*

Returns the size of the unrendered source text of the DTML method in bytes.

- **Permission**—View.

### ObjectManager Constructor

*manage_addDTMLMethod(id, title)*

Adds a DTML method to the current ObjectManager.

# Class *DateTime*

The DateTime object provides an interface for working with dates and times in various formats. DateTime also provides methods for calendar operations, date and time arithmetic, and formatting.

DateTime objects represent instants in time and provide interfaces for controlling its representation without affecting the absolute value of the object.

DateTime objects can be created from a wide variety of string or numeric data, or they can be computed from other DateTime objects. DateTimes support the capability to convert their representations to many major time zones, as well as the capability to create a DateTime object in the context of a given time zone.

DateTime objects provide partial numerical behavior:

- Two DateTime objects can be subtracted to obtain a time, in days, between the two.

- A DateTime object and a positive or negative number can be added to obtain a new DateTime object, which is the given number of days later than the input DateTime object.

- A positive or negative number and a DateTime object can be added to obtain a new DateTime object, which is the given number of days later than the input DateTime object.

- A positive or negative number can be subtracted from a DateTime object to obtain a new DateTime object, which is the given number of days earlier than the input DateTime object.

DateTime objects can be converted to the integer, long, or float number of days since January 1, 1901 using the standard `int`, `long`, and `float` functions. (Compatibility note: `int`, `long`, and `float` return the number of days since 1901 in GMT rather than local machine time zones). DateTime objects also provide access to their value in a float format, which can be used with the Python time module, provided that the value of the object falls in the range of the epoch-based time module.

A DateTime object should be considered immutable—all conversion and numeric operations return a new DateTime object rather than modify the current object.

A DateTime object always maintains its value as an absolute UTC time, and this is represented in the context of the time zone based on the arguments used to create the object. A DateTime object's methods return values based on the time zone context.

Note that in all cases the local machine time zone is used for representation if no time zone is specified.

DateTimes can be created with zero to seven arguments.

- If the function is called with no arguments, then the current date/time is returned and represented in the time zone of the local machine.

- If the function is invoked with a single string argument, which is a recognized time zone name, an object representing the current time is returned and represented in the specified time zone.

- If the function is invoked with a single string argument representing a valid date/time, an object representing that date/time is returned. As a general rule, any date/time representation that is recognized and unambiguous to a resident of North America is acceptable. (The reason for this qualification is that in North America, a date such as 2/1/1994 is interpreted as February 1, 1994, however in some parts of the world, it is interpreted as January 2, 1994.) A date/time string consists of two components: a date component and an optional time component, separated by one or more spaces. If the time component is omitted, 12:00am is assumed. Any recognized time zone name specified as the final element of the date/time string is used for computing the date/time value. (If you create a DateTime with the string `Mar 9, 1997 1:45pm US/Pacific`, the value is essentially the same as if you had captured `time.time()` at the specified date and time on a machine in that time zone):

```
e=DateTime("US/Eastern")
# returns current date/time, represented in US/Eastern.

x=DateTime("1997/3/9 1:45pm")
# returns specified time, represented in local machine zone.

y=DateTime("Mar 9, 1997 13:45:00")
# y is equal to x
```

The date component consists of year, month, and day values. The year value must be a one-, two-, or four-digit integer. If a one- or two-digit year is used, the year is assumed to be in the twentieth century. The month can be an integer, from 1 to 12, a month name, or a month abbreviation, where a period can optionally follow the abbreviation. The day must be an integer from 1 to the number of days in the month. The year, month, and day values can be separated by periods, hyphens, forward slashes, or spaces. Extra spaces are permitted around the delimiters. Year, month, and day values can be given in any order as long as it is possible to distinguish the components. If all three components are numbers less than 13, then a month-day-year ordering is assumed.

The time component consists of hour, minute, and second values separated by colons. The hour value must be an integer between 0 and 23, inclusively. The minute value must be an integer between 0 and 59, inclusively. The second value can be an integer value between 0 and 59.999, inclusively.

The second value, or both the minute and second values, can be omitted. The time might be followed by am or pm in uppercase or lowercase, in which case, a 12-hour clock is assumed.

- If the DateTime function is invoked with a single numeric argument, the number is assumed to be a floating point value, such as that returned by time.time(). A DateTime object is returned that represents the gmt value of the time.time() float represented in the local machine's time zone.

- If the function is invoked with two numeric arguments, then the first is taken to be an integer year and the second argument is taken to be an offset in days from the beginning of the year in the context of the local machine time zone. The date/time value returned is the given offset number of days from the beginning of the given year represented in the time zone of the local machine. The offset can be positive or negative. Two-digit years are assumed to be in the twentieth century.

- If the function is invoked with two arguments—the first argument being a float representing a number of seconds past the epoch in GMT, such as those returned by time.time(), and the second argument being a string naming a recognized time zone—then a DateTime with a value of that GMT time is returned and represented in the given time zone:

```
import time
t=time.time()

now_east=DateTime(t,'US/Eastern')
# Time t represented as US/Eastern

now_west=DateTime(t,'US/Pacific')
# Time t represented as US/Pacific

# now_east == now_west
# only their representations are different
```

- If the function is invoked with three or more numeric arguments, then the first is taken to be an integer year, the second is taken to be an integer month, and the third is taken to be an integer day. If the combination of values is not valid, then a DateTimeError is raised. Two-digit years are assumed to be in the twentieth century. The fourth, fifth, and sixth arguments specify a time in hours, minutes, and seconds—hours and minutes should be positive integers and seconds is a positive floating point value—all of which default to zero if not given. An optional string can be given as the final argument to indicate time zone (the effect of this is as if you had taken the value of time.time() at that time on a machine in the specified timezone).

If a string argument passed to the DateTime constructor cannot be parsed, it raises a DateTime.SyntaxError. Invalid date, time, or time zone components raise a DateTime.DateTimeError.

The module function `Timezones()` returns a list of the time zones recognized by the DateTime module. The recognition of time zone names is not case-sensitive.

## *strftime(format)*

Returns the date/time string formatted according to `format`.

See Python's time.strftime (`http://www.python.org/doc/current/lib/module-time.html`) function.

## *dow()*

Returns the integer day of the week, where Sunday is 0.

- **Permission**—Always available.

## *aCommon()*

Returns a string representing the object's value in the format: `Mar 1, 1997 1:45 pm`.

- **Permission**—Always available

## *h_12()*

Returns the 12-hour clock representation of the hour.

- **Permission**—Always available.

## *Mon_()*

Compatibility: see `pMonth`.

- **Permission**—Always available.

## *HTML4()*

Returns the object in the format used in the HTML 4.0 specification, which is one of the standard forms in ISO8601.

For more information, see HTML 4.0 specification (`http://www.w3.org/TR/NOTE-datetime`).

Dates are output as: YYYY-MM-DDTHH:MM:SSZ where T and Z are literal characters. The time is in UTC.

- **Permission**—Always available.

## *greaterThanEqualTo(t)*

Compares this DateTime object to another DateTime object or to a floating point number, such as that which is returned by the Python time module. It returns true if the object represents a date/time greater than or equal to the specified DateTime or time module style time. It is revised to give more correct results through comparison of long integer milliseconds.

- **Permission**—Always available.

## *dayOfYear()*

Returns the day of the year in context of the time zone representation of the object.

- **Permission**—Always available.

## *lessThan(t)*

Compares this DateTime object to another DateTime object or to a floating point number, such as that which is returned by the Python time module. It returns true if the object represents a date/time less than the specified DateTime or time module style time. It's revised to give more correct results through comparison of long integer milliseconds.

- **Permission**—Always available.

## *AMPM()*

Returns the time string for an object to the nearest second.

- **Permission**—Always available.

## *isCurrentHour()*

Returns true if this object represents a date/time that falls within the current hour in the context of this object's time zone representation.

- **Permission**—Always available.

## *Month()*

Returns the full month name.

- **Permission**—Always available.

## *mm()*

Returns the month as a 2-digit string.

- **Permission**—Always available.

## ampm()

Returns the appropriate time modifier (am or pm).

- **Permission**—Always available.


## hour()

Returns the 24-hour clock representation of the hour.

- **Permission**—Always available.


## aCommonZ()

Returns a string representing the object's value in the format: `Mar 1, 1997 1:45 pm US/Eastern`.

- **Permission**—Always available.


## Day_()

Compatibility: see `pDay`.

- **Permission**—Always available.


## pCommon()

Returns a string representing the object's value in the format: `Mar. 1, 1997 1:45 pm`.

- **Permission**— Always available.


## minute()

Returns the minute.

- **Permission**—Always available.


## day()

Returns the integer day.

- **Permission**—Always available.


## earliestTime()

Returns a new DateTime object that represents the earliest possible time (in whole seconds), that still falls within the current object's day, in the object's time zone context.

- **Permission**—Always available.

### *Date()*

Returns the date string for the object.

- **Permission**—Always available.

### *Time()*

Returns the time string for an object to the nearest second.

- **Permission**—Always available.

### *isFuture()*

Returns true if this object represents a date/time later than the time of the call.

- **Permission**—Always available.

### *greaterThan(t)*

Compares this DateTime object to another DateTime object or to a floating point number, such as that which is returned by the Python time module. It returns true if the object represents a date/time greater than the specified DateTime or time module style time. It's revised to give more correct results through comparison of long integer milliseconds.

- **Permission**—Always available.

### *TimeMinutes()*

Returns the time string for an object not showing seconds.

- **Permission**—Always available.

### *yy()*

Returns the calendar year as a 2-digit string.

- **Permission**—Always available.

### *isCurrentDay()*

Returns true if this object represents a date/time that falls within the current day in the context of this object's time zone representation.

- **Permission**—Always available.

## dd()

Returns the day as a 2-digit string.

- **Permission**—Always available.

## rfc822()

Returns the date in RFC 822 format.

- **Permission**—Always available.

## isLeapYear()

Returns true if the current year (in the context of the object's time zone) is a leap year.

- **Permission**—Always available.

## fCommon()

Returns a string representing the object's value in the format: March 1, 1997 1:45 pm.

- **Permission**—Always available.

## isPast()

Returns true if this object represents a date/time earlier than the time of the call.

- **Permission**—Always available.

## fCommonZ()

Returns a string representing the object's value in the format: March 1, 1997 1:45 pm US/Eastern.

- **Permission**—Always available.

## timeTime()

Returns the date/time as a floating point number in UTC in the format used by the Python time module. Note that it is possible to create date/time values with DateTime that have no meaningful value to the time module.

- **Permission**—Always available.

## *toZone(z)*

Returns a DateTime with the value as the current object represented in the indicated time zone.

- **Permission**—Always available.

## *lessThanEqualTo(t)*

Compares this DateTime object to another DateTime object or to a floating point number, such as that which is returned by the Python time module. It returns true if the object represents a date/time less than or equal to the specified DateTime or time module style time. It's revised to give more correct results through comparison of long integer milliseconds.

- **Permission**—Always available.

## *Mon()*

Compatibility: see `aMonth`.

- **Permission**—Always available.

## *parts()*

Returns a tuple containing the calendar year, month, day, hour, minute, second, and time zone of the object.

- **Permission**—Always available.

## *isCurrentYear()*

Returns true if this object represents a date/time that falls within the current year in the context of this object's time zone representation.

- **Permission**—Always available.

## *PreciseAMPM()*

Returns the time string for the object.

- **Permission**—Always available.

## *AMPMMinutes()*

Returns the time string for an object not showing seconds.

- **Permission**—Always available.

### equalTo(t)

Compares this DateTime object to another DateTime object or to a floating point number, such as that which is returned by the Python time module. It returns true if the object represents a date/time equal to the specified DateTime or time module style time. It's revised to give more correct results through comparison of long integer milliseconds.

- **Permission**—Always available.

### pDay()

Returns the abbreviated (with period) name of the day of the week.

- **Permission**—Always available.

### notEqualTo(t)

Compares this DateTime object to another DateTime object or to a floating point number, such as that which is returned by the Python time module. It returns true if the object represents a date/time not equal to the specified DateTime or time module style time. It's revised to give more correct results through comparison of long integer milliseconds.

- **Permission**—Always available.

### h_24()

Returns the 24-hour clock representation of the hour.

- **Permission**—Always available.

### pCommonZ()

Returns a string representing the object's value in the format: `Mar, 1, 1997 1:45 pm US/Eastern`.

- **Permission**—Always available.

### isCurrentMonth()

Returns true if this object represents a date/time that falls within the current month in the context of this object's timezone representation.

- **Permission**—Always available.

## *DayOfWeek()*

Compatibility: see `aDay`.

- **Permission**—Always available.

## *latestTime()*

Returns a new DateTime object that represents the latest possible time (in whole seconds) that still falls within the current object's day in the object's time zone context.

- **Permission**—Always available.

## *dow_1()*

Returns the integer day of the week, where Sunday is 1.

- **Permission**—Always available.

## *timezone()*

Returns the time zone in which the object is represented.

- **Permission**—Always available.

## *year()*

Returns the calendar year of the object.

- **Permission**—Always available.

## *PreciseTime()*

Returns the time string for the object.

- **Permission**—Always available.

## *ISO()*

Returns the object in ISO standard format.
Dates are output as: YYYY-MM-DD HH:MM:SS

- **Permission**—Always available.

## *millis()*

Returns the millisecond since the epoch in GMT.

- **Permission**—Always available.

## second()

Returns the second.

- **Permission**—Always available.

## month()

Returns the month of the object as an integer.

- **Permission**—Always available.

## pMonth()

Returns the abbreviated (with period) month name.

- **Permission**—Always available.

## aMonth()

Returns the abbreviated month name.

- **Permission**—Always available.

## isCurrentMinute()

Returns true if this object represents a date/time that falls within the current minute in the context of this object's time zone representation.

- **Permission**—Always available.

## Day()

Returns the full name of the day of the week.

- **Permission**—Always available.

## aDay()

Returns the abbreviated name of the day of the week.

- **Permission**—Always available.

# Class *ExternalMethod*

Web-callable functions that encapsulate external Python functions.

The function is defined in an external file. This file is treated like a module, but it is not a module. It is not imported directly, but rather it is read and evaluated. The file must reside in the Extensions subdirectory of the Zope installation, or in an Extensions subdirectory of a product directory.

Due to the way external methods are loaded, it is not currently possible to import Python modules that reside in the Extensions directory. It is possible to import modules found in the lib/python directory of the Zope installation, or in packages in the lib/python directory.

### *manage_edit(title, module, function, REQUEST=None)*

Changes the external method.

See the description of `manage_addExternalMethod` for a description of the arguments `module` and `function`.

Note, that calling `manage_edit` causes the module to be effectively reloaded. This is useful during debugging to see the effects of changes, but it can lead to problems with functions that rely on shared global data.

### *__call__(*args, **kw)*

Calls the external method.

Calling an external method is roughly equivalent to calling the original function from Python. Positional and keyword parameters can be passed as usual. Note, however, that unlike the case of a normal Python method, the `self` argument must be passed explicitly. An exception to this rule is made if:

- The supplied number of arguments is one less than the required number of arguments.
- The name of the function's first argument is `self`.

In this case, the URL parent of the object is supplied as the first argument.

## ObjectManager Constructor

### *manage_addExternalMethod(id, title, module, function)*

Adds an external method to an `ObjectManager`. In addition to the standard object-creation arguments, `id` and `title`, the following arguments are defined:

- **function**—The name of the Python function. This can be an ordinary Python function or a bound method.
- **module**—The name of the file containing the function's definition.

The module normally resides in the Extensions directory, however, the filename might have a prefix of `product.`, indicating that it should be found in a product directory.

For example, if the module is `ACMEWidgets.foo`, then an attempt is first made to use the file `lib/python/Products/ACMEWidgets/Extensions/foo.py`. If this fails, then the file `Extensions/ACMEWidgets.foo.py` is used.

# Class *File(ObjectManagerItem, PropertyManager)*

A File is a Zope object that contains file content. A File object can be used to upload or download file information with Zope.

Using a File object in Zope is easy. The most common use is to display the contents of a File object in a Web page. This is done by referencing the object from DTML, as follows:

```
<dtml-var standard_html_header>
  <dtml-var FileObject>
<dtml-var standard_html_footer>
```

A more complex example is presenting the File object for download by the user. The next example displays a link to every File object in a folder for the user to download:

```
<dtml-var standard_html_header>
<ul>
  <dtml-in "ObjectValues('File')">
    <li><a href="<dtml-var absolute_url>"><dtml-var
    id></a></li>
  </dtml-in>
</ul>
<dtml-var standard_html_footer>
```

In this example, the `absolute_url` method and `id` are used to create a list of HTML hyperlinks to all the File objects in the current ObjectManager.

Also see ObjectManager for details on the `objectValues` method.

## getSize()

Returns the size of the file in bytes.

- **Permission**—View.

## update_data(data, content_type=None, size=None)

Updates the contents of the file with `data`.

The `data` argument must be a string. If `content_type` is not provided, then a content type is not set. If size is not provided, then the size of the file is computed from `data`.

- **Permission**—Python only.

## getContentType()

Returns the content type of the file.

- **Permission**—View.

### ObjectManager Constructor

*manage_addFile(id, file="", title="", precondition="", content_type="")*

Adds a new File object.

Creates a new File object `id` with the contents of `file`.

# Class *Folder(ObjectManagerItem, ObjectManager, PropertyManager)*

A folder is a generic container object in Zope.

Folders are the most common ObjectManager subclass in Zope.

### ObjectManager Constructor

*manage_addFolder(id, title)*

Adds a folder to the current ObjectManager.

- **Permission**—Add Folders.

# Class *Image(File)*

An Image is a Zope object that contains image content. An Image object can be used to upload or download image information with Zope.

Image objects have two properties that define their dimension, `height` and `width`. These are calculated when the image is uploaded. For image types that Zope does not understand, these properties might be undefined.

Using an Image object in Zope is easy. The most common use is to display the contents of an Image object in a Web page. This is done by referencing the object from DTML:

```
<dtml-var standard_html_header>
  <dtml-var ImageObject>
<dtml-var standard_html_footer>
```

This generates an HTML IMG tag referencing the URL to the image. This is equivalent to:

```
<dtml-var standard_html_header>
  <dtml-with ImageObject>
    <img src="<dtml-var absolute_url>">
  </dtml-with>
<dtml-var standard_html_footer>
```

You can control the image display more precisely with the `tag` method. For example:

```
<dtml-var "ImageObject.tag(border=5, align=left)">
```

*tag(height=None, width=None, alt=None, scale=0, xscale=0,*
*yscale=0, \*\*args)*

This method returns a string that contains an HTML IMG tag reference to the image.

Optionally, the `height`, `width`, `alt`, `scale`, `xscale`, and `yscale` arguments can be provided, which are turned into HTML IMG tag attributes. Note, `height` and `width` are provided by default, and `alt` comes from the `title_or_id` method.

Keyword arguments can be provided to support other or future IMG tag attributes. The one exception to this is the HTML Cascading Style Sheet tag `class`. Because the word `class` is a reserved keyword in Python, you must instead use the keyword argument `css_class`. This is turned into a `class` HTML tag attribute on the rendered `img` tag.

- **Permission**—View.

## ObjectManager Constructor

*manage_addImage(id, file, title="", precondition="", content_type="")*

Adds a new Image object.

Creates a new Image object `id` with the contents of `file`.

# Class *MailHost*

MailHost objects work as adapters to *Simple Mail Transfer Protocol* (SMTP) servers. MailHosts are used by DTML `sendmail` tags to find the proper host to deliver mail to.

*send(messageText, mto=None, mfrom=None, subject=None,*
*encode=None)*

Sends an email message. The arguments are

- `messageText`—The body of the mail message.
- `mto`—A string or list of recipient(s) of the message.
- `mfrom`—The address of the message sender.
- `subject`—The subject of the message.
- `encode`—The rfc822 defined encoding of the message. The default of `None` means no encoding is done. Valid values are `base64`, `quoted-printable`, and `uuencode`.

## ObjectManager Constructor

*manage_addMailHost(id, title="", smtp_host=None, localhost=localhost,*
*smtp_port=25, timeout=1.0)*

Adds a MailHost object to an ObjectManager.

# Class *ObjectManager*

An ObjectManager contains other Zope objects. The contained objects are ObjectManagerItems.

To create an object inside an ObjectManager, use `manage_addProduct`:

```
self.manage_addProduct['OFSP'].manage_addFolder(id, title)
```

In DTML this would be

```
<dtml-call "manage_addProduct['OFSP'].manage_addFolder(id, title)">
```

These examples create a new folder inside the current ObjectManager.

`manage_addProduct` is a mapping that provides access to product constructor methods. It is indexed by product `id`.

Constructor methods are registered during product initialization and should be documented in the API documents for each object that can be added.

### *objectItems(type=None)*

This method returns a sequence of (id, object) tuples.

Like objectValues and objectIds, it accepts one argument, either a string or a list to restrict the results to objects of a given meta_type or set of meta_types.

Each tuple's first element is the id of an object contained in the ObjectManager, and the second element is the object itself.

Example:

```
<dtml-in objectItems>
 id: <dtml-var sequence-key>,
 type: <dtml-var meta_type>
<dtml-else>
  There are no sub-objects.
</dtml-in>
```

- **Permission**—Access contents information.

### *superValues(type)*

This method returns a list of objects of a given meta_types contained in the ObjectManager and all its parent ObjectManagers.

The `type` argument specifies the meta_types. It can be a string specifying one meta_type, or it can be a list of strings to specify many.

- **Permission**—Python only.

### *objectValues(type=None)*

This method returns a sequence of contained objects.

Like objectItems and objectIds, it accepts one argument, either a string or a list to restrict the results to objects of a given meta_type or set of meta_types.

Example:

```
<dtml-in expr="objectValues('Folder')">
  <dtml-var icon>
  This is the icon for the: <dtml-var id> Folder<br>.
<dtml-else>
  There are no Folders.
</dtml-in>
```

The results were restricted to folders by passing a meta_type to the `objectValues` method.

- **Permission**—Access contents information.


### objectIds(type=None)

This method returns a list of the contained objects' ids.

Optionally, you can pass an argument specifying what object meta_types to restrict the results to. This argument can be a string specifying one meta_type, or it can be a list of strings to specify many.

Example:

```
<dtml-in objectIds>
  <dtml-var sequence-item>
<dtml-else>
  There are no sub-objects.
</dtml-in>
```

This DTML code displays all the ids of the objects contained in the current ObjectManager.

- **Permission**—Access contents information.


## Class *ObjectManagerItem*

A Zope object that can be contained within an ObjectManager. Almost all Zope objects that can be managed through the Web are ObjectManagerItems.

ObjectManagerItems have these instance attributes:

- `title`—The title of the object. This is an optional one-line string description of the object.
- `meta_type`—A short name for the type of the object. This is the name that shows up in a product add list for the object and is used when filtering objects by type. This attribute is provided by the object's class and should not be changed directly.
- `REQUEST`—The current Web request. This object is acquired and should not be set.

### getId()

Returns the object's id.

The id is the unique name of the object within its parent ObjectManager. This should be a string, and it can contain letters, digits, underscores, dashes, commas, and spaces.

This method replaces direct access to the id attribute.

- **Permission**—Always available.

### title_or_id()

If the title is not blank, it returns the title; otherwise, it returns the id.

- **Permission**—Always available.

### unrestrictedTraverse(path, default=None)

Returns the object obtained by traversing the given path from the object on which the method was called. This method begins with `unrestricted` because (almost) no security checks are performed.

If an object is not found, then the `default` argument is returned.

- **Permission**—Python only.

### absolute_url(relative=None)

Returns the absolute URL to the object.

If the relative argument is provided with a true value, then the URL returned is relative to the site object. Note if virtual hosts are being used, then the path returned is a logical path rather than a physical path.

- **Permission**—Always available.

### this()

Returns the object.

This turns out to be handy in two situations. First, it provides a way to refer to an object in DTML expressions.

The second use for this is rather deep. It provides a way to acquire an object without getting the full context from which it was acquired. This is useful, for example, in cases where you are in a non-item subobject of an item's method, and you need to get the item outside of the subobject's context.

- **Permission**—Always available.

### manage_workspace()

This is the Web method that is called when a user selects an item in an ObjectManager Contents view or in the Zope Management Navigation view.

- **Permission**—View management screens.

### title_and_id()

If the title is not blank, it returns the title followed by the id in parenthesis. Otherwise, it returns the id.

- **Permission**—Always available.

### getPhysicalPath()

Gets the path of an object from the root, ignoring virtual hosts.

- **Permission**—Always available.

### getPhysicalRoot()

Returns the top-level Zope application object.

- **Permission**—Python only.

### restrictedTraverse(path, default=None)

Returns the object obtained by traversing the given path from the object on which the method was called, performing security checks along the way.

If an object is not found, then the `default` argument is returned.

- **Permission**—Always available.

## Class *PropertyManager*

A PropertyManager object has a collection of typed attributes called properties. Properties can be managed through the Web or DTML.

In addition to having a type, properties can be writable or read-only, and they can have default values.

### propertyItems()

Returns a list of (id, property) tuples.

- **Permission**—Access contents information.

### *propertyValues()*

Returns a list of property values.

- **Permission**—Access contents information.

### *propertyMap()*

Returns a tuple of mappings, giving metadata for properties. The metadata includes `id`, `type`, and `mode`.

- **Permission**—Access contents information.

### *propertyIds()*

Returns a list of property ids.

- **Permission**—Access contents information.

### *getPropertyType(id)*

Gets the type of property `id`. It returns `None` if no such property exists.

- **Permission**—Access contents information.

### *getProperty(id, d=None)*

Returns the value of the property `id`. If the property is not found, the optional second argument or `None` is returned.

- **Permission**—Access contents information.

### *hasProperty(id)*

Returns a true value if the PropertyManager has the property `id`. Otherwise, it returns a false value.

- **Permission**—Access contents information.

## Class *PropertySheet*

A PropertySheet is an abstraction for organizing and working with a set of related properties. Conceptually, it acts like a container for a set of related properties and metadata describing those properties. A PropertySheet may or may not provide a Web interface for managing its properties.

## *xml_namespace()*

Returns a namespace string, which can be used as an xml namespace for this property set. This can be an empty string if there is no default namespace for a given property sheet (especially property sheets added in ZClass definitions).

- **Permission**—Python only.

## *propertyItems()*

Returns a list of (id, property) tuples.

- **Permission**—Access contents information.

## *propertyValues()*

Returns a list of actual property values.

- **Permission**—Access contents information.

## *getPropertyType(id)*

Gets the type of property id. Returns None if no such property exists.

- **Permission**—Python only.

## *propertyInfo()*

Returns a mapping containing property metadata.

- **Permission**—Python only.

## *getProperty(id, d=None)*

Gets the property id, returning the optional second argument or None, if no such property is found.

- **Permission**—Python only.

## *manage_delProperties(ids=None, REQUEST=None)*

Deletes one or more properties with the given ids. The ids argument should be a sequence (tuple or list) containing the ids of the properties to be deleted. If ids is empty, no action is taken. If any of the properties named in ids do not exist, an error is raised.

Some objects have special properties defined by product authors that cannot be deleted. If one of these properties is named in `ids`, an HTML error message is returned.

If no value is passed in for `REQUEST`, the method returns `None`. If a value is provided for `REQUEST` (as it is when called through the Web), the object's property management form is rendered and returned.

This method can be called through the Web from DTML or from Python code.

- **Permission**—Manage Properties.


### *manage_changeProperties(REQUEST=None, **kw)*

Changes existing object properties by passing either a mapping object as `REQUEST`, containing `name:value` pairs, or by passing `name=value` keyword arguments.

Some objects have special properties defined by product authors that cannot be changed. If you try to change one of these properties through this method, an error is raised.

Note that no type checking or conversion happens when this method is called, so it is the caller's responsibility to ensure that the updated values are of the correct type.

If a value is provided for `REQUEST` (as it is when called through the Web), the method returns an HTML message dialog box. If no `REQUEST` is passed, the method returns `None` on success.

This method can be called through the Web from DTML or from Python code.

- **Permission**—Manage Properties.


### *manage_addProperty(id, value, type, REQUEST=None)*

Adds a new property with the given `id`, `value`, and `type`.

These are the property types:

- `boolean`—1 or 0.
- `date`—A `DateTime` value, for example, `12/31/1999 15:42:52 PST`.
- `float`—A decimal number, for example, `12.4`.
- `int`—An integer number, for example, `12`.
- `lines`—A list of strings, one per line.
- `long`—A long integer, for example, `12232322322323232323423`.
- `string`—A string of characters, for example, `This is a string`.
- `text`—A multiline string, for example, a paragraph.
- `tokens`—A list of strings separated by white space, for example, `one two three`.
- `selection`—A string selected by a pop-up menu.
- `multiple selection`—A list of strings selected by a selection list.

This method uses the passed in `type` to try to convert the `value` argument to the named type. If the given `value` cannot be converted, a ValueError is raised.

The value given for `selection` and `multiple selection` properties can be an attribute or method name. The attribute or method must return a sequence value.

If the given `type` is not recognized, the `value` and `type` given are simply stored blindly by the object.

If no value is passed in for `REQUEST`, the method returns `None`. If a value is provided for `REQUEST` (as it is when called through the Web), then the object's property management form is rendered and returned.

This method can be called through the Web from DTML or from Python code.

- **Permission**—Manage Properties.

## *propertyMap()*

Returns a tuple of mappings, giving metadata for properties.

- **Permission**—Python only.

## *propertyIds()*

Returns a list of property ids.

- **Permission**—Access contents information.

## *hasProperty(id)*

Returns true if `self` has a property with the given `id`; otherwise, it is false.

- **Permission**—Access contents information.

# Class *PropertySheets*

A PropertySheet is an abstraction for organizing and working with a set of related properties. Conceptually, it acts like a container for a set of related properties and metadata describing those properties. PropertySheet objects are accessed through a PropertySheets object that acts as a collection of PropertySheet instances.

Objects that support PropertySheets (objects that support the PropertyManager interface or ZClass objects) have a `PropertySheets` attribute (a PropertySheets instance) that is the collection of PropertySheet objects. The PropertySheets object exposes an interface, much like a Python mapping so that individual PropertySheet objects can be accessed through dictionary style key indexing.

### *get(name, default=None)*

Returns the PropertySheet identified by `name`, or the value given in `default`, if the named PropertySheet is not found.

- **Permission**—Python only.

### *values()*

Returns a sequence of all of the PropertySheet objects in the collection.

- **Permission**—Python only.

### *items()*

Returns a sequence containing an (`id`, `object`) tuple for each PropertySheet object in the collection.

- **Permission**—Python only.

# Class *PythonScript(Script)*

Python scripts contain Python code that gets executed by:

- Calling the script through the Web by going to its location with a Web browser.
- Calling the script from another script object.
- Calling the script from a method object, such as a DTML method.

Python scripts can contain a safe subset of the Python language. Python scripts must be safe because they can potentially be edited by many different users through an insecure medium, such as the Web. The following safety issues drive the need for secure Python scripts:

- Because many users can use Zope, a Python script must make sure it does not enable a user to do something they are not allowed to do, such as delete an object they do not have permission to delete. Because of this requirement, Python scripts do many security checks in the course of their execution.
- Because Python scripts can be edited through the insecure medium of the Web, they are not allowed access to the Zope server's file system. Therefore, normal Python built-ins, such as `open`, are not allowed.
- Because many standard Python modules break the preceding two security restrictions, only a small subset of Python modules can be imported into a Python scripts with the import statement, unless they have been validated by Zope's security policy. Currently, the following standard Python modules have been validated:
    - `string`
    - `math`

- whrandom and random
- Products.PythonScripts.standard

- Because it enables you to execute arbitrary Python code, the Python exec statement is not allowed in Python methods.

- Because they might represent or cause security violations, some Python built-in functions are not allowed. The following Python built-ins are not allowed:
  - open
  - input
  - raw_input
  - eval
  - execfile
  - compile
  - type
  - coerce
  - intern
  - dir
  - globals
  - locals
  - vars
  - buffer
  - reduce

- Other built-ins are restricted in nature. The following built-ins are restricted:
  - **range**—Due to possible memory denial-of-service attacks, the range built-in is restricted to creating ranges less than 10,000 elements long.
  - **filter, map, tuple, list**—For the same reason, built-ins that construct lists from sequences do not operate on strings.
  - **getattr, setattr, delattr**—Because these can enable Python code to circumvent Zope's security system, they are replaced with custom, security-constrained versions.

- To be consistent with the Python expressions available to DTML, these built-in functions are augmented with a small number of functions and a class:
  - test
  - namespace
  - render
  - same_type
  - DateTime

- Because the print statement cannot operate normally in Zope, its effect has been changed. Rather than sending text to stdout, print appends to an internal variable. The special built-in name printed evaluates to the concatenation of all text printed during the current execution of the script.

### document_src(REQUEST=None, RESPONSE=None)

Returns the text of the read method, with content type text/plain set on the RESPONSE.

### ZPythonScript_edit(params, body)

Changes the parameters and body of the script. This method accepts two arguments:

- **params**—The new value of the Python script's parameters. There must be a comma-separated list of values in valid Python function signature syntax. If it does not contain a valid signature string, a SyntaxError is raised.
- **body**—The new value of the Python script's body. It must contain valid Python syntax. If it does not contain valid Python syntax, a SyntaxError is raised.

### ZScriptHTML_tryParams()

Returns a list of the required parameters with which to test the script.

### read()

Returns the body of the Python script, with a special comment block prepended. This block contains metadata in the form of comment lines as expected by the write method.

### write(text)

Changes the script by parsing the text argument into parts. Leading lines that begin with ## are stripped off, and if they are of the form ##name=value, they are used to set metadata, such as the title and parameters. The remainder of the text is set as the body of the Python script.

### ZPythonScriptHTML_editAction(REQUEST, title, params, body)

Changes the script's main parameters. This method accepts the following arguments:

- **REQUEST**—The current request.
- **title**—The new value of the Python script's title. This must be a string.

- **params**—The new value of the Python script's parameters. There must be a comma-separated list of values in valid Python function signature syntax. If it does not contain a valid signature string, a SyntaxError is raised.
- **body**—The new value of the Python script's body. It must contain valid Python syntax. If it does not contain valid Python syntax, a SyntaxError is raised.

### *ZPythonScriptHTML_upload(REQUEST, file="")*

Passes the text in the file to the `write` method.

### *ZPythonScript_setTitle(title)*

Changes the script's title. This method accepts one argument, `title`, which is the new value for the script's title, and it must be a string.

## ObjectManager Constructor

### *manage_addPythonScript(id, REQUEST=None)*

Adds a Python script to a folder.

# Class *REQUEST*

The REQUEST object encapsulates all the information regarding the current request in Zope. This includes the input headers, form data, server data, and cookies.

The REQUEST object is a mapping object that represents a collection of variables to value mappings. In addition, variables are divided into four categories:

- **Environment variables**—These variables include input headers, server data, and other request-related data. The variable names are as specified in the CGI specification.
- **Form data**—These are data extracted from either a URL-encoded query string or body, if present.
- **CookiesThese**—These are the cookie data, if present.
- **OtherData**—These can be set by an application object.

The REQUEST object can be used as a mapping object, in which case, values are looked up in this order: environment variables, other variables, form data, and then cookies.

The following special variables are set in the REQUEST:

- **PARENTS**—A list of the objects traversed to get to the published object. So, `PARENTS[0]` would be the ancestor of the published object.
- **REQUEST**—The REQUEST object.

- **RESPONSE**—The response object.
- **PUBLISHED**—The actual object published as a result of URL traversal.
- **URL**—The URL of the REQUEST without a query string.
- **URLn**—URL0 is the same as URL. URL1 is the same as URL0 with the last path element removed. URL2 is the same as URL1 with the last element removed, and so forth. For example, if URL=http://localhost/foo/bar, then URL1=http://localhost/foo and URL2=http://localhost.
- **URLPATHn**—URLPATH0 is the path portion of URL, URLPATH1 is the path portion of URL1, and so on. For example, if URL=http://localhost/foo/bar, then URLPATH1=/foo and URLPATH2=/.
- **BASEn**—BASE0 is the URL up to, but not including, the Zope application object. BASE1 is the URL of the Zope application object. BASE2 is the URL of the Zope application object with an additional path element added in the path to the published object, and so forth. For example, if URL=http://localhost/Zope.cgi/foo/bar, then BASE0=http://localhost, BASE1=http://localhost/Zope.cgi, and BASE2=http://localhost/Zope.cgi/foo.
- **BASEPATHn**—BASEPATH0 is the path portion of BASE0, BASEPATH1 is the path portion of BASE1, and so on. BASEPATH1 is the externally visible path to the Root Zope folder, equivalent to CGI's SCRIPT_NAME, but virtual-host aware. For example, if URL=http://localhost/Zope.cgi/foo/bar, then BASEPATH0=/, BASEPATH1=/Zope.cgi, and BASEPATH2=/Zope.cgi/foo.

### get_header(name, default=None)

Returns the named HTTP header, or an optional default argument, or None if the header is not found. Note that both original and CGI header names without the leading HTTP_ are recognized. For example, Content-Type, CONTENT_TYPE, and HTTP_CONTENT_TYPE should all return the Content-Type header, if available.

- **Permission**—Always available.

### items()

Returns a sequence of (key, value) tuples for all the keys in the REQUEST object.

- **Permission**—Always available.

### keys()

Returns a sorted sequence of all keys in the REQUEST object.

- **Permission**—Always available.

### *setVirtualRoot(path, hard=0)*

Alters URL, URLn, URLPATHn, BASEn, BASEPATHn, and `absolute_url()` so that the current object has path path. If hard is true, then PARENTS is emptied.

It provides virtual hosting support. It is intended to be called from publishing traversal hooks.

- **Permission**—Always available.

### *values()*

Returns a sequence of values for all the keys in the REQUEST object.

- **Permission**—Always available.

### *set(name, value)*

Creates a new name in the REQUEST object and assigns it a value. This name and value is stored in the Other category.

- **Permission**—Always available.

### *has_key(key)*

Returns a true value if the REQUEST object contains key, it returns a false value otherwise.

- **Permission**—Always available.

### *setServerURL(protocol=None, hostname=None, port=None)*

Sets the specified elements of SERVER_URL, it also affects URL, URLn, BASEn, and `absolute_url()`.

It provides virtual hosting support.

- **Permission**—Always available.

## Class *Response*

The response object represents the response to a Zope request.

### *setStatus(status, reason=None)*

Sets the HTTP status code of the response; the argument can either be an integer or one of the following strings that is converted to the correct integer value: OK, Created,

322 Appendix B API Reference

Accepted, NoContent, MovedPermanently, MovedTemporarily, NotModified, BadRequest, Unauthorized, Forbidden, NotFound, InternalError, NotImplemented, BadGateway, and ServiceUnavailable.

- **Permission**—Always available.

### setHeader(name, value)

Sets an HTTP return header `name` with value `value`, clearing the previous value set for the header, if one exists. If the literal flag is true, then the case of the header name is preserved; otherwise, word-capitalization is performed on the header name on output.

- **Permission**—Always available.

### redirect(location, lock=0)

Causes a redirection without raising an error. If the `lock` keyword argument is passed with a true value, then the HTTP redirect response code is not changed even if an error occurs later in request processing (after `redirect()` has been called).

- **Permission**—Always available.

### setCookie(name, value, **kw)

Sets an HTTP cookie on the browser.

The response includes an HTTP header that sets a cookie on cookie-enabled browsers with a key `name` and value `value`. This overwrites any previously set value for the cookie in the Response object.

- **Permission**—Always available.

### write(data)

Returns data as a stream.

HTML data can be returned using a stream-oriented interface. This enables the browser to display partial results while proceeding with the computation of a response.

The published object should first set any output headers or cookies on the response object.

Note that published objects must not generate any errors after beginning stream-oriented output.

- **Permission**—Always available.

### expireCookie(name, **kw)

Causes an HTTP cookie to be removed from the browser.

The response includes an HTTP header that removes the cookie corresponding to "name" on the client, if one exists. This is accomplished by sending a new cookie with an expiration date that has already passed. Note, that some clients require a path to be specified—this path must match exactly the path given when creating the cookie. The path can be specified as a keyword argument.

- **Permission**—Always available.

### *appendCookie(name, value)*

Returns an HTTP header that sets a cookie on cookie-enabled browsers with a key name and value `value`. If a value for the cookie has previously been set in the Response object, then the new value is appended to the old one separated by a colon.

- **Permission**—Always available.

### *addHeader(name, value)*

Sets a new HTTP return header with the given value, while retaining any previously set headers with the same name.

- **Permission**—Always available.

### *appendHeader(name, value, delimiter=,)*

Appends a value to a cookie.

Sets an HTTP return header name with value `value`, it appends it following a comma, if there was a previous value set for the header.

- **Permission**—Always available.

### *setBase(base)*

Sets the base URL for the returned document.

- **Permission**—Always available.

# Class *Script*

Web-callable script-based interface.

### *ZScriptHTML_tryAction(REQUEST, argvars)*

Applies the test parameters provided by the dictionary `argvars`. This calls the current script with the given arguments and returns the result.

# Class *Vocabulary*

A Vocabulary manages words and language rules for text indexing. Text indexing is done by the ZCatalog and other third-party products.

## *words()*

Returns a list of words.

## *insert(word)*

Inserts a word in the Vocabulary.

## *query(pattern)*

Queries the Vocabulary for words matching a pattern.

### ObjectManager Constructor

*manage_addVocabulary(id, title, globbing=None, REQUEST=None)*

Adds a Vocabulary object to an ObjectManager.

# Class *ZCatalog*

ZCatalog object.

A ZCatalog contains arbitrary index, such as references to Zope objects. ZCatalog's can index either `Field` values of an object, `Text` values, or `KeyWord` values:

ZCatalogs have three types of indexes:

- `Text`—Text Indexes index textual content. The index can be used to search for objects containing certain words.
- `Field`—Field Indexes index atomic values. The index can be used to search for objects that have certain properties.
- `Keyword`—Keyword Indexes index sequences of values. The index can be used to search for objects that match one or more of the search terms.

The ZCatalog can maintain a table of extra data about cataloged objects. This information can be used on search result pages to show information about a search result.

The metadata table schema is used to build the schema for ZCatalog Result objects. The objects have the same attributes as the column of the metadata table.

ZCatalog does not store references to the objects themselves but rather to a unique identifier that defines how to get to the object. In Zope, this unique identifier is the object's relative path to the ZCatalog (because two Zope object's cannot have the same URL, this is an excellent unique qualifier in Zope).

## schema()

Returns a sequence of names that correspond to columns in the metadata table.

## __call__(REQUEST=None, **kw)

Searches the catalog the same way as `searchResults`.

## uncatalog_object(uid)

Uncatalogs the object with the unique identifier `uid`.

## getobject(rid, REQUEST=None)

Returns a cataloged object given a `data_record_id_`.

## indexes()

Returns a sequence of names that correspond to indexes.

## getpath(rid)

Returns the path to a cataloged object given a `data_record_id_`.

## index_objects()

Returns a sequence of actual index objects.

## searchResults(REQUEST=None, **kw)

Searches the catalog. Search terms can be passed in the REQUEST or as keyword arguments.

Search queries consist of a mapping of index names to search parameters. You can either pass a mapping to `searchResults` as the variable REQUEST, or you can use index names and search parameters as keyword arguments to the method, in other words:

```
searchResults(title='Elvis Exposed',
              author='The Great Elvonso')
```

is the same as:

```
searchResults({'title' : 'Elvis Exposed',
               'author : 'The Great Elvonso'})
```

In these examples, `title` and `author` are indexes. This query returns any objects that have the title *Elvis Exposed* AND also are authored by *The Great Elvonso*. Terms that are passed as keys and values in a `searchResults()` call are implicitly ANDed together. To "OR" two search results, call `searchResults()` twice, and add concatenate the results like this:

```
results = ( searchResults(title='Elvis Exposed') +
            searchResults(author='The Great Elvonso') )
```

This returns all objects that have the specified title OR the specified author.

You can pass some special index names to change the behavior of the search query:

- **sort_on**—This parameter specifies on which index to sort the results.
- **sort_order**—You can specify `reverse` or `descending`. Default behavior is to sort ascending.

There are some rules to consider when querying this method:

- An empty query mapping (or a bogus `REQUEST`) returns all items in the catalog.
- Results from a query involving only Field/Keyword Indexes, for example, `{'id':'foo'}` and no `sort_on` is returned unsorted.
- Results from a complex query involving a Field/Keyword Index and a Text Index, for example, `{'id':'foo','PrincipiaSearchSource':'bar'}` and no `sort_on` is returned unsorted.
- Results from a simple Text Index query, for example, `{'PrincipiaSearchSource':'foo'}` are returned sorted in descending order by `score`. A Text Index cannot be used as a `sort_on` parameter, and attempting to do so raises an error.

Depending on the type of index you are querying, you might be able to provide more advanced search parameters that can specify range searches or wildcards.

### *uniqueValuesFor(name)*

Returns the unique values for a given Field Index named `name`.

### *catalog_object(obj, uid)*

Catalogs the object `obj` with the unique identifier `uid`.

## ObjectManager Constructor

### *manage_addZCatalog(id, title, vocab_id=None)*

Adds a ZCatalog object.

    `vocab_id` is the name of a Vocabulary object this catalog should use. A value of `None` causes the Catalog to create its own private vocabulary.

# Class *ZSQLMethod*

ZSQLMethods abstract SQL code in Zope.

    SQL methods behave like methods of the folders in which they are accessed. In particular, they can be used from other methods, such as documents, external methods, and even other SQL methods.

Database methods support the *Searchable Object Interface*. Search interface wizards can be used to build user interfaces to them. They can be used in joins and unions. They provide metadata about their input parameters and result data.

For more information, see the searchable object interface specification.

Database methods support URL traversal to access and invoke methods on individual record objects. For example, suppose you had an `employees` database method that took a single argument `employee_id`. Suppose that employees had a `service_record` method (defined in a record class or acquired from a folder). The `service_record` method could be accessed with a URL, such as:

```
employees/employee_id/1234/service_record
```

Search results are returned as Record objects. The schema of Record objects matches the schema of the table queried in the search.

### manage_edit(title, connection_id, arguments, template)

Changes database method properties.

The `connection_id` argument is the id of a database connection that resides in the current folder or in a folder higher than the current folder. The database should understand SQL.

The `arguments` argument is a string containing an arguments specification, as would be given in the SQL method creation form.

The `template` argument is a string containing the source for the SQL template.

### __call__(REQUEST=None, **kw)

Calls the ZSQLMethod.

The arguments to the method should be passed through keyword arguments, or in a single mapping object. If no arguments are given, and if the method was invoked through the Web, then the method tries to acquire and use the Web REQUEST object as the argument mapping.

The returned value is a sequence of Record objects.

## ObjectManager Constructor

### manage_addZSQLMethod(id, title, connection_id, arguments, template)

Adds an SQL method to an ObjectManager.

The `connection_id` argument is the id of a database connection that resides in the current folder or in a folder higher than the current folder. The database should understand SQL.

The `arguments` argument is a string containing an arguments specification, as would be given in the SQL method creation form.

The `template` argument is a string containing the source for the SQL template.

# C

# Zope Resources

Aᴛ ᴛʜᴇ ᴛɪᴍᴇ ᴏғ ᴛʜɪs ᴡʀɪᴛɪɴɢ, ᴀ ᴍᴜʟᴛɪᴛᴜᴅᴇ of sources for Zope information is on the Internet—but very little is in print. We collected a number of the most important links that you can use to find out more about Zope.

## Zope Web Sites

Zope.org (http://www.zope.org) is the official Zope Web site. It has downloads, documentation, news, and lots of community resources.

ZopeZen (http://www.zopezen.org) is a Zope community site that features news and a Zope job board. The site is run by noted Zope community member—Andy McKay.

Zope Newbies (http://weblogs.userland.com/zopeNewbies/) is a Weblog that features Zope news and related information. Zope Newbies is one of the oldest and best Zope Web sites. Jeff Shelton started Zope Newbies, and the site is currently run by Luke Tymowski.

## Zope Documentation

Zope.org (http://www.zope.org/Documentation) has lots of documentation, including official documentation projects and contributed community documentation.

Zope Documentation Project (http://zdp.zope.org/) is a community-run Zope documentation Web site. It hosts original documentation and has links to other sources of documentation.

Zope Developer's Guide (http://www.zope.org/DocProjects/DevGuide) teaches you how to write Zope products.

## Mailing Lists

Zope.org (http://www.zope.org/Resources/MailingLists) maintains a collection of the many Zope mailing lists.

## Zope Extensions

Zope.org (http://www.zope.org/Products) has a huge collection of third-party Zope extensions, which are called *products*.

Zope Treasures (http://www.zope-treasures.com/) is a large collection of Zope products.

## Python Information

Python.org (http://www.python.org) has lots of information about Python, including a tutorial and reference documentation.

# Open Publication License

OPEN PUBLICATION LICENSE  Draft v1.0, 8 June 1999

# I. REQUIREMENTS ON BOTH UNMODIFIED AND MODIFIED VERSIONS

The Open Publication works may be reproduced and distributed in whole or in part, in any medium physical or electronic, provided that the terms of this license are adhered to, and that this license or an incorporation of it by reference (with any options elected by the author(s) and/or publisher) is displayed in the reproduction.

Proper form for an incorporation by reference is as follows:

> Copyright ©<year> by <author's name or designee>. This material may be distributed only subject to the terms and conditions set forth in the Open Publication License, vX.Y or later (the latest version is presently available at <http://www.opencontent.org/openpub/>).

The reference must be immediately followed with any options elected by the author(s) and/or publisher of the document (see section VI).

Commercial redistribution of Open Publication-licensed material is permitted.

Any publication in standard (paper) book form shall require the citation of the original publisher and author. The publisher and author's names shall appear on all outer surfaces of the book. On all outer surfaces of the book the original publisher's name shall be as large as the title of the work and cited as possessive with respect to the title.

## II. COPYRIGHT

The copyright to each Open Publication is owned by its author(s) or designee.

## III. SCOPE OF LICENSE

The following license terms apply to all Open Publication works, unless otherwise explicitly stated in the document.

Mere aggregation of Open Publication works or a portion of an Open Publication work with other works or programs on the same media shall not cause this license to apply to those other works. The aggregate work shall contain a notice specifying the inclusion of the Open Publication material and appropriate copyright notice.

SEVERABILITY. If any part of this license is found to be unenforceable in any jurisdiction, the remaining portions of the license remain in force.

NO WARRANTY. Open Publication works are licensed and provided "as is" without warranty of any kind, express or implied, including, but not limited to, the implied warranties of merchantability and fitness for a particular purpose or a warranty of non-infringement.

## IV. REQUIREMENTS ON MODIFIED WORKS

All modified versions of documents covered by this license, including translations, anthologies, compilations, and partial documents, must meet the following requirements:

1. The modified version must be labeled as such.
2. The person making the modifications must be identified and the modifications dated.
3. Acknowledgement of the original author and publisher if applicable must be retained according to normal academic citation practices.
4. The location of the original unmodified document must be identified.
5. The original author's (or authors') name(s) may not be used to assert or imply endorsement of the resulting document without the original author's (or authors') permission.

# V. GOOD-PRACTICE RECOMMENDATIONS

In addition to the requirements of this license, it is requested from and strongly recommended of redistributors that:

1. If you are distributing Open Publication works on hard copy or CD-ROM, you provide email notification to the authors of your intent to redistribute at least thirty days before your manuscript or media freeze, to give the authors time to provide updated documents. This notification should describe modifications, if any, made to the document.

2. All substantive modifications (including deletions) be either clearly marked up in the document or else described in an attachment to the document.

3. Finally, while it is not mandatory under this license, it is considered good form to offer a free copy of any hardcopy and CD-ROM expression of an Open Publication-licensed work to its author(s).

# VI. LICENSE OPTIONS

The author(s) and/or publisher of an Open Publication-licensed document may elect certain options by appending language to the reference to or copy of the license. These options are considered part of the license instance and must be included with the license (or its incorporation by reference) in derived works.

A. To prohibit distribution of substantively modified versions without the explicit permission of the author(s). "Substantive modification" is defined as a change to the semantic content of the document, and excludes mere changes in format or typographical corrections. To accomplish this, add the phrase "Distribution of substantively modified versions of this document is prohibited without the explicit permission of the copyright holder." to the license reference or copy.

B. To prohibit any publication of this work or derivative works in whole or in part in standard (paper) book form for commercial purposes is prohibited unless prior permission is obtained from the copyright holder.

To accomplish this, add the phrase "Distribution of the work or derivative of the work in any standard (paper) book form is prohibited unless prior permission is obtained from the copyright holder." to the license reference or copy.

# OPEN PUBLICATION POLICY APPENDIX

(This is not considered part of the license.)

Open Publication works are available in source format via the Open Publication home page at http://www.opencontent.org.

Open Publication authors who want to include their own license on Open Publication works may do so, as long as their terms are not more restrictive than the Open Publication license.

If you have questions about the Open Publication License, please contact David Wiley, and/or the Open Publication Authors' List at `opal@opencontent.org`, via email.

To subscribe to the Open Publication Authors' List:
Send email to `opal-request@opencontent.org` with the word "subscribe" in the body.

To post to the Open Publication Authors' List:
Send email to `opal@opencontent.org` or simply reply to a previous post.

To unsubscribe from the Open Publication Authors' List:
Send email to `opal-request@opencontent.org` with the word "unsubscribe" in the body.

# Index

# C

# J-K-L

## Q-R

# T

# U

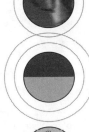

# HOW TO CONTACT US

## VISIT OUR WEB SITE

WWW.NEWRIDERS.COM

On our Web site, you'll find information about our other books, authors, tables of contents, and book errata. You will also find information about book registration and how to purchase our books, both domestically and internationally.

## EMAIL US

Contact us at: **nrfeedback@newriders.com**

- If you have comments or questions about this book
- To report errors that you have found in this book
- If you have a book proposal to submit or are interested in writing for New Riders
- If you are an expert in a computer topic or technology and are interested in being a technical editor who reviews manuscripts for technical accuracy

Contact us at: **nreducation@newriders.com**

- If you are an instructor from an educational institution who wants to preview New Riders books for classroom use. Email should include your name, title, school, department, address, phone number, office days/hours, text in use, and enrollment, along with your request for desk/examination copies and/or additional information.

Contact us at: **nrmedia@newriders.com**

- If you are a member of the media who is interested in reviewing copies of New Riders books. Send your name, mailing address, and email address, along with the name of the publication or Web site you work for.

## BULK PURCHASES/CORPORATE SALES

If you are interested in buying 10 or more copies of a title or want to set up an account for your company to purchase directly from the publisher at a substantial discount, contact us at 800-382-3419 or email your contact information to corpsales@pearsontechgroup.com. A sales representative will contact you with more information.

## WRITE TO US

New Riders Publishing
201 W. 103rd St.
Indianapolis, IN 46290-1097

## CALL/FAX US

Toll-free (800) 571-5840
If outside U.S. (317) 581-3500
Ask for New Riders
FAX: (317) 581-4663

WWW.NEWRIDERS.COM

# RELATED NEW RIDERS TITLES

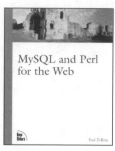

### MySQL and Perl for the Web

Paul DuBois

This book teaches readers the best method for providing information services through the use of Perl, MySQL, and the Web; a powerful system when combined.

*MySQL and Perl for the Web* focuses on Perl scripting combined with the MySQL database because the combination is an important one that has not been adequately documented—even though it is one of the more robust systems available today. This book covers how to put a database on the Web, related performance issues, form processing, searching abilities, security, common e-commerce tasks, and more.

ISBN: 0735710546
500 pages
US $44.99

### Web Application Development with PHP 4.0

Till Gerken and Tobias Ratschiller

*Web Application Development with PHP 4.0* explains PHP's advanced syntax, including classes, recursive functions, and variables. The authors present software development methodologies and coding conventions, which are a must-know for industry quality products and make developing faster and more productive. Included is coverage on Web applications and insight into user and session management, e-commerce systems, XML applications, and WDDX.

ISBN: 0735709971
416 pages with CD-ROM
US $39.99

### MySQL

Paul DuBois

*MySQL* teaches readers how to use the tools provided by the MySQL distribution, by covering installation, setup, daily use, security, optimization, maintenance and troubleshooting. It also discusses important third-party tools, such as the Perl DBI and Apache/PHP interfaces that provide access to MySQL.

ISBN: 0735709211
800 pages
US $49.99

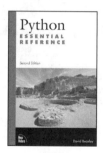

### Python Essential Reference, Second Edition

David Beazley

*Python Essential Reference*, Second Edition, concisely describes the Python programming language and its large library of standard modules—collectively known as the Python programming environment. It is arranged into four major parts. First, a brief tutorial and introduction is presented, then an informal language reference covers lexical conventions, functions, statements, control flow, datatypes, classes, and execution models. The third section covers the Python library, and the final section covers the Python API that is used to write Python extensions. This book is highly focused and clearly provides the things a reader needs to know to best utilize Python.

ISBN 0735710910
416 pages
US $34.99

### PHP Functions Essential Reference

The *PHP Functions Essential Reference* is a simple, clear and authoritative function reference that clarifies and expands upon PHP's existing documentation. The *PHP Functions Essential Reference* will help you write effective code that makes full use of the rich variety of functions available in PHP.

ISBN 073570970X
500 pages
US $44.99

# olutions from experts you know and trust.

## www.informit.com

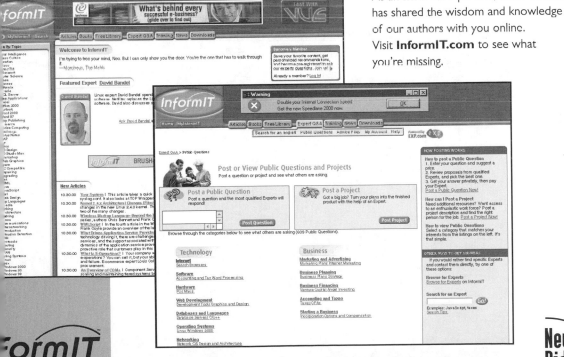

# Colophon

The ruins featured on the cover of this book are those of an aqueduct water system in Merida, Spain—captured by photographer Sami Sarkis.

The design of Merida's aqueduct system, which spans about five miles, is similar to those designed by the Romans dating back as far as 312 B.C. These simple arches relied on gravity to deliver water to the city. Water was collected in a catch basin and then delivered to a fountain or public collecting tank through closed pipes, which ran over a valley picking up pressure through gravity. Aqueducts were constructed from stone, brick, or *pozzuolana*, a mixture of lime and volcanic dust.

*The Zope Book* was written by programmers using programmer tools. Happily, our editors at New Riders adapted to these exotic working conditions, and together we were able to produce the book fairly quickly and painlessly.

*The Zope Book* was written using StructuredText (`http://www.zope.org/Members/millejoh/structuredText`) a simple text markup system. We chose StructuredText because it is simple and easy to write using Emacs (and other lesser text editors). We wrote scripts to translate the book from StructuredText into HTML, DocBook, PDF and a homegrown format used by New Riders.

In addition, we used CVS to collaboratively write and edit the book. CVS works well with StructuredText (it diffs nicely) and provides a reasonable versioning system. You can check the book out of CVS at SourceForge (`http://sourceforge.net/projects/zope-book/`). We used email, comments in the text, and SourceForge's bug tracking system to communicate changes.

This book was laid out in QuarkXPress. The fonts used for the body text are Bembo and MCPDigital. It was printed on 50# Husky Offset Smooth paper at R. R. Donnelley & Sons in Crawfordsville, Indiana. Prepress consisted of PostScript computer-to-plate technology (filmless process). The cover was printed at Moore Langen Printing in Terre Haute, Indiana, on Carolina, coated on one side.